Pitt Latin American Series

THE POLITICS OF WATER

URBAN PROTEST, GENDER, AND POWER IN MONTERREY, MEXICO

Vivienne Bennett

UNIVERSITY OF PITTSBURGH PRESS
Pittsburgh and London

Published by the University of Pittsburgh Press, Pittsburgh, Pa. 15260

Copyright © 1995, University of Pittsburgh Press
All rights reserved
Manufactured in the United States of America
Printed on acid-free paper

Paperback edition, 1996

Library of Congress Cataloging-in-Publication Data

Bennett, Vivienne, 1953–
    The politics of water : urban protest, gender, and power in
Monterrey, Mexico / Vivienne Bennett.
        p.   cm. — (Pitt Latin American series)
    Includes bibliographical references and index.
    ISBN 0-8229-3908-8 (alk. paper).—ISBN 0-8229-5576-8 (pbk.: alk. paper)
    1. Water-supply—Social aspects—Mexico—Monterrey.   2. Water
-supply—Political aspects—Mexico—Monterrey.   1. Title.
II. Series.
HD4465.M6B46   1995
333.91′00972′13—dc20   95-32779
                                                              CIP

A CIP catalogue record for this book is available from the British
Library
Eurospan, London

To my parents, James and Simone

CONTENTS

FIGURES

TABLES

ACRONYMS AND GLOSSARY

Aquifer • Water-bearing layer of permeable rock, sand, or gravel (underground).

BANHUOPSA • Banco Nacional Hipotecario Urbano y de Obras Públicas, S.A. (National Hipothecary Bank for Public Works, changed its name to BANOBRAS in 1966).

BANOBRAS • Banco Nacional de Obras y Servicios Públicos, S.A. (National Bank of Public Works and Services).

CAPM • Comisión de Agua Potable de Monterrey (the Potable Water Commission of Monterrey, called the Commission in this book).

CNA • Comisión Nacional de Agua (National Water Commission). The CNA was formed within the SARH in 1989.

Groundwater • Water within the earth that supplies wells and springs (for example, the water in an aquifer).

Grupo Monterrey • The Monterrey Group is the elite entrepreneurial bourgeoisie of Monterrey, Nuevo León. The Grupo Monterrey consists of a small number of families, interlocked through marriage and joint ventures, who own and control vast networks of industry, real estate, and finance across Mexico, with strong links to the international economy as well.

IDB • Inter-American Development Bank.

Infiltration gallery • A type of water collection alongside a river or a lake or under a dry riverbed that allows water to filter through a sandy layer (natural or manmade) and enter a conduit (such as a pipe or tunnel).

kilometer • One kilometer equals approximately 0.62 mile.

liters per day (lpd) • Liters per day is derived from liters per second (see below), one of the units of measurement used in Mexico to measure volume of water. Liters per day equals liters per second times sixty seconds, times sixty minutes, times twenty-four hours: lpd = lps $\times$ 60 $\times$ 60 $\times$ 24. Dividing the liters per day by total population gives the liters per day per capita.

liters per second (lps) • One liter equals 1.056 quarts. Liters per second is one of the two units of measurement used in Mexico to measure volume of water. The second unit of measurement is the cubic meter (see below under M³).

M³ (cubic meter) • One cubic meter equals 1,000 liters or 264.12 gallons. The cubic meter is one of the two units of measurement used in Mexico to measure volume of water (see also liters per second above). A flow of 1M³ per second translates into approximately 25,550 acre-feet per year.

PAN • Partido de Acción Nacional (National Action Party, the most important conservative opposition party in Mexico).

Parshall meter • A type of open channel flow meter.

PRI • Partido Revolucionario Institucional (the Institutional Revolutionary Party, the official party of the Mexican government having held the presidency for over sixty years).

SADM • Servicios de Agua y Drenaje de Monterrey (the Water and Sewerage Services of Monterrey, called the Water Service in this book).

SARH • Secretaría de Agricultura y Recursos Hidráulicos (the Secretary of Agriculture and Hydraulic Resources).

SEDUE • Secretaría de Desarrollo Urbano y Ecología (the Secretary of Urban Development and Ecology)

SRH • Secretaría de Recursos Hidráulicos (the Secretary of Hydraulic Resources, supplanted by the SARH in 1977).

Surface water • Water that lies above the surface of the ground in rivers, lakes, and other catchments and impoundments such as dams.

Wastewater treatment plant • Sewage treatment plant.

ACKNOWLEDGMENTS

Thirteen years after first setting foot in Monterrey I remain passionately interested in the city's problems of water delivery and urban public services, and in the process of sociopolitical change in Mexico. My most profound gratitude lies with the Regiomontanos who so generously shared their city, their troubles, and their hopes with me. The subject matter of this book has traveled with me for many years, in Monterrey, Austin, San Diego, and Santa Cruz. I therefore have many individuals to thank both in Mexico and in the United States.

IN MEXICO

This book was possible because I was given unlimited access to primary material (reports, minutes of board meetings, and other internal documents) by the two government agencies responsible for providing water to the city of Monterrey. At Servicios de Agua y Drenaje de Monterrey, I warmly thank C. P. José Chávez Gutiérrez and Ing. Francisco Cantú Ramos for the many hours of discussion about Monterrey's water history and the hydraulics of urban water service, and for being so generous with their time and archival resources. I also thank Ing. Sergio Sedas Rodriguez and Ing. Enrique López Torres (directors of SADM), Ing. Raúl García Treviño, Ing. Rogelio González Rodríguez, Raúl García Cruz, and Laura E. Solís. At the Comisión de Agua Potable de Monterrey I especially thank C. P. Raúl Cisneros Ramos and Ing. Federico Villareal, as well as Ing. Enrique Lavalle, Ing. Eliseo Segovia, and Guadalupe Rodríguez. I am particularly grateful to C. P. Don Ramón Cárdenas Coronado, long-time financial advisor to Servicios de Agua y Drenaje de Monterrey, who first opened the doors for me.

At the Universidad Autónoma de Nuevo León, I deeply thank Lic. María de los Angeles Pozas and Lic. Meynardo Vázquez for sharing their knowledge of Monterrey and helping me organize my research. Lic. Artemio Benavides at the Universidad de Monterrey; Lic. Efraín Pérez Güemes and Lic. Alma Rosa Garza del Toro of the Oficina de Información y Difusión del Movimiento Obrero S.A.; Ing. Ramón de la Garza and Ing. Carlos Gil of the Laboratorio e Ingeniería de la Calidad del Agua S.A.; and Lic. Graciela Salazar all contributed at critical moments to furthering my research. Lic. Jesús Escalante, director of the newspaper *El Porvenir*, and Lic. Pedro Muñóz and Manuel Yarto of the newspaper's archives facilitated my archival work.

For six months in 1983 I carried out a survey in twenty Monterrey neighborhoods. I thank Lic. Beatriz de la Vega, director of the Escuela Cervantes de Trabajo Social, for letting me use her school as a weekly meeting place for the survey team. The wonderful trio, Lic. Genoveva Rodríguez, Lic. Etelvina Sáenz, and Lic. Lilia Herrera, were invaluable research assistants for more than two years.

Friends in Monterrey who encouraged me and contributed to my understanding of the region include Leticia Parra, María de los Angeles Pozas, Fernando Elizondo, Jorge Vargas, Magda Martínez, Arturo Salinas, María Palacios, and especially Javier Palacios.

In the United States

While I was working on my doctorate at the University of Texas at Austin, I received invaluable intellectual guidance and support from Harry Cleaver, Michael Conroy, and Antonio Ugalde. I am grateful to the Institute of Latin American Studies for awarding me a dissertation research grant and providing office space upon my return from Monterrey.

After my fieldwork in Monterrey, the Center for U.S.-Mexican Studies, University of California, San Diego, funded six months of writing time. For providing a nurturing and stimulating climate for scholarly work on Mexico I thank Wayne Cornelius, director of the center, and his staff. At the University of California, Santa Cruz, my colleagues in the Study Group on New Social Movements in Latin America, Sonia Alvarez, Arturo Escobar, Cathy Schneider, and Teresa Carrillo, provided support, inspiration, and a broader context for my work. Alejandro Portes encouraged my continued work on this topic.

I thank Jeffrey Rubin, Maria Cook, and Paul Haber, close friends and colleagues, who spent long hours discussing my work with me and who challenged me with insights from their work on Mexico. I am deeply grateful to Jeffrey Rubin, Leslie Sklair, and Lawrence Herzog, who read the entire manuscript, providing invaluable feedback and constructive critiques. Brian Loveman, Michael Conroy, and Peter Ward provided good advice and support during the publication process. I thank John Bailey and Roderic Camp, the two reviewers for the University of Pittsburgh Press, whose comments were extremely helpful and insightful. Arq. Alejandro Joulia Lagares and Leah Hewitt drew the maps of the Monterrey region used in this book. Catherine Marshall and Elizabeth Detwiler of the University of Pittsburgh Press provided outstanding editorial guidance with their reliable, efficient, and caring approach throughout the process of publication.

Family and friends have provided love and encouragement as I progressed through the different stages of this long project. My parents, James and Simone, instilled in me a sense of humanism and taught me to be intellectually curious and to risk seeking answers. Danielle Jaussaud, María Elena Cisne, and Sara Hill in Austin; Kitty and Nico Calavita, America Rodríguez, Cathryn Thorup, and Fay Englemayer in San Diego; Jean Korner; and especially my long-distance friends Tessa Wardlaw, Deedy Mishler, Anne Archer, Kim Korner, and my sister Dina Bennett, provided the essential nourishment of close friendship and intellectual challenge. My husband and colleague, Lawrence Herzog, knows better than anyone the struggles and satisfactions embodied in this manuscript. I thank him most of all, for believing in me and believing in my work.

This book is dedicated to Kim Korner, who shared the love of academe, the quest: in memoriam.

THE POLITICS
OF WATER

1 INTRODUCTION

THE first time I visited Monterrey, Mexico, in August 1980, I was struck by two phenomena: the intense heat, and the water shortages that left the entire city with only a few hours of running water each day. The more time I spent in the city the more I realized the scope of the water problem. The squatter settlements and shantytowns on the outskirts of Monterrey either had no piped water whatsoever or shared public faucets that were dry more often than not. All other neighborhoods in the city, even the affluent ones, had only a few hours of water service daily, and that was not predictable either.

Monterrey is Mexico's second most important industrial city and the third largest in population, with two million inhabitants in 1980. The city concentrates heavy industry such as steel, iron, chemical, and paper works, which are all heavy users of water in the production process. Preliminary research showed that water had been rationed to the entire population of the city on and off since 1978, and permanently since 1980. Up to one quarter of the population (the poor) did not have running water in their homes.

The water crisis of the 1980s in Monterrey reveals tremendous inadequacies in the planning of water services. The objective of this book is to use Monterrey's water crisis as a lens through which to explore the political process of public service provision in Mexico. Among public services, water is of particular interest because it is both an essential component of the production process and vital for human survival. My research on the evolution of Monterrey's water system during the twentieth century reveals that three political actors were key to the process of planning water services for the city: the executive branches of the federal and state governments, the regional private sector elite known as the Grupo Monterrey, and women living in low-income neighborhoods in Monterrey. The history of Monterrey's water problems is a history of changing relations of power between these political actors.

For decades, the conflictive relationship between the Grupo Monterrey and the government contributed to constraining public-sector investment for water infrastructure. The long-term outcome of this was the citywide water crisis of the 1980s. In addition, years of deteriorating water service along with a rapidly growing population and the harsh semiarid environment of Monterrey resulted in citywide public protests that were shaped by gender, class, and territoriality. The protests reached their peak during the years when the government and the Grupo Monterrey were developing a more cordial and even cooperative relationship. Both the protests and changing private sector–government relations contributed to a major reversal in public-sector spending as the government for the first time made Monterrey's water sector a high priority.

Furthermore, two key features of the Mexican political system, fiscal centralization and presidentialism, are illustrated in the political history of Monterrey's water services. While both of these features strongly enhance presidential power, in the case of Monterrey they served to constrain public spending for water infrastructure and contributed to the looming water crisis.

This book also addresses the issue of private versus public sector ownership or management of public services. An increasingly frequent response by Latin American governments to the economic crises in their countries has been the sale of state-owned enterprises, including not only industries but public services. Chile, for example, sold its national telephone company and its electricity service. Mexico has granted private firms the right to build and collect tolls on new superhighways. Recently, some medium-sized cities in Mexico have considered selling their water services to the private sector in order to increase their capital base and improve service.[1] Monterrey's history includes two periods of private sector control of the city's water services. During the first, from 1909 to 1945, a Canadian company actually owned the water system, while during the second, from 1971 to 1976 (and partially during the 1960s), the Grupo Monterrey controlled the board of directors of the city's Water Service. The status of water services in Monterrey at the end of each of these periods suggests that privatization does not guarantee either an improvement in service or a more rational organization of service than occurs under government control.

In sum, the astonishing lack of infrastructure development in a major industrial city in Mexico raises questions about the process of planning urban services. The history of water service provision in Monterrey is a political history. This book unravels the politics of water in Monterrey by following three threads of inquiry over time. The first thread is the history of Monterrey's water services themselves: what was built, when, why, and funded by whom. The second thread is the response of the urban poor in Monterrey to the growing water crisis: who participated in the protests over water, what strategies did they use, and why. In turn, this leads to an analysis of the government's response to the protests. The third thread considers the dynamics of planning water services for Monterrey: the roles of the private sector and the government, and their changing relations of power.

Urbanization in Latin America

Water service problems plague most Latin American cities, but not to the point of crisis experienced in Monterrey. In other cities, poor neighborhoods typically suffer because they are not linked to the municipal water system and must rely instead on public standposts or on water trucks that deliver water. Usually, middle-income and affluent neighborhoods are connected to the water system and receive water normally twenty-four hours a day. What distinguishes Monterrey is that it is a major industrial city with several million inhabitants, with water rationed to its entire population on a permanent basis, a phenomenon that does not exist elsewhere in Latin America. Yet Monterrey experienced a pattern of urbanization similar to other Latin American cities and very similar to other major cities in Mexico.

During the postwar period, Latin America underwent a significant transition from being a primarily rural society to an urban, industrial society. By 1960, 49 percent of Latin America's population lived in cities; by 1987, the proportion had risen to 69 percent (Inter-American Development Bank 1988: 535). Urban population growth was caused by two concurrent trends: rural to urban migration and high rates of natural population growth. Rural to urban migration occurred when millions of poor peasants lost their livelihood as a result of distorted rural development and sought a better life in the cities. At the same time, the rate of natural population growth increased as public health systems expanded their vaccination programs, preventing infant deaths from childhood diseases, and as improved health care for the population as a whole lowered the mortality rate of the general population.

Latin American cities were unprepared for the rapid increases in their populations (Herbert 1979: 7). The development policies of many Latin American governments were based on channeling investment into industrialization and limiting social spending. Tax incentives, long-term low interest rates, tariff barriers, and overvalued domestic currencies were among the mechanisms used to encourage and protect domestic investment for industrial production (Sheahan 1987: 84). As a result, in the postwar period, the rate of growth of the manufacturing sector in Latin America was impressive. From 1960 to 1965, manufacturing production grew at an average annual rate of 5.2 percent, compared to 5.7 percent for the industrialized nations; and from 1965 to 1970, manufacturing production in Latin America grew at an average annual rate of 6.3 percent, compared to 5.7 percent for the industrialized countries (85).

Industrial growth fueled rural to urban migration by raising expectations that jobs were to be had in the cities. However, investment in residential infrastructure did not keep pace with the growth of the productive sector. Urban housing stocks and public services such as water and sewerage systems were inadequate to cover burgeoning urban populations. Yet, while government policies to stimulate investment in productive infrastructure were in place by the 1950s, most Latin American countries did not have urbanization policies until the 1970s. To this day, municipal governments in Latin America do not have the revenue base to generate the significant funds necessary to resolve local housing and public service needs (Herbert 1979: 8–9). The result has been a massive shortfall of housing and services, and growing polarity between rich and poor (Roberts 1978: 5, 137; Gilbert and Ward 1985: 251). In response to the lack of housing, large numbers of poor urban residents resorted to invading vacant plots of land and setting up squatter settlements. In 1961, squatters represented 20 percent of the population of metropolitan Peru; by 1972 that had risen to 25 percent, or over 800,000 people. The figures for Peru are standard for Latin America and the rest of the Third World. In 1970, squatters constituted 30 percent of the population of Cali, 33 percent of Karachi, 35 percent of Caracas, and 45 percent of Ankara (Collier 1976: 27–28).

Together with housing shortages there were widespread deficiencies in public services, particularly water, sewerage, roads, and transportation, but also in education and health care. For example, in São Paulo only 63 percent of the population had access to the municipal water system in 1974 (Jacobi Neru 1987: 75), only 61 percent of Peru's urban population was connected to municipal water systems in 1980 (Zolezzi and Calderón 1985: 74), and only 50 percent of the population had access in Buenos Aires in 1980 (Braunstein 1985: 20).

Urban population growth in Mexico followed the Latin American pattern. The extensive rural to urban migration that took place in Mexico after 1940 was a response to development policies implemented by the government. The Mexican import-substitution model pursued after 1940 emphasized rapid industrialization financed by foreign credits and by the export earnings of the rural sector of the economy. The Mexican government fomented, through regulation and the construction of infrastructure, the transformation of the agricultural sector, emphasizing cattle and crops for export. The emphasis on agriculture for export had a profound impact on the rural employment structure. Many small landholders, who produced mainly staple crops, were forced to sell their land when inadequate financial, infrastructural, technical, and price supports from the government left them and their families at below subsistence level. Their lands were absorbed by large commercial producers, and they were left depending on waged jobs for survival. Other peasants found that over time their small plots of land could no longer support their families, so family members were forced to look for waged jobs elsewhere. The collective farms, or *ejidos*, were undermined by corruption and the systematic inefficiency of the Ejidal Bank and supporting ministries, so that by 1980, 80 percent of *ejidos* in northern Mexico had rented their land to commercial producers and the *ejidatarios* had also joined the waged labor market (Adler Hellman 1983: 99).

The rural poor had three choices: find a waged job in the countryside, move to the cities, or migrate illegally to the United States. While commercial farms controlled more and more of the countryside, they were not able to absorb the growing numbers of rural inhabitants needing waged jobs. Consequently, between 1930 and 1980 there was a radical shift of the population from rural to urban.[2] Whereas in 1930 two-thirds of Mexico's population lived in the countryside, by 1980 two-thirds lived in urban areas. From 1940 to 1950 rural to urban migration was the primary cause of city growth, but after 1950 migration took second place to natural increase (Scott 1982: 117). As health care improved in the cities, infant mortality dropped and age at death rose. In other words, more people survived infancy and lived to old age. In addition, the typical migrant was young and began or continued building a family upon arrival in the city. And, despite rapid industrialization, job opportunities in the cities did not keep pace with urban population growth, or with the growing number of high school and university graduates seeking professional employment. A growing sector of the urban population was underemployed, with family wages insufficient to cover the cost of home ownership or even rental.

Between 1940 and 1970, Mexico's population grew an average of 3.5 percent per year, doubling over the thirty-year period (Adler Hellman 1983: 59). The urban population increased even faster, so that during the same period the population of Mexico City more than quadrupled, and the populations of Monterrey and Guadalajara more than quintupled (see table 1.1).[3] Yet, until the mid-1970s, the Mexican government paid little attention to urban planning (Herzog 1990: 215).

It was not until 1976, with the Law of Human Settlements and the creation of a new Ministry of Settlements and Public Works (Secretaría de Asentamientos Humanos y de Obras Públicas, or SAHOP), that recognition was given to the need for the systematic regulation and planning of urban areas. A National Urban Development Plan was written, which had

TABLE 1.1

Population: Mexico City, Guadalajara, and Monterrey Metropolitan Areas, 1940–1980

Year	Mexico City	Guadalajara	Monterrey
1940	1,802,679	274,733	206,152
1950	3,137,599	440,528	375,040
1960	5,251,755	851,155	708,300
1970	8,799,937	1,491,085	1,246,181
1980	13,354,271	2,192,557	1,913,075

Source: Estadísticas históricas de México (Mexico City: Instituto Nacional de Estadística, Geografía, e Informática, Secretaría de Programación y Presupuesto, 1985), 24–28.

as one of its goals to restrict the growth of Mexico City, Monterrey, and Guadalajara (Ward 1990: 118–19). However, urban planning in Mexico tended to be oriented toward meeting the needs of the dominant economic sectors, even if that meant ignoring or contradicting the mandates of the National Urban Development Plan (119). SAHOP itself was given neither the necessary funding nor the institutional support to implement its plans (Herzog 1990: 215–16). The SAHOP ministry barely lasted the six years of President López Portillo's administration before being replaced with an even less effective ministry in terms of urban planning— the Secretaría de Desarrollo Urbano y de Ecología (SEDUE) established in 1983 after President de la Madrid came to power.

The result was that Mexico's largest cities grew in an unplanned manner, sprawling out in poverty-ridden, unregulated settlements often formed by illegal squatting or illegal development. Cities were characterized by housing shortages, low-income and impoverished neighborhoods of very high density, and inadequate public services due to lack of planning and investment in infrastructure. Garza and Schteingart (1978: 26–35) estimate the deficit of urban housing in 1970 to have been 1.6 million homes, with an average deficit per city of 45.3 percent of existing housing stock. By 1980, the Ministry of Planning and Budget estimated a country-wide housing deficit of four million homes affecting 30 percent of the population (Schteingart 1985–86: 170). In that same year, 21 percent of homes in Monterrey had only one room (Villarreal and Castañeda 1986: 188), while the average number of occupants per home was 5.53 persons (Instituto Nacional 1983). Approximately half the homes nationwide did not have running water or sewerage service (Instituto Nacional 1985: 127). Sustained high urbanization rates unaccompanied by adequate government spending on social welfare meant that an urban crisis was brewing by the 1960s. The crisis erupted in the late 1970s in Monterrey, where a series of political factors had combined to further distort public spending, and where daily life had therefore deteriorated below an acceptable threshold for thousands of city residents.

Monterrey: The Setting for the Study

Monterrey, a highly polarized city, a city checkered with impoverished shantytown neighborhoods and dominated by an eminently successful bourgeoisie that has held its own in a conflict-ridden relationship with the federal government, is the setting for this study of the politics of water (see figure 1.1).

Monterrey was founded in 1596 after two previous attempts failed, one in 1577 and one in 1583 (Vizcaya Canales 1971: v). It is notable that the archival documents recording the foundation in all three years refer to the availability of water as a critical factor in the decision to settle in the area. During its first three centuries of existence Monterrey was considered an oasis within a generally semiarid region (Servicios 1981: 13). Viscaya mentions that the availability of water in Monterrey as compared to other cities in the north of Mexico contributed to its early industrialization.[4]

Before Mexico's independence in 1821, Monterrey was little more than a village, a pastoral and agricultural community that also served as a defensive post against the Indian population (Saragoza 1988: 17). The Wars of Independence, the Texas War of 1836, and the U.S.-Mexican War

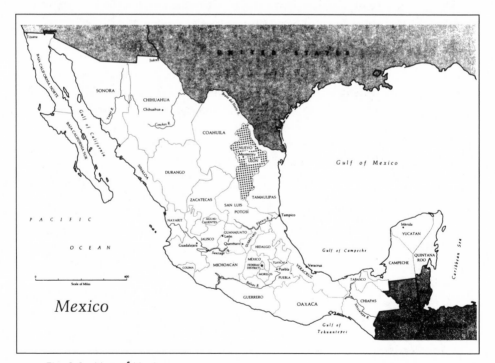

Fig. 1.1. Map of Mexico

of 1846 served to increase commercial traffic through Monterrey. The population grew from about six thousand inhabitants in 1803 to over twenty thousand in 1850 (17, 40). As a result of losing the U.S.-Mexican War, Mexico lost about half its territory to the United States. All of a sudden, Monterrey found itself close to the new U.S.-Mexico border. This further stimulated Monterrey's growth as a commercial center for the region.

The roots of Monterrey's industrialization lie in the sixty-year period 1850–1910. The years 1850 to 1890 were of mercantile capital accumulation, while 1890 to 1910 saw the switch to investment in mining, banking, and industry.[5] The mining sector first developed to fill the growing needs of heavy industry in the northeastern United States. Beginning with the construction of three smelters and four foundries between 1890 and 1900, Monterrey became a center of mining-related activities (Saragoza 1988: 37–39). Between 1890 and 1910 numerous other industries, including brickyards, cement plants, glassworks, and a major brewery, were established. Commercial activity continued expanding, and local financial institutions were created.

A significant characteristic of industrialization in Monterrey was the early and rapid development of industry both horizontally and vertically. As transportation and communication networks within Mexico improved under the Porfirian regime, the early Monterrey industrialists expanded their operations into new regions. At the same time, they diversified, creating fully integrated industries. For example, the brewery spawned bottle works, a cork industry, and a packaging industry.

A second important characteristic of Monterrey's industrialization was the early formation of a very cohesive regional bourgeoisie. The original smelting, foundry, and brewery industries had been founded by a handful of local families. By the early 1900s these families began to cooperate in joint ventures, and they consolidated their wealth and relationships through intermarriage. Until 1910, they received important fiscal incentives from the state government under their ally, Governor Bernardo Reyes (Vellinga 1988: 32–33). The economic development of the city stimulated an increase in migration to Monterrey from other Mexican states, as well as from within the state of Nuevo León, to fill the new demand for labor. While the population of Nuevo León grew 54.7 percent between 1883 and 1910, the population of Monterrey grew 106 percent (from

41,842 residents in 1883 to 86,294 in 1910). By 1900, 56.6 percent of the out-of-state population residing in Nuevo León lived in Monterrey (in absolute figures, 24,059 persons) (Cerutti 1983: 137–38).

The Revolution had a devastating impact on Monterrey. Rail service was interrupted over long periods of time, impeding continued trade with other regions of Mexico (Montemayor Hernández 1971: 327). The city itself was invaded three times, causing destruction to property including industries and commercial establishments. From 1915 to 1925 the state government of Nuevo León changed hands fifteen times, and state budgets were highly limited. However, most of the leading entrepreneurs removed themselves, their families, and their money to the United States for the duration of the war (Nuncio 1982: 67). As the state government settled down after 1925, they brought their money back to Monterrey and renewed industrial investment, this time with production oriented primarily for the internal market (Vellinga 1988: 36–39). Their strategy received a boost in the 1930s as the Great Depression forced Latin American nations away from a strategy of importation to one of import substitution.

After the Second World War, from 1945 to 1950, industrial investment in Monterrey quadrupled. State laws provided incentives such as tax exemptions of 75 percent for up to twenty years for existing industries that wanted to expand, as well as for new industries (Rojas Sandoval and Rodríguez 1988: 59). Over the next fifteen years, 1950 to 1965, the Monterrey entrepreneurs, who came to be known as the Grupo Monterrey, invested heavily in advanced technology and began producing capital goods. Investment in the industrial sector multiplied ninefold. Modern industries were opened, including petrochemical plants, plastics, electronics, and heavy machinery. Metalworking continued to be the single most important sector of the economy, accounting for 50 percent of total industrial investment (Vellinga 1988: 42–43).

Since 1950, industrialization in Monterrey has been distinguished by the increasing concentration and centralization of investments. Between 1974 and 1980 the number of companies owned by the Grupo Monterrey jumped from 100 to 375 (Nuncio 1982: 22). By 1984, 2.6 percent of Monterrey's industries accounted for 88.6 percent of total capital investment and 63 percent of industrial employment. In some sectors, the level of concentration was even more extreme. In metalworks, 1.6 percent of firms represented 90 percent of total invested capital and 60 percent of labor employed in the sector. In textiles, two companies accounted for 90 percent of capital investment and 60 percent of workers (Vellinga 1988: 45–46). In the 1970s, the concentration and centralization of industry into conglomerates took two forms. On the one hand, there were conglomerates consisting of subsidiaries whose products were unrelated to each other (for example, Alfa). On the other hand, there were conglomerates whose subsidiaries formed an integrated industry (for example, Vitro). Heavy investments in financial services gave the Grupo Monterrey even greater strength and independence as their banks attracted capital from other regions of Mexico that did not have strong regional banks (47–50).

Ever since the consolidation of the Mexican Revolution in the 1920s, the Monterrey bourgeoisie has opposed state involvement in the Mexican economy. The Grupo Monterrey has sustained a vision of the state as subsidiary to the private sector. The role of the state was to maintain social and political stability, and to finance and construct infrastructure, but not to direct the economy or play a major role through direct investment. The Grupo Monterrey's vision brought the Monterrey bourgeoisie into conflict with the state as direct state involvement in the economy grew. The relationship between the Grupo Monterrey and the government reached levels of open hostility during the presidencies of Cárdenas (1934–1940), López Mateos (1958–1964), and Echeverría (1970–1976), and during the last years of the López Portillo presidency (1981–1982) (Vellinga 1988: 63–64).

As Vellinga (1988: 62–67) points out, the Grupo Monterrey has sustained an ideological discourse embracing not only economics and the role of the state, but religion, the family, labor, law and order, and patriotism. This ideology has become embedded in the character of the city itself, differentiating it from other Mexican cities. For example, the Monterrey industrialists' opposition to state regulation of school texts brought them into conflict with the state in the 1950s. They also refused the state-controlled labor unions and instead created their own independent unions, called *sindicatos blancos.* Strongly Catholic, they drew from papal encyclicals to support the sanctity of private property. They used the rhetoric of patriotism to transcend their regionalism and soften the constant tension in their relations with the national government. Thus all of their investments, and all of their ideology, was "for the national good." Until recently, the Grupo Monterrey did not participate directly in politics. Instead, they counted on intermediaries, such as the employer confederations that they controlled, to carry their opinions and negotiate on their behalf with the government on issues of concern to them.[6] The Grupo Monterrey sustained an autonomy from the state as much as possible, including actively supporting the right-wing opposition party, the Partido de Acción Nacional.

As Monterrey industrialized, its population grew. The city was a magnet for migrant flows from northern and central Mexico, growing 8.7 percent each year during the 1950s, 7.3 percent each year during the 1960s, and 6 percent per year in the 1970s (Pozas Garza 1990: 20). The city's population almost doubled each decade. From 206,152 people in 1940, it jumped to 1,913,075 in 1980 (Instituto Nacional 1985: 24–28). Despite great industrial wealth, income distribution in the city has remained highly stratified. In 1965, the wealthiest 5 percent of the city's population received 32.33 percent of gross family income, and the poorest 5 percent received 0.80 percent (Puente Leyva 1976: 17). By 1985, the polarization between the richest and the poorest had barely changed: the richest 5 percent received 33.0 percent of gross family income and the poorest 5 percent received 0.63 percent (Vellinga 1988: 90). A study of the absolute changes in real income between 1965 and 1985 showed that real income had increased for all income groups, but the lower the income group, the smaller the increase. Thus, real income rose 12 percent for the poorest 30 percent of the city's population, while it rose by 56 percent for the wealthiest 15 percent (104).

The pace of urban growth in Monterrey together with the income stratification of the population had dire consequences for the urban landscape, especially in a sociopolitical context of very limited urban planning. By 1965, more than half the population lived in inadequate housing (Puente Leyva 1976, as cited in Vellinga 1988: 142). Homes were constructed out of flimsy material, such as adobe or mud, roofed with tin, palm fronds or cardboard, and had dirt floors. Thirty-seven percent of homes did not have a bathroom; 30 percent were not connected in any way to the sewerage system (Montemayor 1971: 416). The poor lived in conditions of high density, often with more than one family to a dwelling, and an average of three to four persons per room (Tijerina Garza 1965, as cited in Vellinga 1988: 142–43). Financing for low-income housing was highly limited. As a result, in the early 1970s thousands of poor families began participating in land invasions on the outskirts of the city, setting up cardboard and tin shelters on vacant plots of land. While many of the land invasions faced government repression in the form of violent evictions from the invaded land or police barricades surrounding the new invasion settlement, most land invasions succeeded in consolidating as illegal settlements because the city and the government simply did not have alternative housing to offer. Some of the land invasions had an overtly militant character and were organized with block leaders, block meetings, and neighborhood-wide assemblies for decision-making purposes.

In 1976, more than two dozen militant land invasion neighborhoods joined forces to create an umbrella organization called the Frente Popular Tierra y Libertad, with a constituency estimated at 150,000 to 300,000, or 5 to 10 percent of Monterrey's total population. In response both to the acute housing shortage and to the alternative militant organizations that were gaining strength by organizing squatter settlements, the state government of Nuevo León created a housing authority, Fomento Metropolitano de Monterrey (Fomerrey), to regularize illegal settlements. A 1973 Fomerrey census determined that two hundred thousand people were living in irregular settlements—one-sixth of the city's population (Pozas Garza 1990: 28). In addition to negotiating the legalization of these irregular settlements, Fomerrey also opened up new land for legal settlement. As a result, by the late 1970s, land invasions had become sporadic in Monterrey. However, the Fomerrey neighborhoods were also characterized by inadequate standards of living. Usually, families were given plots of land and were expected to build their own homes. When the neighborhoods were more than half occupied they could petition for water and electricity services. In the meantime, they relied on water truck deliveries (at inflated prices) and strung wires from their neighborhood out to the main power lines. Streets remained unpaved, children had to attend schools in other neighborhoods, health care services were distant, and transportation was cumbersome and expensive.

By the early 1980s, Fomerrey had provided lots to 54,000 families—an estimated 324,000 people. Yet even Fomerrey could not keep up with the growth of the poor urban population. By 1981, another 300,000 people were estimated to be living in irregular settlements (Pozas Garza 1990: 30). A total of almost one-third of the population was living in substandard conditions. A study by the city's Department of Urban Development found that in the early 1980s, 176,000 homes were deficient based on quality of construction material, 124,000 homes did not have potable water in the home, and 126,000 homes were without sewerage service.

ORGANIZATION OF THE BOOK

Chapter 2 takes a step back to explore the role of water in the urban environment more generally and to posit theoretical frameworks for discussing the planning of public services in Latin America. Chapter 3 responds to the first thread of inquiry by presenting the history of Monterrey's water services since the first municipal water system was built in 1909. This chapter demonstrates that the roots of the water crisis of the 1980s go back to the 1930s, and that the crisis was the result of decades of inadequate planning.

Chapters 4 and 5 follow the second thread of inquiry by analyzing the popular protests that constituted the response of the population in Monterrey to the critical water shortages and unreliable water service. Chapter 4 describes the protests over water in Monterrey and situates them in the comparative context of social movements and urban protest in Latin America. Drawing from theoretical and empirical work on women's activism in Latin America, chapter 5 uses the variables of gender, class, and territoriality to explain why women were the primary participants in the protests and why they chose the strategies that were used in the protests.

Chapter 6 weaves together all three threads of inquiry. Addressing the government's response to the protests over water, chapter 6 provides more detail on government planning and investment for water services in Monterrey. In so doing, the chapter exposes the centrality of the private sector–government relationship to the planning process in Monterrey, and illustrates how changes in that relationship were accompanied by changes in government investment patterns. At the same time, relations of power between the Grupo Monterrey and the government were bounded by two prevailing features of the Mexican political system, fiscal centralization and presidentialism, both of which contributed in a variety of ways to constraining local-level decision making and to shaping federal-level investment decisions for Monterrey.

By way of conclusion, chapter 7 considers in further empirical and theoretical detail the issue of relations of power in Mexico, the impact of protest on planning water services in Monterrey, and the trade-offs between public and private ownership or management of urban water services.

2 URBAN WATER SERVICES
Theory and Planning

A S urbanized areas have expanded in Latin America, so has the need for the development of new water resources and the extension of urban water systems. Urban water services have technical, political, and social dimensions. On the one hand, the provision of water to a city comprises a technical puzzle that usually has more than one set of technical solutions (Etherton 1980). Water for cities comes from wells tapping underground aquifers, from dams, from infiltration galleries, from rivers, and so on. Each city has a finite number of sources for its water. While decisions about the siting of wells or dams, about the quantity of water to be extracted, and about water main layout can be resolved technically, these decisions often also have political components. Dam location, for example, can become highly controversial as landowners fight to save their land. At the same time, the urban area served by a new dam will develop more quickly than unserved areas, with urban landowners reaping profit from land development. Forces promoting and opposing a new dam site can impinge on decision making. Or, in a city like Monterrey, where the municipal water authority and private industry have separate wells drawing water from the same aquifer, decisions on the amount of water extracted from the aquifer can be influenced by the relationship between the private sector and the government.

In the city, water is provided to a variety of consumers who use water for different purposes. When there is scarcity of water in an urban environment, as is often the case in Latin American cities, it can provoke competition for water between different water users (Herbert 1979; Jacobi Neru 1987; Zolezzi and Calderón 1985). Industry may have around-the-

18

clock water service while residential customers are rationed. Water rationing may vary from neighborhood to neighborhood. Some neighborhoods may have reliable, part-time water service; others may experience an erratic schedule of water availability. Technical problems with the water system itself—pump breakdowns, leaks, broken or worn-out valves—may contribute to unreliable water service. When there isn't enough water for all users to consume as much as they want, then water services become an embodiment of the social structure and the social dynamic of the city. Planners and other decision makers decide who gets water when, and their decisions may reflect the power and relationships of different groups of water users. This is as visible in southern California, where residential customers were threatened with fines if they did not voluntarily reduce their water consumption by 30 percent in the early 1990s while developers continued to build new housing developments, as it is in Monterrey, where the urban poor have organized protests to demand water while industries have their own wells drawing water twenty-four hours a day.

The analysis of water in the urban environment therefore begins by considering the significance of water for different groups in the city. Water in the city is a commodity: it is extracted from its source, purified, transported, and sold. There are producers, sellers, and consumers of water. Urban water consumers include residential users, heavy and light industry, commercial establishments, and public institutions such as schools, hospitals, and government buildings. In an industrialized city, the two biggest groups of water consumers are the city's residents and industry.

Residential Water Use

Water has a variety of uses for urban residents. These can be tentatively ranked according to urgency of need. The primary use of water is for physical survival. Without adequate intake of water the human body dies. However, enough water to insure survival does not constitute an adequate supply of water. Beyond the survival level an increase in water supply is necessary for health and hygiene. Urban residents who do not have in-house water connections store water in barrels and tubs. These receptacles are usually not cleaned appropriately and are often left uncovered. As a result, the water used by family members for drinking can easily become contaminated and can carry a variety of pathogenic organisms that cause diseases such as typhoid, giardiasis, and parasitic or bacterial dysenteries. Reducing the incidence of these diseases depends on increasing both the quantity and the quality of water (Bradley 1978).

Limited availability of water also has an impact on hygiene. Water is needed to wash clothes, to clean the house, for waste disposal, and for bathing. Inadequate water supplies can impede proper hygiene, and thereby contribute to the incidence of skin and eye infections, as well as infections carried by fleas, ticks, and lice. The incidence of these diseases is usually reduced by increasing the quantity of water available for each family. Finally, some diseases are spread by insects that either breed in water or bite near water. Examples include malaria, yellow fever, and dengue. The strategy for preventing such diseases is to eliminate the breeding sites of insects. This is problematic when people do not have running water in or near their homes, and so must continually store water in large containers.

While the amount of water needed for purposes of hygiene may to a certain extent be culturally determined, there is a minimal level that must be met or health problems ensue. In the poor neighborhoods of Latin American cities, women need to have sharp management skills and time to organize household water use in such a way so as to prevent the inadequate water supplies from fostering infection and disease in their homes. However, rarely do they have the combination of education, time, and energy necessary to avoid completely the negative health effects of their water supply. If water supplies cannot be increased then solutions must focus on household strategies for water use, otherwise health problems are sure to ensue.

The usefulness of water is a function both of its qualities and its quantity. In determining usefulness, the particular qualities of water must be considered before determining its quantity: the need for water arises first and foremost from its quality as sustainer-of-life. The quantity of water ultimately determines life or death. However, the ranking of usefulness of water is based on increasing quantities of water. First we need water to survive, then we need more water to maintain our health and hygiene, and finally, when we have a lot of water we can use some to sprinkle lawns or wash cars.[1] But quantity alone is not enough to guarantee either survival or good health—we need a certain amount of water with certain qualities. If the water is for drinking it must not be contaminated. If it is for cooking its level of contamination must not exceed that which can be eliminated through the application of heat. If the water is for washing clothes it does not need to be potable, but it should not be muddy. If the water is for bathing it should not have aquatic snails in it because they are the intermediate hosts for schistosomiasis, which can infect humans through the skin. In short, each use of water requires distinct qualities as well as distinct quantities. Thus the ranking of use built on ever-increasing amounts of water assumes, a priori, that the water has the qualities needed for each of its uses.

Apart from the uses of water itself, the different types of water service are also important (White 1978). Accessibility and availability of water affect the quantity of water used by a family, and thus the family's well-being: the more accessible the water, the more is used, until the limit for water consumption is reached. Poor urban residents are willing to pay for upgraded water services, even when the cost in proportion to their income is very high, precisely because of the usefulness of better service.

A hierarchy of water services can be established. At the bottom of the scale of urban water services in Latin America is water-truck service. At this level, neighborhoods are not connected to the city's water system and residents depend on trucks delivering water house by house. The next level of service is the public standpipe: neighborhoods are connected to the city's water system but in the most rudimentary way possible with pipes laid over the ground leading to single faucets that may serve as many as one to two hundred families. The next level of service is a patio connection. Here, either a group of families shares a faucet in a common patio, or the families share a meter but each has a faucet in the home. Finally, there is private home service, wherein each home has its own meter and its own faucet (or multiple faucets).[2] Each level up of service implies greater amounts of water available per person, greater control over water use, more flexibility in the use of water, and a positive impact on household work, hygiene, and health.

In the urban context water is sold to most consumers. Water is a wage good; people must work in order to pay for it. In fact, because water is a fundamental necessity of life, water can be considered a pillar of the capitalist system: the transformation of water into a commodity forces people to work in order to insure their very survival. The price of water and of different levels of water service determines the nature of survival. For impoverished families the price does not permit them to meet their needs—they survive, but live in unhygienic conditions. Paradoxically, poor urban residents in Latin America with the worst water service often pay up to ten times more for their water than wealthy families with the best water services.[3] Thus, the price of water can undermine the family budget, while insufficient quantity and a low level of service undermines health. In addition, as water services are upgraded in low-income neighborhoods, residents must pay for the new infrastructure, often over long periods of time.

That water is a commodity with a price also creates a source of income for some of the low-income population. Some poor urban residents living in neighborhoods that do not have piped water service invest in building storage tanks to hold water, which they can sell to their neighbors at higher than purchase price when their neighbors have run out of water. Second, it is common for water truck drivers, who are poorly paid, to demand a tip before pouring water from the truck into the storage barrels of families with no direct water supply. Commonly, the tip per barrel of water is as much as ten times greater than the cost of the same amount of water coming from an in-house faucet connected directly to a city's pipelines (White 1978: 107). The families who need water are forced either to pay the tip or remain without water.

Industrial Water Use

Water in the production process is part of constant capital. Water can be a raw material for production or it can be an auxiliary substance. As an auxiliary substance for production, water may temporarily lose its usefulness in the production process. For instance, water used in cooling must not exceed a certain temperature. As it is used its temperature rises, it temporarily loses its suitability as a cooling agent, and some of it evaporates (Kollar and Brewer 1975). Similarly, when water is used to wash minerals, it eventually becomes too saturated with waste matter to serve as a cleaning agent.

Water is also used as a raw material for production. During the production process water is transformed along with other raw materials into a finished product. Water loses its initial form in the production process but may reappear in the properties of the final product, as is the case with sodas, juices, and beer.

Just as for residential water use, the qualities of water are the first determinant of the usefulness of water for industry. The particular qualities of water that are needed depend on water's role in production. When water is used in cooling, the significant quality is temperature. When water is a raw material, as in the beverage industry, then potability is important. Industry must ensure the quality of water before it enters the production process. However, the quality of water as it exits the production process is also critical, although often neglected by industry, especially in the Third World. Water that is heated through use as a cooling agent may be dumped back into rivers where plant and fish life become threatened or die in the altered environment. Water used as a cleaning agent may carry chemicals or other destructive substances into the outside environment when it exits the factory (CEPAL 1980).

Industry generally ignores the public health implications of residential water service discussed above. Although industry depends on a steady supply of healthy workers, its efforts to assure or protect their health are limited. Sometimes industries in Latin America build neighborhoods for their workers and try to provide a minimum standard of living, including water service. This, however, is less and less common. Decades ago, in Monterrey, Mexico, for example, some industrialists built working-class neighborhoods right next to their factories and connected the neighborhoods to the private factory water supply. In the 1980s, when it became popularly known that the same factories had water around the clock while nearby neighborhoods had water only a few hours a day, the factory opened its gates every afternoon so housewives with buckets could collect water from its garden faucets.

The quantity of water used in production varies with its role in the production process and with its price. Modern systems of production, which usually operate twenty-four hours a day, require a reliable and continuous supply of water. Since water is part of constant capital, its cost is important: as constant costs decrease, profits increase. Most industries that use water as an auxiliary substance in production have a number of different technologies available using differing amounts of water. When the price of water rises too high, industries may switch to more water-efficient production technology. If water is abundant and the price is low, then industry can use technologies that employ greater amounts of water.

The Production of Water for the City

Water is one of several public services that fall under the rubric of collective consumption (Castells 1979; Jaramillo 1988a). The means of collective consumption are services that are considered essential for capitalism, such as water, health care, education, and highways. Although these services are consumed individually, they are provided collectively. Thus, a school is built for a neighborhood, not for one family. A highway is built for all drivers, not for any particular vehicle owner. A water system is built for an entire section of the city and expanded neighborhood by neighborhood, not house by house. The means of collective consumption require large initial investments in infrastructure. In modern capitalist economies, the responsibility for providing the means of collective consumption has fallen to the state, for three reasons. The first is that it takes a long time to make a profit on the initial investment in infrastructure, if a profit is ever made, which has eliminated the appeal of such investments for the private sector.[4] The second reason is that some public services, such as water and sewerage systems, are provided more efficiently by one central administrative bureaucracy than by a number of competing firms.[5] Finally, under the ideology of the welfare state, the means of collective consumption have come to be considered fundamental human rights (Coing 1991: 16), with the state as the guarantor of the provision of those services.

While large water infrastructure projects represent a sizeable investment for the government, they provide returns to investment that are both monetary (through tariffs) and nonmonetary in nature. Governments often use infrastructure projects to obtain popular support and to legitimate themselves (Ward 1986: 3). For example, water services may be extended into an urban neighborhood when a grassroots movement is forming there, as a method of co-opting the movement. The government's investment may preempt the grassroots movement, if one of its objectives was to improve water service to the neighborhood. Residents who see the government providing a badly needed service may feel renewed loyalty to the government and increased hesitation about participating in the grassroots movement. Or the government may actually require neighborhood residents to join, participate with, support, or vote for the ruling regime in exchange for providing needed infrastructure.

Another source of leverage for the government is the decision to upgrade water services in low-income neighborhoods. Poor urban neighborhoods usually go through different stages of water service. They may start with water truck service. Eventually, public standposts are installed. Later, the number of public standposts may be increased. Finally, but not always, each house may receive individual faucets. At each stage of the process families pay for the improvements, and specialized construction companies are awarded contracts to do the work.[6] Each level of improvement in the water service can be used as a bargaining chip by the government. This would not be possible if the best service were installed right away. With each upgrade the government demonstrates anew its commitment to the social welfare of the urban poor and can derive the benefits described above.

Water services provide the government with ongoing mechanisms of social control. Once water infrastructure is built, the government water authority can control the flow of water into specific neighborhoods. Having a pipeline does not necessarily mean having water. Under conditions of water scarcity, the government can actually decide which neighborhoods will get water when. By opening and closing pipeline valves, the water authority can direct water to certain neighborhoods and away from others. While this is usually a technical decision it can also be a political one—more water being allocated to wealthier neighborhoods, to less militant ones, or even to more militant ones as a form of co-optation.

Water rates also can be used as a means of social control. For example, an increase in tariffs greater than the yearly increase in wage levels constitutes a net transfer of income from the working class to the government.[7] In the case of a heavily industrialized city, if water tariffs are not scaled to reflect type of usage (residential, commercial, government, or industry), then the government is effectively subsidizing not only residential but commercial and industrial water use as well. However, while water rates are so low as to be insignificant in proportion to the incomes of the dominant classes in Latin American cities, for low-income families who constitute the urban majority the cost of water, even when subsidized by the government, is a significant part of household expenses.

The analysis of water as a commodity has direct implications for empirical research because it indicates which groups are likely to be involved in conflicts over urban water services when such services are inadequate. Different sectors within the urban setting have different relationships with the water system. City residents need water for survival and health. Industry needs water for the production process. Governments are responsible for providing, distributing, and regulating urban water services. Under conditions of scarcity, water is not only a commodity needed by different groups in society, it is also a commodity whose distribution reflects social dynamics and political processes.[8] Thus the varying quality of water infrastructure in different neighborhoods in Latin American cities may be due to technical issues, but it may also be a reflection of class biases in the planning bureaucracy or may reflect the varying abilities of different neighborhoods to have their voices heard by the planning bureaucracy. Similarly, the existence of unlicensed, unmetered, private wells owned by large industries in direct defiance of national laws raises questions about the relationship between industrialists and the government.

Given the inadequate water services of many Latin American cities, residential and productive water needs come into competition, and the government must manage competing claims for water. In doing so, the government juggles more than one goal: it must provide sufficient water services to insure a minimum health level for the population, while adequately supplying the process of production. When there is insufficient water to meet both goals then the government has to balance the needs of the population against the needs of the private sector. This balancing act can be very complex when both groups use the government as the terrain for their competing claims for water. Each decision about water supply and distribution comes to have political meaning as it either reflects or creates new power relations within sectors of civil society or between civil society and government. The analysis thus far suggests that the study of water problems in Latin American cities should begin by looking at residential water service, industrial water use, and government policy, planning, and investment for the urban water sector.

PLANNING URBAN PUBLIC SERVICES IN LATIN AMERICA

Public service deficiencies in Third World cities are of a scale previously unknown to mankind because city populations are so much larger, the sheer numbers of urban poor so much greater, and city budgets proportionately smaller than in the cities of the advanced nations at any time during their urban development. There is a vast literature on planning that intersects with a limited literature on the politics of public service provision in the United States and Great Britain, but planning public services in Latin America (or Asia or Africa) is significantly different than in advanced industrialized nations. Little has been written about the process of public service provision in Latin America.

Planning itself can have different objectives. One objective is social reform. Social reformers perceive the capitalist system to have engendered inequalities, and they use policy making and planning as tools for perfecting society through incremental change (Friedmann 1987: 87–136). Another objective stems from defining social ills as technical problems; policy making and planning can then focus on finding "optimal solutions" to technical puzzles. Such an approach, called policy analysis by Friedmann (137–80), is geared to providing solutions to fine-tune the workings of the market as the supreme allocator of resources. Both of these planning traditions have in common that they do not challenge the structure of society, even though social reformers admit that the social system itself is the cause of the problems they seek to solve. No matter how serious social problems may be, these traditions of planning assume that they can be resolved by planning within the existing socio-political-economic structure. Both traditions fit into the general category of top-down planning, whereby policies and plans are decided by bureaucrats and politicians on behalf of the population in general.[9]

The approaches to planning described above can also be termed state centered. In state-centered models, policy choices stem from "the perceptions and interactions of policy elites and from the broad orientation of the state more generally" (Grindle and Thomas 1991: 20). For example, Heclo (1974) posits that social change comes from bureaucracies learning and evolving over time. State-centered models can be contrasted with society-centered models, which posit that policy elites do not act autonomously but rather choose policies that reflect "relations of power among individuals, groups, or classes in society" (Grindle and Thomas 1991: 19). Grindle and Thomas suggest that a merging of the state-centered and society-centered explanations comes closest to explaining what policy making is all about. While policy choices are in fact the result of decisions made within the state bureaucracy, policy makers are indeed influenced by relations of power among groups in society. While policy analysis, as analyzed by Grindle and Thomas (1991), is a tradition of planning with a more profound understanding of the links between state and society than Friedmann (1987) suggests, it is still a tradition rooted in perfecting the structure of society rather than challenging it.

Much of the literature on public service provision fits into the tradition of planning as social reform or as policy analysis. In this literature (see, for example, Linn 1983), the public sector is expected to have primary responsibility for planning urban services. Economies of scale, externalities such as the public health impacts of inadequate water and sewerage service, and the potential for monopolies if urban services were in the hands of the private sector are the most common reasons for assigning provision of urban services to the public sector. Bridging the social reform and the policy analysis traditions, Linn (1983) acknowledges the inequality of public service provision across income groups and suggests technical solutions within a framework of social reform. Appropriate technology should be used to provide service to the poor commensurate with their ability to pay for the installation of infrastructure. As their lot improves, poor urban neighborhoods can upgrade to better levels of service. This approach characterized World Bank projects in the Third World during the late 1970s and the 1980s.

While such policies appear to redress social inequities by envisioning a stepwise progression of service levels, with the urban poor gradually but inevitably reaching middle-class living standards, actual conditions do not follow this logic. While some among the urban poor have improved their living standards, many have not. For structural reasons (employment, wages, inflation, rural outmigration, population growth, and so on), the ranks of the urban poor keep growing, as does the number of households with only baseline infrastructure (collective faucets, no sewerage service, unpaved streets, and so on). Unless the structural causes of urban poverty are addressed, the steps envisioned in reformist policies such as those recommended by Linn will not take place. In addition, neither the public health dangers nor the negative consequences of monopolies have been avoided by the public sector provision of water and sewerage services.

In a radical departure from conventional theories of planning, Friedmann (1987: 225–316) pursues the idea of planning as a challenge to the social system. A fundamental contradiction of the capitalist system is that it is characterized by the unprecedented creation of wealth with the simultaneous creation of growing socioeconomic disparities. Under such circumstances, reforms to the system are useless. Reforms can only lead to an endless chain of more reforms because they do not address the real cause of social problems: the social system itself. Friedmann suggests that individuals and groups who seek to transform society should be called planners. He therefore posits another planning tradition, called social mobilization, whose objective is social transformation. In this tradition, planning occurs from below, as a form of politics, when disfavored groups in society mobilize to obtain social goods that the state on its own would not provide.

Annis and Hakim (1988) and Hirschman (1984) provide examples from across Latin America of grassroots organizing that has circumvented traditional planning bureaucracies and resulted in lasting improvements and stronger autonomous organizations among the poor. Annis and Hakim (210) observe that small-scale grassroots organizations that initially operated only at the local level are forming regional and national networks by sector (rural versus urban, coffee growers, cotton growers, et cetera). These networks of grassroots organizations have connected with the official public sector and with nongovernmental organizations and both influence and are influenced by policies formed at the national level. Pinch (1985) places social mobilizing at the center of planning and suggests that the public sector has assumed responsibility for certain urban services not for technical reasons but to meet social demands. And Castells (1980: 322) concludes that the "mere existence of a crisis situation in the urban system does not necessarily trigger off the intervention of the planner: it must be expressed socially at first, then it is transcribed into the terms of the political apparatus."

Case studies on the provision of urban services in Latin American cities indicate that even when planning occurs in government bureaucracies that have a top-down approach (reformist and technology oriented), planning decisions for certain services occur in a context of social mobilization and pressure. Gilbert and Ward (1985), in their studies of Bogotá, Valencia, and Mexico City, show that government involvement in public service provision can take different forms. The government can own the service outright, it can provide subsidies to a privately owned service, and it can regulate the service. The form of government involvement can be different for different services within the same city, and can vary from city to city, even within the same country. For example, Ward's research (1986: 87–101) on water and electricity provision for Mexico City concludes that, while electricity provision is governed primarily by technical criteria, the provision of water and sewerage services is more prone to be affected by political influences. All the electrical service to the Valley of Mexico is provided and managed by a single government agency. Most of the employees of this agency have permanent jobs and are not affected by the widespread changes in government employment that accompany each new president every six years. Consequently they are less vulnerable to outside manipulation by either consumers or politicians.

On the other hand, water provision for the Valley of Mexico is carried out by a number of government agencies. Certain agencies work on increasing total water supply for the city as a whole, while others manage the supply and distribution of water to individual consumers (commercial, industrial, public, and residential users) within the city. The agencies in charge of water distribution are "more open to partisan political influence," particularly in the distribution of water to poor residential consumers (Ward 1986: 91).

> Whether they are serviced depends on the political priority given to satisfying their needs and the pressures that local groups exert on the government. The agency continues to act in a technically responsible way, but political rationality becomes more influential. In the case of water supply politicians influence the priorities much more than in the case of electricity. (Ward 1986: 93)

Under President Echeverría, from 1971 to 1976, the political influences observed by Ward took the form of patron-client links between the government and the urban poor population. The poor urban communities that were the best organized and had the strongest ties to the government received water service; but usually the services they received were partial at best, either the installation of a collective faucet or the delivery of water by a water truck. After 1977, under President López Portillo, many of the city's public services were decentralized, so that local city districts (the *delegaciones*) became wholly responsible for activities previously managed by the mayor's office. Each neighborhood that wanted to negotiate services with its district office was obligated to do so through representatives elected to a local neighborhood association (the *junta de vecinos*). The creation of a formal institutional structure for government-resident relations increased the control of each district over its residents while decreasing the responsibility of Mexico City's mayor (Ward 1986: 99). Ward concludes that, although the water system is run efficiently for business, commerce, and upper- and middle-income groups, service for the lower-income groups depends on a combination of community mobilization and government commitment to provide service (106).

Watson's (1992) study of water and sanitation service provision in São Paulo, Brazil, illustrates how social mobilization can produce changes in policy, investment, and infrastructure construction by reshaping relations of power between and within different government agencies. Watson (10–11) identifies three forces that came together to create significant changes in water policy for the poorest neighborhoods in São Paulo. The first was user pressure through neighborhood mobilizations. The second was indirect pressure on the water and sewerage authority from outside agencies and politicians. The third was pressure from within the water and sewerage authority by subgroups who wanted to develop unorthodox infrastructure programs for poor urban neighborhoods.

> In sum, community mobilizations were crucial in getting water and sewer services in irregular settlements, but were not sufficient to bring about institutional learning within [the water authority]. Rather, pressure from community mobilizations was channeled through the more receptive municipal agencies . . . and through elected officials—two mayors and the state governor—that in turn put pressure on [the water authority] to improve service delivery. (Watson 1992: 88)

The research in São Paulo also underscores the importance of the larger political context to policy formulation and implementation. While municipal authorities responded favorably to community mobilization in the 1980s, at a different time in Brazilian history or in other Latin American countries similar mobilizations could have been met with violent repression. During the period of political liberalization in Brazil, poor urban residents understood that there was an opening to get basic needs met as well as to contribute to social transformation through citizen mobilization (Watson 1992: 88). This is made particularly clear by Alvarez (1990), who demonstrates the contribution of local women's movements across Brazil to shaping that country's transition to democracy.

A theory of urban public service provision, then, must draw from the social reform and policy analysis traditions as well as from the social mobilization approach. As long as governments hold primary responsibility for the construction and management of public service infrastructure, then key investment decisions will be made or influenced by government policymakers and planners. At the same time, investment decisions occur within political and financial contexts that influence and permit particular choices to be made. Elite groups within civil society (such as industrialists, bankers, and land developers), important politicians, key technical personnel in government bureaucracies, and organized groups of urban residents may all have voices that contribute to shaping government policy and investment for public sector infrastructure. An understanding of the dynamics of public service provision for a given city is achieved by exploring the voices and relations of power of actors in government and civil society. Planning occurs from above and from below. Planning from below through social mobilization can lead to the resolution of sectoral problems (such as water services or health care), and it can become a form of politics leading to social transformation.

The next four chapters examine the role of regional elites, government planners, and the urban poor in the development and resolution of a major water crisis in Monterrey, Mexico. In Monterrey, planning new water services was rarely, if ever, a purely technical exercise. Despite government control over policy implementation through the centralization of budgeting and planning, the relationship between the Monterrey elite and the government worked to obstruct the necessary expansion of water service infrastructure. Massive new infrastructure projects were authorized by the government only after citywide social mobilizations by the urban poor that lasted several years, and after a significant change in the relationship between the government and the regional elite.

3 BUILDUP OF A CRISIS
The Evolution of Monterrey's
Water Service, 1909–1985

INTRODUCTION

WATER availability has been a necessary condition for the emergence of cities since the first communities appeared on this planet. No town or city of any significance, either present or past, could survive without access to water, be it from a river, a lake, an oasis in the desert, or an underground aquifer (Mumford 1961; Jones 1966). Typically, at the moment of initial settlement, the source of water appears to be bountiful. Over the decades, as the course of history shapes regions, towns may grow into major metropolises. The transition from settlement to town to city takes on a life of its own, responding more to market forces than to those of ecology. Whether there is enough water to sustain population growth, or whether air currents can clear away pollution, are questions left unanswered in periods of rapid economic growth. By the late twentieth century, many megacities were wedged into inappropriate ecological settings. Mexico City sprawls out in a valley surrounded by mountains that impede the air flows necessary to combat air pollution. Monterrey, the second largest industrial center in Mexico and the third largest population center, lies in a semiarid zone lacking the basic regional water resources needed to sustain the economic and population expansion of the city.

Most large Latin American cities have inadequate water infrastructure and do not provide home water service to all their residents. In Buenos Aires, half the population was not connected to the municipal water system in 1980 (Braunstein 1985: 20). About one-quarter of the population of Belo Horizonte, Brazil (total population of 2.4 million), was not connected to piped water in 1979 (Penfold 1979: 10). Monterrey, however, stands out as the only major industrial city in Latin America to have its water service permanently rationed to less than twelve hours of service per day. Monterrey's water problems are only partly linked to natural causes—the city is located in a semiarid zone with periodic multiyear droughts. More critical to the analysis in this book, the expansion of the city's water infrastructure throughout the first three-quarters of this century was inadequate, the result of a set of structural problems within the system set up for planning and implementing water infrastructure projects.

THE ORIGIN OF STATE INVOLVEMENT IN MONTERREY'S WATER SECTOR

Until the early 1900s the people of Monterrey used water from nearby streams and rivers, or from wells on their own or neighboring property. There was no municipal water system whatsoever. However, the growth of the city required a more organized and efficient method of assuring a constant water supply for its industries as well as for its population. In 1896 the state government of Nuevo León contracted with J. A. Robertson of the United States to build a dam west of Monterrey and develop a water distribution system for the city. Robertson was never able to begin the project and returned the concession to the state in 1901. The first waterworks were finally built between 1905 and 1909 by MacKenzie, Mann, and Company of Toronto, Canada (the same firm that owned and operated the Monterrey Power, Light, and Public Transportation Company). The original system was planned to serve an eventual population of up to 200,000 (the 1910 population was 86,294) allowing for an average daily per capita consumption of 200 liters per day (lpd) (Servicios 1973: 2).[1] For the first twenty years of its existence the municipal water service of Monterrey was the best in Mexico. In fact, all the original pipes, tanks, and other installations were still functioning seventy-five years later.

During the thirty years after the construction of the original waterworks the foreign-owned water company failed to increase its service in proportion to the city's growth. Instead, it limited new construction to areas of the city that for geographic and economic reasons would permit the rapid recuperation of investment. In addition, many of the new extensions of the distribution network did not adhere to the norms and regulations developed by the company itself for its original distribution system. For example, smaller pipes made out of galvanized iron were used instead of cast iron, limiting the lifetime of the new extensions (Servicios 1973: 5).

By 1940 the population of Monterrey had risen to 212,000 inhabitants. The original waterworks plan had called for 200 liters per day per person, but by 1940 the waterworks were supplying only 164 liters per day per person.[2] In addition, while the city's population grew 146 percent from 1909 to 1949, the water distribution system had increased only 64 percent—from 110 kilometers of pipeline to 180 kilometers (Saldaña 1965). Even worse, a 1949 study demonstrated that the city's water needs had changed since the original per capita needs were calculated in 1909. With the increase in industrial and commercial activity, Monterrey really needed 450 lpd per capita, not the 200 lpd fixed in 1909 ("Anteproyecto" 1949: 4). Using this new criterion, the city's real supply of water in 1940 was only 37 percent of what was needed.

Thus, it is not surprising to see in a 1946 chamber of commerce report that only 50 percent of Monterrey's inhabitants received potable water from the municipal system (Cámara Nacional de Comercio de Monterrey 1946: 3, 12). In addition, many industries in Monterrey had bypassed the municipal water system by building their own water facilities consisting of deep wells and distribution networks. Some industries developed their water systems before the Monterrey Water and Sewerage Company existed. Others built their systems after 1909, either to increase autonomy over their water supply or because the water company did not extend pipelines into their area. By 1940, neither the city's inhabitants nor its industries were adequately served by the water company.

In the early 1940s the state government of Nuevo León confronted the water company over its failure to meet its contractual obligations.[3] Article 8 of the contract signed by the two parties in 1904 stated that once the original waterworks were completed the company was required to build further works as necessary to extend the water distribution system to all inhabited areas of Monterrey.[4] In Article 30 the state government guaranteed a minimum yearly income to the water company for ninety-nine years, consisting of 10 percent of its accumulated investment. If the yearly income of the water company fell below 10 percent of its accumulated investment, the state government had to make up the difference. On the other hand, any income above that 10 percent was to be shared equally with the government. Article 30 applied even if a deficit was caused by water shortages or other uncontrollable events. The water company was in charge of keeping the books and turning the accounts over to the state government every six months.

Effective private ownership of a city's water service depends on adequate government regulations enforced through a binding contract. The contract between the water company and the state government was expected to assure efficient water and sewerage service for the city from 1909 to 2008. However, the government had neglected to include in the contract effective sanctions against the water company in case it failed to build the waterworks needed to extend the system. As the city grew and the company did not extend the system sufficiently, the government could do little more than urge the company to meet its obligations.

At the same time that the water company was negligent about extending the water and sewerage system, it was fraudulent in its bookkeeping. Since the contract also failed to establish the accounting method used to determine the total investment by the water company, the two parties had not been able to agree on what that total was. When the water company made more per year than 10 percent of accumulated investment, it adjusted its books so that they showed a deficit. Then it asked the government to fulfill Article 30 by paying the guaranteed 10 percent of total accumulated investment, using the figure calculated by the water company, which was often highly inflated.

In 1921, 1928, and 1936 the government set up commissions to resolve the conflict, but to no avail. From 1909 to 1944 the two parties were unable to come to agreement either on how much the government owed the water company to compensate its alleged inadequate income, or on how much the company owed the government due to higher income. By 1944 the company claimed that it was owed thirty million pesos ($6,185,567 in 1944 U.S. dollars) compensation by the government, and the government claimed it was owed more than two million pesos ($412,371 in 1944 U.S. dollars) of unpaid back profits by the water company.

In 1943 the government set up a fourth commission, which fixed total investment by the water company at 7,347,027 pesos. Since the company's income up to November 1943 was already 1,527,197 pesos, or more than 20 percent of its accumulated investment, the commission intervened to confiscate further earnings until a settlement could be reached. According to Articles 39, 41, 42, and 44 of the contract, the state government was responsible for bill collection, but the collector was to turn in the payments daily to the water company. In its action of November 1943 the government broke the contract by ordering that the bill payments be deposited in the general treasury of the state of Nuevo León instead of at the water company.

The water company responded by filing an injunction against the state government in early 1944, claiming that the government was dispossessing it of its rightful earnings. A prolonged legal battle ensued, reaching the Supreme Court of Mexico, which ruled in favor of the state government. At that point the relationship between the water company and the state government broke down completely, and the state began negotiating the purchase of the water company.

1945–1960: The Creation of the Potable Water Commission and the Water and Sewerage Service

In 1945 the state government of Nuevo León bought the water company from its Canadian owners for 8,270,000 pesos ($1,705,154 in 1945 U.S. dollars), using a loan from Nacional Financiera, the federal government's development bank (Torres López and Santoscoy 1985: 80). From 1945 to 1956 the daily financial and administrative business of water services for Monterrey was managed by the trust department of the Banco Mercantil de Monterrey. However, "the good intentions leading to the nationalization of the water company did not see the light of day due to the deficient functioning of the new administration" (Servicios 1981: 18). A bank was not the appropriate manager for a municipal water system.

In the late forties and early fifties the city suffered a severe drought. As a result, the water level of the aquifer under the dry Santa Catarina River (which cuts Monterrey in half) declined sharply. One of the two major sources of water for the city was put out of operation—the San Jerónimo infiltration gallery, located to the west of the city under the dry riverbed. Monterrey was left with only the lesser source—the La Estanzuela infiltration gallery, to the south, which produced a minimal 30 liters per second (lps). As an emergency measure the state government decided to drill surface wells within the city itself. In 1948, water rationing was imposed for the first time in the history of the city. In 1950 the Secretary of Hydraulic Resources (SRH) began construction of an infiltration gallery at La Huasteca, which in 1954 began supplying about 770 lps to the city.

By the early 1950s the population of Monterrey had risen to 450,000 inhabitants, and the real supply of water was only 43 percent of the amount recommended per capita in 1949.[5] Only 55 percent of the population was being served by the municipal water system. A historical overview of that period says:

> In the early 1950s there was a sense of discouragement in Monterrey provoked by the suffering due to the tremendous water shortages of the past years. The population, interested in the progress of the city, asked itself whether there was enough water in its sterile surroundings to meet the city's needs. Or would they have to resign themselves to face enormous investments in order to bring water from far away, occasioning excessively high water rates? (Servicios 1981: 25)

By 1954, the city was living through the worst water crisis in its history (Elizondo 1977: 78). The view back into the early 1950s indicates that Monterrey had serious infrastructure bottlenecks even before its period of rapid population growth and industrial expansion. Thus, the infrastructure problems of today's Third World cities not only accompany development as population, commerce, and industry grow faster than the public service infrastructure does, but these problems may actually precede the period of rapid development.

The water crisis in Monterrey had the potential to severely limit the city's industrial growth as well as to discourage migration from other states.[6] At the same time, the type of comprehensive planning necessary to overcome the water crisis was not taking place. The trust department of the Banco Mercantil de Monterrey had not been mandated to carry out the studies necessary to expand the city's water system. On the other hand, neither the city nor the state government maintained public works offices dedicated solely to hydraulic infrastructure planning. Finally, in 1954, the president of Mexico decreed the creation of the Comisión de Agua Potable de Monterrey (CAPM, the Potable Water Commission of Monterrey). The Commission was mandated to have exclusive responsibility for the technical and financial planning necessary to improve the supply and distribution of water for the city of Monterrey. It was governed by a board of directors composed of five government representatives (one each from the Nuevo León state government, the Monterrey city administration, the Banco Nacional Hipotecario Urbano y de Obras Públicas, S.A., the Secretary of Hydraulic Resources, and the Secretary of Health and Welfare), three representatives from the private sector of Monterrey (one each from the chamber of commerce of Monterrey, the chamber of industry of Monterrey, and the chamber of real estate of Monterrey), and one representative of the residents of Monterrey (a purely token position, as this member of the board was appointed directly by the state governor).[7]

Throughout the 1950s Monterrey suffered from a severe deficit in the supply of water. From its inception the Commission was running to catch up. The first problem was the lack of detailed information necessary for effective planning. Initially then, the Commission moved ahead with several smaller projects while carrying out the studies needed to plan larger waterworks. The smaller projects could be completed while a larger one was designed, thus increasing the city's water supply in the interim (Elizondo 1977: 2). It was apparent that water resource development had to take place in as many zones as possible, because no single source was large enough to guarantee the supply of water Monterrey needed. Since the 1950s Monterrey's water had come from four distinct regions: La Huasteca–Buenos Aires, to the west of the city; Villa de Santiago–San Francisco, to the south of the city; Mina, to the north of the city; and from wells within the city limits (see figure 3.1). The first projects designed by

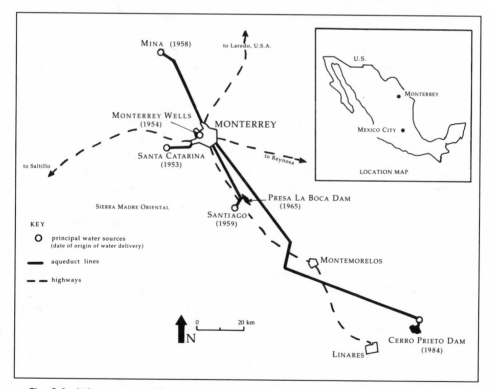

Fig. 3.1. Water sources, Monterrey region

the Commission were a small infiltration gallery in the La Huasteca area, which was completed by the late 1950s, and two infiltration tunnels in the San Francisco area, finished in 1959. Meanwhile, the Secretary of Hydraulic Resources (SRH) began exploratory drilling at Mina, despite the Commission's initial opposition, and was able to add two hundred lps to the city's water supply in 1958 (Hernández Terán 1983: 5).

In 1954, the SRH also began work in the Villa de Santiago area, building a dike to dam water for agricultural purposes. But in 1956, the Commission, together with a consortium of Monterrey industrialists, developed a project to expand the dike into a dam, called Presa La Boca, that would provide water for industrial use. The industrialists in turn would cede some of their wells and springs to the city to add water to its desperately deficient water supply. In 1956, President Ruiz Cortines approved the La Boca project and authorized thirty-five million pesos to build La Boca's sustaining wall. The industrialists, in turn, were to contribute sixty million pesos to build the water treatment plant, the pumping stations, and the aqueduct to bring the water to Monterrey (Torres López and Santoscoy 1985: 105; Comisión de Agua Potable de Monterrey 1981: 8). Due to construction delays, the La Boca dam did not actually come on line until 1965.

While the Commission's responsibilities covered the areas of research and planning, there was still no coordination of the day-to-day running of Monterrey's water system. In 1956, the Commission suggested that a separate agency be set up to take these responsibilities over from the trust department of the Banco Mercantil de Monterrey, and from the various city and state offices that had been involved until then. In May 1956, the governor of Nuevo León signed the bill creating Servicios de Agua y Drenaje de Monterrey (the Monterrey Water and Sewerage Service, called the Water Service from here on) ("Actas," 4-30-1956). The Potable Water Commission would continue to design projects to increase Monterrey's water supply, find financing, and supervise project execution, but once the water reached the city pipelines it would come under the jurisdiction of the Water Service. The Water Service was in charge of water distribution, the maintenance of the city's distribution network, and bill collection.

The Water Service became Monterrey's water authority, and the Commission its research and planning arm. The Commission's budget was approved by, and came from, the Water Service. The Water Service was controlled by a board of directors, with representatives from exactly the same government and civic groups as the Commission's board. Both the Commission and the Water Service were decentralized state agencies,[8] which meant that although they were government agencies they were autonomous and their boards could not be controlled by any other government institution from either the state or federal level. Nevertheless, government control, specifically by the federal level, was achieved through local dependence on federal budget allocations. As long as local public services depended on federal financing of infrastructure, they were limited in their autonomy no matter what their official designation was.

At the time it was created, the Water Service was already in debt to the federal government for forty-two million pesos ($3,360,000 in 1956 U.S. dollars). This debt was the result of the 1945–1956 period, when the city's water system could draw in only 150,000 pesos per year of income, which was insufficient to cover operating costs, let alone to pay for the small projects that were being carried out to try to contain the water crisis.[9] In a show of good faith, President Ruiz Cortines authorized the federal government to absorb thirty-six million pesos ($2,880,000 in 1956 U.S. dollars) of the Water Service's debt, leaving it with six million owed to BANHUOPSA (Banco Nacional Hipotecario Urbano y de Obras Públicas, S.A., the federal public works development bank) for construction of the aqueduct from La Huasteca to Monterrey. At the same time, he authorized a new sixty-one-million-peso BANHUOPSA loan to be used for the two water tunnel projects in the San Francisco region and for expanding the distribution system within the city (see table 3.1) (Torres López and Santoscoy 1985: 106).

Throughout the 1950s, water was rationed in Monterrey all year round (Comisión 1976b: 6). In the midfifties the gap between supply of and demand for water grew larger as the population grew, because the smaller water projects mentioned above did not come on line until 1958–1959. In 1957 the lack of water caused uprisings in one of Monterrey's most populous lower-class neighborhoods. As an emergency measure, the state government borrowed steel pipes from PEMEX, which were laid on top of the ground to bring to Monterrey whatever water was available from the two San Francisco infiltration tunnels as they were being constructed (1981). By 1961, both the Commission and the SRH projects were finished. Between 1950 and 1960 the city's water supply had slightly more than doubled, but its population had almost doubled as well, and its industrial

TABLE 3.1
Construction for Water Supply, Monterrey, 1954–1960

Year	Region	Projects	Cost (pesos)	lps Gained
1954–56	Santa Catarina	Infiltration Gallery (Morteros), pipelines, 2.8 km.	4,650,000	250
1954–60	Villa de Santiago	2 infiltration tunnels, Parshall meter, aqueduct, 37.8 km.	62,260,000	850
1956[a]	all	President Ruiz Cortines authorizes absorption of Water Service debt	36,000,000	na
1954–58	Mina	4 deep wells, pumping and electrical equipment, aqueduct, 40.6 km.	53,631,063	420
1954–60	Metropolitan Area	storage tanks (43,000 M³ capacity), pipelines, 82.2 km.	31,040,000[b]	na

Source: Leobardo Elizondo, "Comisión de Agua Potable de Monterrey: abastecimiento de agua potable" (Monterrey: Comisión de Agua Potable, 1977), cuadros 22–24 (after p. 93), anexos a-8-d, a-8-e.

[a]The source for this data is Enrique Torres López and Mario A. Santoscoy, *La historia del agua en Monterrey desde 1577 hasta 1985* (Monterrey: Ediciones Castillo, 1985), 106.
[b]For example, this was the equivalent of roughly $2.5 million U.S., averaging the exchange rates for the 1954–1960 period.

na = not applicable

and commercial base had expanded. There was slightly more water per person in 1960 than in 1950, but still only 55.9 percent of the population was being served by the municipal water system.[10]

1961–1967: THE GRUPO MONTERREY CONSOLIDATES ITS CONTROL OVER MONTERREY'S WATER SERVICES

The 1960s were characterized by high population growth and insignificant spending on Monterrey's water infrastructure. The city's population had grown at an average rate of 6.5 percent during the 1950s and it continued to grow by an average of 5.4 percent a year in the 1960s. The rate of growth of Monterrey's population was higher than for any other city in Mexico. The industrial base of the city continued to grow as well, so that by the mid-1960s there were 4,525 industries registered in Monterrey (Torres López and Santoscoy 1985: 110). This growth continuously put more pressure on the city's already inadequate water system. In mid-1960 BANHUOPSA approved a forty-one-million-peso loan ($3,280,000 in 1960 U.S. dollars) requested by the Commission for water infrastructure expansion. However, for the next nine months, a stream of obstacles arose to impede the disbursement of the loan ("Actas," 6-20-1960 to 7-24-1961). President López Mateos refused a request from the Commission to grant a 30 percent subsidy of the loan ("Actas," 3-22-1960). The Secretary of Hydraulic Resources also refused to grant a subsidy, stating that its budget had been reduced ("Actas," 4-4-1960). The state governor of Nuevo León required that the Commission rewrite the loan proposal so that all infrastructure projects would be finished by the end of his term in 1961 ("Actas," 8-15-1960). These financial problems may have been the beginning of a power struggle between the Commission and the federal government that lasted until 1977 (*El Porvenir*, 2-7-1983).

Finally, in March 1961, the Banco Hipotecario disbursed a five-million-peso loan ($400,000 in 1961 U.S. dollars)—barely enough to keep the Commission going. That was supplemented by another 3.5 million from the SRH in July 1961—also the product of much negotiation. By 1961, the Water Service's debt to BANHUOPSA had risen to 85 million pesos ($6,800,000 in 1961 U.S. dollars), a factor often cited by the latter as an impediment to further loans. The result was that in 1960 and 1961 there was no construction of water infrastructure of any kind for Monterrey ("Actas," 10-30-1961). In 1961, the board members of the Commission began discussing the possibility of converting the La Boca dam from a source of untreated water for industrial use to a source of potable water for the city system.

In 1962, the Banco Hipotecario's reluctance to lend to the Commission continued (Comisión 1981: 18). As a result, only two small projects were completed in 1962–1963: the extension of the Huasteca infiltration gallery, and the enlarging of one of Monterrey's storage tanks. By 1963, Monterrey was again suffering from a severe shortage of water. The Commission began looking elsewhere for funds and for the first time the Inter-American Development Bank (IDB) was considered as a possible source. In addition, the Commission reached an agreement with the consortium of industries involved in the La Boca dam project to trade the dam water for wastewater from the city system. Consequently, the new state governor, Eduardo Livas Villarreal, was able to obtain a thirty-four-million-peso loan from BANHUOPSA for the construction of a water treatment plant to make the dam's water potable.[11] Nevertheless, by then the water crisis had become chronic; the governor and local industrialists agreed on the need for urgent action. They decided to meet with President López Mateos to explain that the water infrastructure needed for Monterrey was beyond the Commission's and Nuevo León's financial capabilities and to ask for his personal intervention with their funding problems (19).

Apart from the water treatment plant that was under construction using the 1963 BANHUOPSA loan for thirty-four million pesos, no new water infrastructure construction was undertaken in 1964. This suggests that the president did not respond positively to their plea—possibly because he was in the lame-duck phase of his presidential term, which was ending in 1964. At the federal level, the Secretaría de Hacienda y de Crédito Público (SHCP) authorized the Commission to initiate loan negotiations with the Inter-American Development Bank (Comisión 1981: 19).

In 1965 the La Boca water treatment plant was completed, which meant that some water from the dam could be sent to Monterrey. However, once again, no new projects were undertaken by either the Commission or the SRH, and no funding was authorized for water projects in Monterrey. By 1965, the water problems, and the lack of apparent solutions, were perceived as having a potentially negative impact on industrial expansion. Whereas the gross regional product of metropolitan Monterrey had grown at least 10 percent a year from 1955 to 1965, in 1965 a study carried out by the Department of Economics of the Universidad de Nuevo León concluded that further growth would be seriously hampered by the inadequacies of Monterrey's water service (Centro de Investigaciones Económicas 1965: 1).

During President López Mateos's term in office, from 1959 through 1964, Neuvo León received an average of 3.49 percent of total federal public investment in the thirty-two states (including the Federal District). During that period, Nuevo León averaged tenth among the states in federal public investment received. Other states received significantly larger percentages of federal public investment. For example, Veracruz averaged more than twice as much as Nuevo León, Tamaulipas averaged almost twice as much, Sinaloa averaged 50 percent more, and neighboring Coahuila averaged one-third more (Palacios 1989: 165). The level of federal public investment for Nuevo León indicates that even during a phase of government-promoted industrial expansion, the Mexican government did not finance the infrastructure needed for development in a consistent manner in all states with important industrial zones.

The only way that Monterrey's industrial base was able to expand was to bypass the municipal water system. In 1950 the Water Service had 250 industrial contracts. By 1965, after fifteen years of continuous expansion of industry, it had dropped to 118 industrial contracts. As demand for water rose during those years, many industries turned to drilling their own wells (Centro de Investigaciones Económicas 1965: 15–16). The concern of the industrialists was already manifest in 1962, when several who had factories to the west of the city and had drilled their own wells in the Huasteca region approached one of the influential members of the Commission's board of directors, Roberto Garza Sada, to express their concern that continued city exploitation of the Huasteca site would lower the water level in their wells. Garza Sada, himself a leader of Monterrey's industrial oligarchy, brought up the issue at a board meeting of the Commission and suggested that the Commission limit extraction of water from Huasteca ("Actas," 4-30-1962). A pattern was emerging where industrial water needs had higher priority than domestic water needs.[12]

One crucial but unplanned consequence of the continuously inadequate municipal water system in the forties, fifties, and sixties was the development of a dual water system for the city of Monterrey. On the one hand there was the municipal water system, which provided deficient service to residential consumers, to small commercial and industrial concerns, and to government institutions. On the other hand there was the vast, uncontrolled, and unmeasured industrial extraction of water from private wells. Industrial autonomy over its own water supply in Monterrey began in the 1950s and continues to this day in the face of federal legislation opposing it.[13]

In the mid-1960s, Monterrey's private sector elite consolidated its control over the Commission and the Water Service. In 1965, the Commission and the SRH experienced a series of disagreements over future water infrastructure projects for Monterrey. The Secretary of Hydraulic Resources distributed the results of its technical evaluation of the Monterrey region, recommending a group of three dams: the Independencia dam, the Cerro Prieto dam, and the Libertad dam (Hernández Terán 1983: 6).[14] However, in an August 1965 meeting with the state governor, the Commission recommended construction of a different dam, El Cuchillo ("Actas," 8-2-1965). In the fall of 1965, the directors of the Commission and the Water Service met in Mexico with the Secretary of Hydraulic Resources, who proposed building the Las Blancas dam, considered much too small by the Commission (11-8-1965). When a congressman suggested that the Commission work more closely with the SRH, even the SRH representative on the Commission's board protested, explaining that the SRH favored projects that the Commission's technicians had previously studied and rejected (6-21-1965).

Earlier, in August 1965, the secretary of SRH had met with Garza Sada of the Commission's board. According to Garza Sada's report of the meeting, the secretary informed him that the SRH could not help in resolving Monterrey's water problems because the 1954 decree that created the Commission mandated that it have exclusive responsibility for planning Monterrey's water system. Unless the Commission reorganized, forming an executive committee with three representatives designated by the SRH and three representatives from Monterrey's private sector, the SRH would have nothing more to do with Monterrey's water problems ("Actas," 8-26-1965). The secretary's statement referred to a decree that had been in existence for eleven years, during which time the SRH had planned, funded, and constructed water infrastructure for Monterrey. His ultimatum reflected increasing discord between the SRH and the Commission, as well as the decreasing control of the SRH over the Commission's board as the Monterrey oligarchy became more entrenched.[15] Yet the Commission's exclusive rights over planning were useless without the SRH's cooperation, because under federal law the SRH had to approve, finance, and supervise construction of all water infrastructure projects for Monterrey.

While initially the Commission's board paid lip service to the SRH's ultimatum, it never created the requisite six-man executive committee. Instead, in early 1966 it replaced its executive director ("Actas," 1-24-1966). The outgoing executive director had been the SRH representative to the board. The new executive director was the representative from the Monterrey chamber of real estate, Carlos Maldonado. Two months later, the Commission's board created a two-member executive committee to act on important issues in between board meetings (3-4-1966). The new executive committee consisted of the representatives from the Monterrey chambers of real estate and commerce—both members of the Grupo

Monterrey. The Grupo Monterrey had cemented its control over the city's water sector. The conflict between the SRH and the Commission's board as it came to be controlled by Monterrey's private sector elite explains, at least partially, the inadequacy of water infrastructure development in Monterrey during the sixties.[16]

Even as early as 1965, water was a preoccupation among high government officials in the Monterrey region. In September 1965, in his fourth annual report, Governor Livas Villarreal stated that water was the only major problem of Monterrey as yet unresolved (*El Norte*, 9-18-1965). In December 1965, the Banco Hipotecario came through with an emergency loan of twelve million pesos to rehabilitate wells at Mina, where the water level had been dropping steadily since 1959 (as a result of unusually low rainfall from 1959 to 1964). Two exploratory wells were also drilled to the south of the city (Hernández Terán 1983). But that was the end of funding for waterworks under Governor Livas Villarreal, whose term ended in 1967 ("Actas," 12-10-1965).

In August 1966, the SRH submitted a new list of recommendations for the Monterrey area prioritizing a group of dams: the Prudencia dam, the Cerro Prieto dam, and the La Libertad dam ("Actas," 8-29-1966). The Commission disagreed with the SRH's recommendations, claiming that those particular dams would be too costly. In October, the technical staff of the Commission submitted its recommendations: the Salinas dam, a small dam on the San Juan River, a dam on the confluence of the San Fernando and Purificación rivers, and an aqueduct to bring water from the Falcón dam on the Río Grande (10-31-1966). The first two dams were smaller projects suggested by the technical staff to allow time for further study of larger projects. When the board reviewed these recommendations it voiced concern that if the smaller projects were undertaken, the larger ones would be forgotten. In November, Maldonado met with the secretary of SRH. The only agreement that could be reached was to continue studying Monterrey's hydraulic resources. The agreed-upon goal was to find groundwater sources that could provide water quickly while further studies were made of the surface water options, including the dam sites suggested by both the Commission and the SRH (11-28-1966). In September 1966, Governor Livas Villarreal gave his fifth annual report. The section on water services was a virtual repeat of his fourth report: "Only the water problem of Monterrey remains unsolved" (*El Norte*, 9-18-1966). The inability of the SRH and the Commission to reach agreement on a large dam project illustrates the bottlenecks created when funding for large infrastructure projects comes from the federation (or from international lending agencies with federal approval) but project selection requires agreement between federal and local institutions. The conflicting outcomes of the SRH and Commission technical studies prevented the appropriate infrastructure from being built for Monterrey.[17]

Nineteen sixty-seven was the third year of the sixties when absolutely no construction was carried out to improve Monterrey's water services. The SRH began new ground and surface water studies. Meanwhile, in May, the Commission produced yet another set of recommendations: building the Icamole dam, bringing water from the existing Falcón dam on the Río Grande, and extending the distribution system ("Actas," 5-2-1967). In June, Maldonado and the technical director of the Commission met with the PRI's candidate for governor of Nuevo León (elections were to be held in July 1967), and the three concluded that the Falcón project was the best (2-26-1967). Maldonado met with the secretary of the SRH to urge authorization of the Falcón project, and again agreement could not be reached. According to the secretary of the SRH, the Falcón dam was too far away. In addition, taking water from Falcón could create conflicts with the agriculturalists of the lower Río Grande irrigation district. The SRH continued to favor other dam sites closer to Monterrey (8-3-1967). Nevertheless, in his sixth and last annual report, Governor Livas Villarreal announced that the long-term solution to Monterrey's water problems was the Falcón dam—a project that would add five thousand lps to Monterrey's water supply at a cost of 628 million pesos. Without the Falcón project Monterrey's water needs were only secure until 1969—two years away (*El Norte*, 9-18-1967). The Falcón project was never approved by the SRH.

When Governor Livas Villarreal left office in 1967 the population of Monterrey, at 1,022,907, was 1.37 times larger than when he took office in 1961. The total water supply (2,834 lps) was 1.42 times the 1961 supply—implying a parallel growth of the population and the water supply. However, water lost to leaks still consumed at least 20 percent of the total supply, leaving a real supply of water that had not matched population growth.[18] Only 66.8 percent of the population was connected to the city's water system (leaving 340,000 people dependent on standpipes and water trucks), and rationing was enforced throughout the city during the summer months (Elizondo 1977; 69, cuadro 11). Major industry had augmented its independent water supply by 627 lps through the construction of four wastewater treatment plants. Spending for water infrastructure under Governor Livas Villarreal was at most one-third of spending under his predecessor, Governor Rangel Frías (compare table 3.1 with table 3.2). By the end of Livas Villarreal's term, the Commission, seemingly with his support, was in a standoff with the SRH.

1968–1973: THE TRANSITION TO THE CONTEMPORARY PERIOD IN MONTERREY'S WATER HISTORY

The new governor of Nuevo León, Eduardo A. Elizondo, was a tax lawyer and a member of the Grupo Monterrey. Previously the rector of

TABLE 3.2

Construction for Water Supply, Monterrey, 1961–1967

Year	Region	Projects	Cost (pesos)	lps Gained[a]
1961	all	nothing	0	0
1962–63	Santa Catarina	extension, Huasteca Gallery 1.21 km.	6,950,000[b]	670
1962–63	Metropolitan Area	expansion of storage tank	na	0
1964	Santiago	water treatment plant for La Boca dam, aqueduct extension, 4 km.	37,700,000	500
1965	all	nothing	0	0
1966	Mina and Metropolitan Area	rehabilitate wells	9,775,078	215
		drill wells	2,224,922	NA
1967	all	nothing	0	0

Sources: For 1966, Comisión de Agua Potable de Monterrey, "Manual de organización" (Monterrey: 1981), 22; for all years (including 1966), Leobardo Elizondo, "Comisión de Agua Potable de Monterrey: abastecimiento de agua potable" (Monterrey: Comisión de Agua Potable, 1977), cuadros 21–24 (after p. 93), and anexo a-8-d.

[a]Due to supply variations month by month during the year, these figures may not match those given in the text.
[b]For example, this is the equivalent of $556,000 U.S., given the exchange rate of this period.

na = not applicable
NA = not available

the Universidad de Nuevo León, Elizondo had no government experience. Despite having an ally in the Governor's Palace, the Commission continued to be unable to reach an accord with the SRH.

The Commission persisted in recommending the Falcón dam project through 1967 and 1968, despite the fact that in early 1968 the secretary of the SRH insisted that such a project was impossible (now referring to a national policy of moving water only from south to north—the Falcón dam would mean transferring water from north to south). The SRH continued to emphasize groundwater projects, which were closer to Monterrey and less expensive to carry out ("Actas," 10-31-1967, 2-1-1968, 3-4-1968, 5-27-1968). The secretary of the SRH also suggested that if the Commission wanted surface water the SRH could offer ten thousand lps from Presa Las Adjuntas, a new dam that it was building in the neighboring state of Tamaulipas ("Actas," 2-1-1968).

During the first months of 1968 there was a growing sense of desperation at the Commission (evidenced in the written minutes of the meetings of its board of directors) as the board noted that half the term of President Díaz Ordaz had already passed and no projects or funding had been approved for Monterrey ("Actas," 4-29-1968). The board acknowledged that the cause was its disagreements with the SRH (4-1-1968), because President Díaz Ordaz had indicated a willingness to help resolve Monterrey's water problems (3-4-1968).

Finally, in May 1968, agreement was reached on an SRH plan in a meeting between the Commission, Governor Elizondo, and the secretary of SRH. The project proposed to develop sources of groundwater near existing aqueducts: ten deep wells in the Huasteca region, three in Mina, and an extension of one of the water tunnels in the Santiago region. These groundwater projects were to guarantee Monterrey's water supply until 1980, with the ten thousand lps promised from the Las Adjuntas dam to be a backup source in case of emergency ("Actas," 5-27-1968). No new dams were approved. In September of 1968, the Banco Nacional de Obras Públicas (BANOBRAS, the new name for BANHUOPSA) approved funding for the groundwater development projects as well as for the extension of Monterrey's water distribution and sewage systems. Half of the funding for these projects was to come from the Inter-American Development Bank.

For the next year, the Commission worked on designing a master plan for the city's water and sewage systems and on the details of its loans with BANOBRAS and the IDB. The IDB approved its first loan to Monterrey in October 1969, for 12.5 million dollars (or its equivalent in other currencies). The contracts were signed in early 1970, but the first disbursements were not made until November 30, 1970. The IDB had agreed to finance 53.1 percent of the total costs of the SRH-Commission projects (Villatoro et al. 1983: 27). The rest would come from BANOBRAS and from local private banks ("Actas," 3-27-1969).[19]

In 1969, the Commission was able to start the extension of the Santiago tunnel, the drilling of new wells at Huasteca, and the expansion of the distribution system in Monterrey, using the BANOBRAS and local bank loans. Polyethylene pipes, instead of copper, were used to replace worn-out pipes in the city's distribution system and for new house connections. Unfortunately, it was clear by the early seventies that the polyethylene material had been unusually sensitive to careless installation and thus prone to massive leakages.

In early 1969 the secretary of SRH announced that the SRH was going to increase its investment in the Las Adjuntas dam in order to guarantee five thousand lps for the city of Monterrey (*El Norte*, 2-6-1969). Consequently, Governor Elizondo triumphantly announced in his second annual report that "the most fundamental problem of Monterrey—whose solution conditioned development on all levels—has been resolved. A secure source of water has been promised by President Díaz Ordaz, the Las Adjuntas dam" (3-2-1969, 11B). For the rest of 1969 the Las Adjuntas proposal was left untouched, and no mention of it was made in Governor Elizondo's third report in March 1970. Then, in April 1970 President Díaz Ordaz again confirmed that five thousand lps was available for Monterrey from Las Adjuntas and stated that he wanted to sign a contract guaranteeing this water for Monterrey before he left office on November 30 (*El Porvenir*, 4-4-1970). In May 1970, the secretary of SRH also confirmed the Las Adjuntas water for Monterrey (5-28-1970).

It appears, however, that the Las Adjuntas proposal did not exist beyond the realm of political expediency. The state of Nuevo León had traditionally complained that major dams in Tamaulipas were being filled with water from Nuevo León. Promising water from Las Adjuntas in Tamaulipas for Monterrey was a way for the federal government to avoid quarrels and accusations.[20] In 1983 the engineer who had been secretary of the SRH under President Díaz Ordaz referred to the Las Adjuntas proposal in his first public appearance in Monterrey since the 1960s: justifying the fact that no water from Las Adjuntas ever became available for Monterrey, he said that the fault lay with the Commission, which had never requested the water formally in writing (Hernández Terán 1983: 13). Such a weak explanation, given in a public speech fourteen years after the fact, indicates the extent of discord and disrespect that existed between the SRH and the Commission in the late 1960s.

Monterrey entered the 1970s as it had entered the 1950s and 1960s: with a vastly deficient water system. Monterrey's population had more than tripled between 1950 and 1970, while industrial investment multiplied ninefold (Vellinga 1988: 42–43). However, during the 1960s, three years of the decade saw no spending on water infrastructure, four years saw negligible spending, and only two years had moderate spending (see table 3.3). Since 1967 alone, when Governor Elizondo had taken office, the city's population had grown by 17 percent. The water supply had grown by 30 percent, yet the population served had grown by only 6.8 percent, so that in 1970, 71.4 percent of the population was connected to the municipal water system. While the percentage of the population without service decreased, the absolute numbers of people without service increased. In 1960, the 44.1 percent of the Monterrey population who

TABLE 3.3
Spending for Water Infrastructure for the Monterrey Metropolitan Area, 1961–1969

Year	Amount (pesos)
1961	0
1962–1963	6,950,000[a]
1964	37,700,000
1965	0
1966	12,000,000
1967	0
1968	16,600,000
1969	22,870,000

Source: Leobardo Elizondo, "Comisión de Agua Potable de Monterrey: abastecimiento de agua potable" (Monterrey: Comisión de Agua Potable, 1977), cuadro 21 (after p. 93).

Note: Figures include spending for water sources, aqueducts, tanks, distribution systems, and pumping and electrical equipment.

[a]For example, this is the equivalent of $556,000 U.S., given the exchange rate of the 1960s.

were not connected to the municipal water system numbered 313,427 people. In 1970, 28.6 percent were not connected to the municipal water system; however, they numbered 341,761 (Elizondo 1977: 69, cuadro 11).[21]

The significant inadequacy of Monterrey's water system in the early 1970s was not unique in the Third World. Other Latin American cities also had experienced rapid industrial and population growth unmatched by equal growth of infrastructure. International development banks and foundations, including the World Bank, the Inter-American Development Bank, and the Ford Foundation, had working groups studying the water and sewerage problems of Third World cities. What is notable about the case of Monterrey is that two highly qualified technical groups, the SRH and the Commission, had already spent more than fifteen years studying the region's water resources and designing complex water infrastructure, almost none of which had been built. In addition, the federal government was committed to a model of development based on import substitution industrialization, and federal public investment was being channeled to other Mexican states to support their industrialization efforts. Throughout the 1960s and 1970s, despite the size of its industrial sector and its population, and despite its need for infrastructure development, Nuevo León received a disproportionately low share of federal public investment (Scott 1982: 112–15; Secretaría 1980: 151).

In 1970 and 1971 work continued on the SRH groundwater projects, and more water was slowly incorporated into the city's supply. Funds from the IDB loan were used to improve the city's distribution system, with emphasis on the construction of regulating tanks to expand the city's water storage capacity. Meanwhile, problems were developing between Governor Elizondo and the federal government under President Echeverría over a different issue: the university. University students in Monterrey were demanding university autonomy, meaning that the state and federal governments would no longer be involved in university business—they could no longer name rectors, set student quotas, and so forth. The fight for autonomy was raging at the Universidad de Nuevo León. Governor Elizondo presented, and then approved, a law granting autonomy to the Universidad de Nuevo León (Montemayor Hernández 1971: 423–24). However, it was a law designed to stymie true autonomy, and it exacerbated the conflict between Governor Elizondo and the university community (Farías 1992: 125–31). The students accused Governor Elizondo of sabotaging university autonomy by reducing the university's budget, controlling the selection process for the new rector, and dictating the content of the new charter and internal statutes. This ran counter to President Echeverría's support of the university autonomy process (Montemayor Hernández 1971: 424).[22]

In the first few months of 1971, conflicts over university autonomy divided the Monterrey community. The Grupo Monterrey supported Governor Elizondo, while most of the university community was against him, as was a substantial group of government bureaucrats who supported President Echeverría (Montemayor Hernández 1971: 427). The conflicts came to a head when, at one point, there were two rectors and two boards of directors in power simultaneously (426). In June 1971, Elizondo resigned as governor. President Echeverría chose Luis M. Farías, then senator from Nuevo León, to replace Elizondo and complete the term in office that would end in October 1973. Farías's first action was to support the university autonomy movement.

State politics now served to impede progress in Monterrey's water sector. Because he had only two years and four months in office, Farías was not able to do much with the water sector beyond finishing projects designed under Governor Elizondo. By late 1972, the Commission was again voicing the urgent need to find new sources of water ("Actas," 10-3-1972). In 1973, the newspapers began reporting water shortages on the front pages of the local news sections (*El Norte*, 5-29-1973; *El Porvenir*, 4-26-1973). The Monterrey industrialists requested that the government act to prevent water shortages that could constrain industrial development (*El Porvenir*, 6-7-1973). In June 1973, the federal and state governments and the Commission signed an agreement to maintain a minimum reserve of six thousand lps of water for Monterrey. However, nothing ever came of this, and the reserve of water was never created.

In 1972 the Commission discussed the possibility of contracting a team of Israeli water experts to develop a master plan for the Monterrey area ("Actas," 3-7-1972). This came after almost twenty years of studies by both the SRH and the Commission that had not resulted in a master plan that could be agreed upon by the two institutions. In 1973, the Commission, the Water Service, and the SRH signed a new groundwater agreement. Exploration of groundwater potential would be undertaken in a number of areas near Monterrey. The Water Service would pay for the productive wells, while the SRH would absorb the cost of the nonproductive ones (8-7-1973). With increases in Monterrey's water supply rest-ing on this project, Governor Farías ended his term in office in October 1973. At that time, Monterrey's population had climbed to over 1.4 million. The population of Monterrey had grown by 37 percent since Governor Elizondo took office in 1967, while real water supply had increased by 65 percent.[23] Almost 80 percent of the population was connected to the water system, a significant 12 percent increase in the population served since 1970 (Elizondo 1977: 69, and cuadro 11).

The groundwater projects authorized in 1968, funded by BANOBRAS, the Inter-American Development Bank, and local banks, were responsible for these improvements in supply. Without them, Monterrey's water supply would have remained at the 1967 level. Table 3.4 gives a summary of projects, costs, and supply gained from 1968 to 1972. It is, of course, impossible to know how much better off Monterrey might have been in 1973 if the Commission and the SRH had not had a relationship of disagreement and conflict in the 1960s. During the six years from 1967 through 1972, for a state of its importance Nuevo León ranked very low in federal public investment received by the Mexican states. In 1970, Nuevo León was the ninth largest state in terms of population, and fourth in terms of population employed in manufacturing (Scott 1982: 220–22). Yet, in 1967 and 1970 it ranked fifteenth out of thirty-two in federal public investment received; in 1968, thirteenth; in 1969, eleventh, in 1971, eighth; and in 1972, fourteenth (Scott 1982: 112–15; Secretaría 1980: 151).[24] In terms of federal public investment in the social welfare sector, which included urban public service infrastructure, Nuevo León also ranked low, falling to sixteenth place in 1971 and 1972 (Secretaría 1980: 154–55).

In 1973, improvements to the water system notwithstanding, 282,000 people still were not connected to the water system, and many of those who were connected were subject to rationing, at least in the summer months.

1974–1985: CRISIS IN THE WATER SECTOR

In 1973, Pedro Zorrilla Martínez, chosen by President Echeverría, was elected to the governorship of Nuevo León for the usual six-year term. During his tenure in office water shortages in Monterrey became severe. Investment for water infrastructure, which in 1973 was only 5 percent of what was spent in the previous six years combined, peaked in 1974 and declined each year thereafter (see tables 3.5 and 3.6). From 1973 to 1977

TABLE 3.4

Construction for Water Supply, Monterrey, 1968–1972

Year	Region	Projects	Cost (pesos)	lps Gained[a]
1968–72	Santa Catarina	wells, aqueduct 13 km., pumping and electrical equipment	66,929,000[b]	650
1969–71	Metropolitan Area	wells, pumping equipment	21,043,709	230
1969–72	Santiago	extending infiltration tunnel, Cola del Caballo	14,800,000	50
1969–72	Metropolitan Area	storage tanks (10), pumping stations, distribution network 169.5 km. or 105 km.[c]	175,200,000	0
		sewage system, 44.5 km. or 14 km.[c]	98,378,000	0
1970–71	Mina	wells, aqueduct 5.7 km., electrical and pumping equipment	24,601,805	416

Source: Leobardo Elizondo, "Comisión de Agua Potable de Monterrey: abastecimiento de agua potable" (Monterrey: Comisión de Agua Potable, 1977), cuadros 21–24, and anexos a-8-c, a-8-d, a-8-f.

[a]Due to supply variations month by month during the year, these figures may not match those given in the text.
[b]For example, this is the equivalent of roughly $5,350,000 U.S., given the exchange rate of this period.
[c]The source for this data is Enrique Torres López and Mario A. Santoscoy, La historia del agua en Monterrey desde 1577 hasta 1985 (Monterrey: Ediciones Castillo, 1985), 111.

the only water supply project that was carried out for Monterrey was the joint SRH-Commission groundwater program. Over three years the program found 3,500 lps of water, which would have almost doubled Monterrey's real supply of water ("Actas," 9-2-75; Servicios 1971–1976: 12). However, due to the limited capacity of the aqueducts transporting water from the sources to the city, the new supply was barely tapped (Anson 1978; Comisión de Agua Potable 1976a, 1977; Diario Oficial, 2-28-1980; Elizondo 1977: 69; Villatoro et al. 1983: app. 7). Water services deteriorated for the majority of the population.

In 1974, the Commission requested a loan of four hundred million

TABLE 3.5
Investment for Water Supply and Aqueducts, Monterrey, 1973–1976 (pesos)

Year	Santa Catarina	Santiago	Mina	Monterrey Metropolitan Area	Total
1973	5,200,000	—	5,000,000	11,200,000	21,400,000
1974	70,000,000	6,200,000	31,900,000	25,850,000	133,950,000
1975	42,300,000	—	24,000,000	20,400,000	86,700,000
1976	10,600,000	—	16,225,000	11,600,000	38,425,000
Total	128,100,000	6,200,000	77,125,000	69,050,000	287,475,000[a]

Source: Leobardo Elizondo, "Comisión de Agua Potable de Monterrey: abastecimiento de agua potable" (Monterrey: Comisión de Agua Potable, 1977), table 21.

[a]For example, this is the equivalent of roughly $23,000,000 U.S., given the exchange rate of this period.

pesos (thirty-two million in 1974 U.S. dollars) from the Banco Nacional de Obras Públicas (BANOBRAS) to increase aqueduct capacity and to drill and equip new wells ("Actas," 4-1-1974). BANOBRAS responded by authorizing the Commission and the Water Service to submit a proposal to the Inter-American Development Bank (IDB) for a second loan (6-4-1974). Approval of the second IDB loan the the Water Service came two years later in April 1976, but the first loan disbursement actually was not made until 1978.[25] From 1973 through 1977, Nuevo León continued to receive a disproportionately low share of federal public investment, and its share of monies designated for social welfare was also low—the state ranked tenth in 1974, fifteenth in 1975, and eleventh in 1976 (Secretaría 1980: 154–55).

During this period, the Water Service's financial situation deteriorated. In 1973, the Water Service used 11 percent of its total income to make interest payments on outstanding loans; by 1977 that figure had jumped to 60 percent.[26] At the same time, inflation was creeping upward, and in 1976 President Echeverría devalued the peso 83 percent, with the result that the Water Service's foreign currency debt as expressed in pesos nearly doubled. In 1976, the Water Service also had to begin its interest payments on the second IDB loan—although the first disbursement of the loan would not be made until 1978 (*El Norte*, 3-31-1979).[27] Yet, while its costs were rising, the Water Service was losing a significant share of its revenue due to losses in the water distribution system. By 1976, 45 percent

TABLE 3.6
Other Investments in the Water Sector, Monterrey, 1973–1977

Project	Cost (pesos)
Storage tanks[a, d]	
total new capacity 190,700 cubic meters	64,215,000
Pumping stations[a, b]	
total new horsepower, 3200	25,600,000
Distribution system[b, c]	
42.3 kilometers	46,825,000
Sewage system[b, d]	
61.1 kilometers	89,272,000
Subtotal	225,912,000
Water supply and aqueducts	
(from table 3.5)	287,475,000
Total 1973–1977	513,387,000

Sources:
[a]Servicios de Agua y Drenaje de Monterrey, "Informe al gobierno del estado" (Monterrey: 1976).
[b]Comisión de Agua Potable de Monterrey, "Consideraciones sobre los ingresos que corresponden a Servicios de Agua y Drenaje de Monterrey" (Monterrey: 1976), 19.
[c]Leobardo Elizondo, "Comisión de Agua Potable de Monterrey: abastecimiento de agua potable" (Monterrey: 1977), annex a-8-e.
[d]Ibid., annex a-8-f.
[e]Servicios de Agua y Drenaje de Monterrey, "Pasado, presente, futuro" (Monterrey: 1981), 69.

of the water supplied to the city was unaccounted for at billing time.[28] This meant that almost half of the water supplied by the Water Service, which cost money in wages, equipment, material, and depreciation, was either lost through leaks, was being distributed free of charge through illegal tapping of water mains, or was not being billed because of faulty meters. Citing the precariousness of its financial situation the Water Service raised water rates three times, in 1973, in 1975, and in 1977 ("Actas," 12-3-74, 8-19-75; *El Norte*, 8-23-1975, 12-15-1977).

Despite the increase in water rates, the Water Service's financial status continued to deteriorate. By the end of 1977 the Water Service had a deficit of 144 million pesos (6.4 million dollars) (*El Porvenir*, 5-7-1977; Servicios 1977: 3–4). In the meantime, the IDB made disbursement of the second IDB loan contingent on the improvement of the Water Service's finances. In mid-1977, the federal government stepped in with a rescue package including short-term loans and an agreement to guarantee larger long-term loans (*El Norte*, 7-13-1977; *El Porvenir*, 5-18-1977).

In the summer of 1977 Monterrey suffered from extreme water shortages (*El Norte*, 6-6-1977; *El Porvenir*, 7-7-1977). When the Commission's board of directors met in November 1977, the primary topic was the need to get new waterworks projects underway rapidly. If the first disbursement of the IDB loan, which had been approved in April 1976, was not made by January 1978, the loan would be canceled. The board agreed to proceed with a series of projects approved by the IDB that would increase the city's water supply, expand aqueduct capacity, and extend the distribution network and sewage system. Concurrently, the Water Service would finally embark on a leak reduction program that planned to reduce the 45 percent of the water supply that was unbilled (because it was lost through leaks, clandestine taps, and faulty meters) to 20 percent of total supply ("Actas," 11-28-1977).

In the summer of 1978 the real supply of water was only 58 percent of demand (*El Norte*, 8-2-1978). Because bidding on the IDB loan projects only began in the fall of 1978, the projects themselves were not completed until 1980 ("Actas," 11-13-1978). In fact, the projects from the second IDB loan were by themselves insufficient. They might have constituted a useful intermediary step in the early 1970s, but by the late 1970s the magnitude of the deficiencies in Monterrey's water services required projects on a larger scale. In the last year and a half of Governor Zorrilla's term, the most that could be done was of a short-term nature. The initial IDB loan disbursements were used for an emergency program consisting of a number of small projects (2-20-1978). In the summer of 1978, the Water Service was forced to announce that water would be cut off throughout the city between 10 p.m. and 6 a.m. (*El Porvenir*, 7-2-1978).

Alfonso Martínez Domínguez followed Zorrilla Martínez as governor of Nuevo León for the term running from 1979 to 1985. When Martínez Domínguez took office Monterrey had a population of almost two million. During Zorrilla Martínez's term, Monterrey's population had grown by 37 percent, while the real increase in the city's water supply was 30 percent.[29] Monterrey's water deficit had thus continued to grow during the 1970s.

In 1979 and 1980 the second IDB loan projects were completed but barely made a difference in the by-then critical status of Monterrey's water services. Table 3.7 details the investments made with the second IDB loan, showing that most of the expenditures went to increasing aqueduct capacity. By 1980 water shortages were so acute that over half of Monterrey was rationed year round (*El Porvenir*, 2-17-1980). Even some of the private wells used by industry were running dry, threatening the water supply in the sphere of production for the first time (*El Norte*, 5-16-1980; *El Porvenir*, 5-22-1980).

In July 1980 President López Portillo appointed a cabinet-level commission to formulate a long-term solution to Monterrey's water problems (*El Norte*, 7-24-1980; *El Porvenir*, 7-24-1980). One month later, the commission turned in its recommendations, and in early September the president authorized the Plan Hidráulico de Nuevo León (the Hydraulic Plan of Nuevo León) (*El Norte*, 9-3-1980; *El Porvenir*, 8-28-1980). In a complete

TABLE 3.7

Investment in the Water Sector, Monterrey, 1978–1980

Year	Activity	Cost (pesos)
1978	Emergency program: equip, maintain, and rehabilitate wells; leak correction; water use campaign	na
1978	Leak reduction program	na

Projects initiated under Governor Zorrilla Martínez, using the second IDB loan, but finished under Governor Martínez Domínguez

Year	Activity	Cost (pesos)
1977–80	Storage tanks: 2 tanks, 57,000 cubic meters total	31,000,000[a]
	7 tanks, 12,450 cubic meters total	14,680,463
1979–80	Second Mina-Monterrey Aqueduct	265,000,000
1979–80	Equip Mina wells	35,000,000
1979–80	Extend Huasteca Aqueduct (Santa Catarina)	26,000,000
1979–80	Extend Buenos Aires pipeline and equip six wells (Santa Catarina)	160,000,000

Source: Servicios de Agua y Drenaje de Monterrey, "Pasado, presente, futuro" (Monterrey: 1981), 69, 87.

[a]For example, this is the equivalent of roughly $1,360,000 U.S., given the exchange rate of this period.

na = not available

reversal of twenty years of weak federal support for Monterrey's water sector, the Plan Hidráulico was a multibillion-peso, comprehensive water management program consisting of projects to the south, east, north, and northeast of Monterrey.[30] The first phase of the Plan Hidráulico, which began in the fall of 1980, included the Cerro Prieto dam to the south, a 150-kilometer-long aqueduct connecting the dam to Monterrey, five pumping stations, electrical lines, and a water treatment plant (see figure 3.1). The dam would be the largest ever built for urban residential water supply in Mexico, and the aqueduct the longest of its kind in Latin America (Servicios 1981: 102–07).[31]

The Plan Hidráulico dominated Monterrey for the next five years. However, a project of the scope of the Plan Hidráulico could not be completed overnight. The Cerro Prieto dam and aqueduct would not be ready until 1984. In the meantime, Monterrey had to survive with its existing supply and infrastructure. The deficiencies in Monterrey's water services reached crisis proportions after 1980, when supply fell to only 50 percent of demand (where it remained until mid-1984).[32]

The government's response in the early 1980s was not limited to the federal level. While the federal government had agreed to finance the dam and related infrastructure to bring water from Cerro Prieto to the Monterrey city limits, the state government was responsible for financing the waterworks necessary to effectively distribute the Cerro Prieto water within the city limits (Torres López and Santoscoy 1985: 128). In 1981, the commission and the Water Service began designing the Anillo de Transferencia (the Transfer Ring). This project would build a pipeline around the perimeter of Monterrey, finally interconnecting all the city's sources of water (see figure 4.5). The Transfer Ring project also included large storage tanks, pumping stations, and extensions of the distribution and sewage networks (Servicios 1980: 11).

The Transfer Ring projects were beyond the financial capability of either the Water Service or the state. Once again the authorities turned to the IDB. However, 1982, the year that the third IDB proposal was submitted, was the year that Mexico's economy collapsed. With the federal government taking emergency measures to adjust its balance of payments, such as cutting spending in the public sector and reducing foreign debt, a new IDB loan for Monterrey became temporarily impossible and the proposal had to be withdrawn (Villatoro et al. 1983: 1). By the time the loan proposal was resubmitted in 1983, the Water Service was so financially unstable that the IDB imposed two conditions that had to be met before it would authorize the loan. First, the Water Service had to increase water rates; and second, the IDB required that the federal government absorb the Water Service's foreign currency debt. Thus, in early 1983, Governor Martínez Domínguez authorized a 75 percent increase in water rates that would be followed by a 2 percent monthly increase as long as inflation remained high (*El Porvenir*, 1-18-1983).

The second condition imposed by the IDB was met in May 1983. In a historic visit to Monterrey, newly inaugurated President de la Madrid announced that the Secretary of the Treasury and Public Credit (SHCP) would absorb all of the Water Service's foreign currency debt,[33] that the federal government would restructure the Water Service's peso debt, and that he was authorizing 1.462 billion pesos ($9,000,000 in 1983 U.S. dollars) more for the Plan Hidráulico (on top of seven billion he had authorized four months earlier). Furthermore, he added four hundred million pesos for an Emergency Water Plan, and another eight hundred million for the first phase of the Transfer Ring (*El Norte*, 5-24-1983; *El Porvenir*, 5-24-1983, 6-27-1983). The federal government was clearly living up to its claims that Monterrey's water crisis was a national priority. A new era of federal investment in Monterrey had been ushered in. Even the change in the presidency in December 1982, and the corresponding turnover in cabinet ministers, had not halted or slowed down the federal government's support for the Plan Hidráulico. The new president, Miguel de la Madrid Hurtado, had been Secretary of Planning and Budget (SPP) under President López Portillo and consequently knew, as well as anyone could, the details and history of the Plan Hidráulico.

At the end of June 1983 the IDB authorized its third loan to Monterrey to build the Transfer Ring and complementary infrastructure. Due to the reduction in public spending following the onset of Mexico's economic crisis, the size of the project had been reduced from 160 to 112 million U.S. dollars, with the IDB financing sixty-one million dollars and the Mexican government financing fifty-one million dollars. The federal government assumed the foreign exchange risk of the loan—the Water Service was thus responsible only for the peso equivalent of its foreign currency debt as calculated in the summer of 1983 (Villatoro et al. 1983: 1–2). Given the disastrous decline in the value of the peso in the mid-1980s, this provision saved the Water Service from bankruptcy.

The following year, 1984, was a turning point for water services in

Monterrey for all sectors of the population. In March 1984 Governor Martínez Domínguez gave his fifth annual report to the people of Nuevo León. In it he announced a landmark project, Agua Para Todos (Water for All) (*El Porvenir*, 3-10-1984). Agua Para Todos would use part of the third IDB loan to extend the water distribution system to the low-income neighborhoods that depended on collective faucets and water trucks. Initially, Agua Para Todos included 121 neighborhoods with an estimated population of three hundred thousand. Later, more neighborhoods would be included. Without Agua Para Todos the water from the Cerro Prieto dam would hardly have benefited Monterrey's poor neighborhoods. At best, there would have been more hours of service at the collective faucets, but women would still have had to wait in line and carry heavy buckets home. Water truck service would still have been constrained by the limited number of trucks available to make the rounds.

During 1984 and 1985 work was going on all over Monterrey to expand and improve the city's water system. The Plan Hidráulico and Agua Para Todos had to be completed by the time Governor Domínguez left office in the summer of 1985.[34] While work proceeded at a feverish pace, the water services themselves were still in crisis. The continued drought had affected aquifer levels so that until mid-1984 Monterrey had a 40 percent deficit in its water supply. In July 1984 the long-awaited water from Cerro Prieto finally arrived. As the Transfer Ring was completed water services slowly began improving throughout the city. By the spring of 1985, 60 percent of the city no longer had its water rationed. The Water Service forecasted that by the summer 100 percent of the population connected to the municipal system would have water twenty-four hours a day. In addition, ever since the federal government had absorbed the Water Service's debt and agreed to assume the foreign exchange risk of the third IDB loan, the Water Service's finances had remained healthy. In August 1983 the Water Service's accounts showed a surplus for the first time in fifteen years (*El Norte*, 3-24-1983); one year later it still had a surplus (9-24-1984).

CONCLUSION

While Monterrey's water system was one of the most advanced in Mexico at the time it was built in 1909, by 1940 it was already woefully inadequate. Neither the supply of water nor the distribution system had

kept pace with population growth and industrial expansion. The private
company that ran the water service had failed to meet its contractual obligations in terms of expanding the water system. Once the state government of Nuevo León purchased the water company from its private
owners in 1945, it took more than a decade for the new state-owned enter-
prise to be set up in its final form: a water planning commission (the
Commission) and a separate water authority to manage water distribution (the Water Service). While the water system was being reorganized
between 1945 and 1956, Monterrey's water problems worsened. The population, and the industrial and commercial base of the city, continued
to grow, as did the need for more water and more pipelines, while the
government did the studies that were needed and organized the institutions that could evaluate the studies and decide on new water infrastructure. Throughout the 1950s water was rationed in Monterrey all year long.
Insufficient infrastructure was not a *product* of unexpectedly rapid industrial and population growth (although both exacerbated the insufficien-
cies); rather, deficient service was a constant feature of Monterrey's
industrialization from the 1920s on.

From the mid-1960s to 1976, representatives of Monterrey's big business interests (the Grupo Monterrey) were in control of the board of directors of the Water Planning Commission. The board consisted of
representatives of various government agencies and local business sectors. However, by 1965 the only regular participants in the board meetings (where all major decisions affecting the expansion of Monterrey's
water services were made) were the representatives of the Grupo Monterrey, the representative of the government-owned Bank of Public Works
(himself a member of the Grupo Monterrey), the engineer who headed
the Commission, and the representative of the Ministry of Hydraulic Resources (who, however, stopped attending meetings after 1971). During
the 1960s and 1970s the Commission carried out a number of small projects that increased both the water supply and the distribution system, but
not sufficiently. Given the inadequacies of the water system inherited by
the government in 1945, and the massive population and industrial
growth of the 1950s and 1960s, Monterrey needed major new infrastructure. Instead, the Commission and the Ministry of Hydraulic Resources
(the SRH) both spent years carrying out studies and coming to differing
conclusions about the hydraulic projects that would work best. As a re-

sult, no major project was agreed upon, and both organizations continued to commit themselves to further studies while excecuting only small waterworks projects as stopgap measures.

Furthermore, during the 1960s and 1970s, the state of Nuevo León received a disproportionately low share of federal public investment allocated to the states relative to the state's population size and total income (Palacios 1989). Nuevo León's share of federal public investment for social welfare, which included spending on urban public service infrastructure, was also disproportionately low. Despite its designation as a decentralized state agency with a certain degree of autonomy, the Water Commission was controlled by the federal government, because local infrastructure projects were financed with federal funds and thus required authorization at the federal level. Federal financing was not guaranteed even during a period of heavy government investment in infrastructure to support industrialization. In 1961, 1962, 1965, and 1968 there was no investment in Monterrey's water sector, and investment was very low from 1973 to 1977, despite the city's desperate need for expanded infrastructure.

The Grupo Monterrey and the federal government had a history of hostile relations dating back to the 1930s, due to the elite group's outspoken criticism of the government on issues ranging from national economic policy to the use of standardized school textbooks. The continuous disagreements between the Commission's board, controlled by members of the Grupo Monterrey, and the SRH in Mexico City appear to be part of a larger pattern of conflict between Monterrey elites and the federal government. This history of conflict not only underlay the relationship between the board of directors of the Commission and the SRH, it may help explain the low levels of federal investment in water infrastructure for Monterrey.

By 1980, Monterrey's water problems had become a national priority—so stated President López Portillo in his third State of the Nation speech. In a new spirit of support for Monterrey, the president authorized a multibillion-peso project to construct a massive dam and aqueduct to bring water to the city. In 1984, President de la Madrid authorized a second major project designed to bring water service into the homes of all the residents of poor neighborhoods who had relied on collective faucets or water-truck deliveries. Federal investment in major water infrastructure for Monterrey changed significantly during López Portillo's presidency, and the high level of investment has continued through the 1980s and into the 1990s.

Why did the federal government finance major new water infrastructure for Monterrey starting in 1980 when government investment had been so restrained over the previous twenty years? And why especially did the government sponsor the Water for All project in 1984, during the worst years of Mexico's economic crisis, when social welfare spending was slashed? In order for federal investment to increase as it did, and for high levels of investment to be sustained for more than a decade, the management of the Commission had to change, as did the relationship between the Commission and the SRH. Even with increased investment, the new water infrastructure took years to complete. In the meantime, water service for the residents of Monterrey deteriorated.

By the late 1970s, the Walter Service had to ration water to the whole city for months at a time, and severe rationing became a year-round phenomenon in 1980. In the late 1970s, residents began complaining about, and then protesting, the unreliable and insufficient water service they received. Chapters 4 and 5 explore the protests over water in Monterrey. Chapter 6 discusses the reorganization of Monterrey's water sector undertaken by the state and federal government, as well as the government's response to the protests and to the water crisis more generally.

4 THE VOICE OF THE PEOPLE

Protests Over Water Service in Monterrey Between 1973 and 1985

F ROM 1940 to 1970, the decades that constitute the "Mexican Miracle" in terms of economic growth, the expansion of Monterrey's water services did not keep pace with the city's population, industrial, and commercial growth. By the early 1970s, over three hundred thousand residents, almost 30 percent of the population, were not connected to the municipal water system. In addition, shortfalls in the water supply itself forced the Water Service to implement rationing in neighborhoods that did have municipal service. As water service deteriorated, city residents responded with outrage. Complaints poured in to the Water Service and to local newspapers, and protests broke out across the city. While water service in Monterrey was worse than in other major Latin American cities because of the widespread rationing, the protests in Monterrey fit into a pattern of popular mobilization by the urban poor in Mexico and other Latin American countries dating back at least to the 1970s.

Latin American cities have become physical respresentations of unbalanced economic development, where beautiful homes complemented by the latest leisure technology (satellite dishes and jacuzzis, for example) spread out along tree-lined streets in some neighborhoods, while plywood shacks with no running water sprawl along arid hillsides in others. By the 1970s, urban population growth in Latin America had far outstripped available housing. Garza and Schteingart (1978: 17) estimate a shortage of 1.6 million homes in urban Mexico in 1970. Of that total, 634,000 represented families without homes, 516,000 families living in highly deteriorated housing, and 428,000 families living in conditions of severe overcrowding. Roberts (1978: 137) suggested that the shortage of urban housing in Mexico would be five million homes by 1980. Thousands of people lived with families or friends in crowded housing or rented substandard apartments in deteriorated downtown buildings or in courts with shared facilities. As a result, in the early 1970s, mobilizing efforts by the poor centered on housing. When they couldn't find low-rent units or purchase low-income housing, more and more poor families turned to land invasions or bought into fraudulent low-income developments far outside of town that were abandoned by land developers before any services were installed (Cornelius 1975; Perlman 1976; Collier 1976; Castells 1983; Gilbert and Ward 1985). Estimates of the proportion of the urban population living in such settlements in Latin American cities range from 20 to 80 percent, depending on the city (Portes and Walton 1976: 44).

By participating in land invasions, many among the urban poor in Latin America discovered that it was possible to achieve improvements in living conditions by bypassing the legal housing market. Land invasions were carried out by families selecting a vacant plot of land (preferably government land) and rapidly setting up provisional shelter.[1] For a land invasion neighborhood to be established, squatters had to successfully resist government efforts to dislodge them. As soon as a group of families carried out a land invasion they had to organize themselves. They had to divide the land into plots for each family, deciding how big each plot should be and agreeing on each family's location. They had to be able to incorporate newcomers as word of mouth brought new families streaming in to join them. Leaders and patterns of decision making emerged and meetings were held, all during the difficult first days and weeks of the neighborhood's life, when the government was most likely to try to oust the squatters from the land. From their very beginnings, squatter settlements had a higher degree of organization than any other urban neighborhood, because they had to.[2]

Typically, once the poor secured shelter they sought to meet their needs for potable water and electricity. In the case of squatter settlements, municipal governments usually refused to extend services because doing so would legitimate the settlements' existence. The fraudulent low-income developments did not fare any better, because local governments claimed that it was up to the developer to connect the developments to water, sewerage, and electrical service. In short, once the fight for housing was over, the fight for services began. Life in these low-income and squatter settlements consisted of surmounting innumerable challenges on a daily basis—the high cost of living, lack of jobs, inadequate water supply, transportation, sewerage, and health care. Friends and relatives helped each other through informally organized reciprocal exchange networks providing loans and in-kind services (Lomnitz 1975). Entire neighborhoods participated in community building projects, constructing a school or a health clinic during a Sunday of community labor (Pérez Güemes and Garza del Toro 1984). Some poor urban neighborhoods held open assemblies to discuss community problems and decide on tactics for resolving them, such as sending a delegation from the neighborhood to negotiate with government officials, or inviting officials into the neighborhood itself (Perlman 1976; Haber 1992; Watson 1992). Often, however, meetings between neighborhood committees and government officials did not lead to the desired solution. Committees would be given the runaround by uninterested or class-biased bureaucrats. Endless red tape delayed action. In response, residents turned to strategies of disruption, such as mass mobilization and civic protest, to get the attention of the government and to get their needs met.

Starting in the 1980s, scholars began reporting and analyzing the spread of grassroots organizing in Latin American cities (Hirschman 1984; Slater 1985a; Eckstein 1989; Foweraker and Craig 1990; Camacho 1990). Unequal development had resulted in unequal standards of living and unequal access to power. Part of the response to unequal urbanization was the surge in nonelectoral political activity by the urban poor. There are two principal forms of grassroots or popular organizing. The first consists of actions taken to resolve an immediate problem: neighborhoods organize only to the extent necessary to cope with a pressing need—for example, water, a bus route, or garbage collection. Once the particular issue is resolved there is no further organizing activity. Such short-term actions are a constant feature of daily life in Latin American cities. The second form of popular organizing consists of the consolidation of actions into ongoing social movements with long-term goals. In the last two decades, social movements arose not only among the urban poor in Latin America, but among peasants (Starn 1992; Fox and Gordillo 1989), human rights activists (Navarro 1989), church groups (Burdick 1992; Levine and Mainwaring 1989), women and feminists (Alvarez 1990), and environmentalists (García 1992).

In poor urban neighborhoods, because living conditions are substandard, collective consumption needs (water, sewerage, transportation, et cetera) motivate most protests and community organizing. Protest over urban public services can occur for different reasons: the absolute lack of service, a sudden deterioration of the level of service, a threat of service disruption, the wearing down created by constantly inadequate levels of service, and opposition to urban policy (Borja 1975: 18). Because collective consumption goods, such as water and sewerage services, urban transportation systems, and health care, are either provided or regulated by the government, protests over services confront government representatives or agencies. This calls for some level of organization within the neighborhood, whether it be forming a delegation of neighborhood residents to meet with government bureaucrats, holding a mass rally at a government office, or creating a civic organization to lead and guide the neighborhood in its struggles for improved services. Piven and Cloward (1979, as cited in Eckstein 1989: 6–7) suggest that even without formal or lasting organizations, the urban poor are more likely to effect change if they choose strategies that cause disruption—disruption of government offices through sit-ins, disruption or traffic through street blockades, and so on. The protests over water in Monterrey are evidence of the effectiveness of disruption as a strategy.

Recent studies have documented large-scale protests over water service in Latin American cities (on São Paulo, Brazil, see Jacobi Neru 1987 and Watson 1992; on Lima and Chimbote, Peru, see Zolezzi and Calderón 1985). In greater São Paulo, approximately 35 percent of the 1970 population of six million were not connected to the city's water system and had access only to contaminated water (Jacobi Neru 1987: 76). Protests and popular mobilizing over water services began in São Paulo in the 1970s. In response to the serious public health problems occasioned by the use of contaminated water, in the mid-1970s the city water authority embarked on a massive expansion of the water network, reaching over three million people by the end of the decade.

Despite the improvements, thousands of families in neighborhoods on the periphery of São Paulo still did not have water service. These happened to be neighborhoods with a history of community organizing, who turned their experience to protesting their inadequate water service. Protesting neighborhoods worked together, holding rallies that frequently attracted more than one thousand participants and putting continuous pressure on the water authority to expand the water system (Jacobi Neru

1987: 77). They received support from church groups, militant students, and opposition political parties. They were successful in getting the São Paulo water authority to change its policies and extend the water system to their areas. Watson (1992: 9) states that while "these mobilizations were not solely responsible for transformations within government agencies, pressures from social mobilization influenced the pace, timing, and nature of government policy and program initiatives." In fact, there was a dialectical relationship between the water authority and the protests. While the protests influenced government policy and programs, the fact that the government was investing heavily to improve the water system encouraged the protestors to continue protesting. Jacobi Neru (1987: 80) concludes that it was not so much the lack of water service that motivated the protests as the concrete possibility of obtaining service during a phase of government investment in the water system.

In Lima, Peru, more than 20 percent of the population in 1970 (over one million people) were not connected to the water system and received water from water delivery trucks. Zolezzi and Calderón (1985) report on protests carried out by a low-income sector of the city with a population of fifty thousand. Forty-two percent of the area's population was connected to the water system, and 37 percent was not (the remainder were awaiting completion of new pipelines). In 1980, Lima residents began a battle to obtain water service for the whole area by organizing a march to the President's Palace. The march drew ten thousand participants. Two years of protests, meetings, and negotiations followed, culminating in a major new water infrastructure project, funded by the government and the World Bank, to extend Lima's water system to the protesting area.

In short, popular mobilization and sustained protest by residents of poor urban neighborhoods in São Paulo and Lima resulted in significant government investment for improved water services to those neighborhoods. In both cases, the neighborhoods had preexisting community organizations and some history of popular organizing. If social transformation is defined as achieving sustained changes in relations of power between groups in society, obtaining better water service through protest cannot be equated with social transformation. At the same time, it is unlikely in either case that the governments would have extended the cities' water systems to the protesting neighborhoods if they had not been able to sustain their mobilizing efforts over time and consistently demonstrate sizeable constituencies. If we narrow our focus to relations of power within the water sector in Lima and São Paulo, the sustained mass protests increased the voice, visibility, and therefore the power of the poor urban residents who participated in the protests. The protests altered relations of power sufficiently that decision makers in the government decided to allocate investment funds to meet the residents' demands for improved water service. However, the protests by these particular neighborhoods did not alter relations of power in general between city government and all poor residents of the city. The decisions to extend the water systems of Lima and São Paulo to certain neighborhoods were not sweeping policy changes designed to reorganize water services for all neighborhoods, let alone to reorganize all urban public services.

Nevertheless, protest movements such as the ones in Lima and São Paulo can contribute to social transformation by helping to redefine citizens' rights. When reliable and convenient access to urban public services is perceived as the right of each resident of the city, then there is a foundation on which to base demands. The voicing of citizens' demands in and of itself constitutes a change in relations of power, because it adds a new voice to discussions on the distribution of resources—the old voices being the government and private sector elites. In turn, if the voice of poor urban residents becomes a consistent voice in city politics, even if it is through repeated protest over different needs (water today, transportation tomorrow), the entire definition of citizens' identities and citizens' rights can change, and protest over basic needs can evolve into protest over the organization of politics and further into the demand for democratization (Alvarez 1990; Slater 1985a).

Urban Popular Movements in Mexico

Mexico stands out among Latin American countries because of the strength of its urban popular movements. There are, or have been, movements in most Mexican cities. Several of the strongest movements are now almost twenty years old, and many others are reaching the ten-year mark. The most important movements have constituencies numbering in the tens of thousands. Their longevity, large constituencies, and geographic dispersion in cities across Mexico have made urban popular movements a social actor that the government has had to acknowledge and negotiate with.[3]

Urban protests and popular movements began in the early 1970s in response to the inability of Mexico's development model to provide a minimum standard of living for the majority of the population.[4] As in the rest of Latin America, there were dramatic housing shortages in Mexican cities, leading to severe overcrowding.[5] Garza and Schteingart (1978: 28–33) estimated the 1970 housing deficit for Mexican cities by totaling the number of families without housing, families living in heavily deteriorated housing, and families living in severely overcrowded homes. The total for all Mexican cities was a deficit of 45.3 percent, or 1,577,697 homes. Guadalajara had an estimated housing deficit of 62.6 percent, or 109,569 homes. Mexico City had a deficit of 43.6 percent, or 577,301 homes. Monterrey had a deficit of 50 percent, or 82,000 homes.

In the 1970s, families desperate to have a home of their own, no matter how miserable it might be at first, took part in land invasions on the periphery of cities throughout Mexico. Land invasions by poor urban residents constitute the roots of urban popular movements in Mexico. Most of those who took part in land invasions did so not because they wanted to organize a popular movement, make a political statement, or challenge the government, but because the housing deficits left them no choice.

Since the late 1930s, the Mexican government had tried to channel the needs of the people—peasants, workers, and popular sectors—through the mass organizations of the ruling party, the PRI (the Partido Revolucionario Institucional).[6] The purpose of the mass organizations was to be the voice of a defined sector of the population, to reflect and channel that sector's needs to decision makers in Mexico City, and to mediate the government's response. However, as Mexico's development model led the country to higher under- and unemployment, and as the government's economic policy continued to favor large-scale industrialization and the commercialization of agriculture, the mass organizations acted less and less as representatives of the people and more and more as representatives of the capital-state alliance. This meant that basic needs were addressed in a minimal and haphazard fashion within an overall policy of trickle-down modernization. The land invasion communities and the urban popular movements that emerged from them constructed new channels for expressing the needs of the urban poor in order to bypass the traditional channels, which were seen as incapable of resolving the growing urban crisis. Through the direct appropriation of land the squatters bypassed the government as guarantor of social welfare. In addition, by setting up their own leadership and decision-making mechanisms, the squatters bypassed the mass organizations of the PRI as the voice of the people.

In some cities, land invasions were led by militant students who had left the universities after the demise of the student movement in 1968.[7] In the early 1970s, militant students were particularly important as leaders of land invasions in Monterrey, Chihuahua, and Durango. Land invasion neighborhoods in these cities had in common a high level of internal organization. Once the lots were laid out and families had set up shelter, block leaders were elected for each block. Block leaders transmitted the concerns of the residents of their block to the overall leadership of the neighborhood. In addition, general assemblies open to all residents were held where issues and strategy could be debated. These land invasion neighborhoods developed their own code of internal behavior and created honor and justice committees to enforce the code. For example, prostitution was forbidden, as was adultery or spousal abuse. Violators of the behavior code were evicted from the settlements. In order to establish a viable neighborhood, special work days were designated, when all able-bodied residents would turn out to build needed infrastructure.

In the 1970s, the Mexican government responded to the housing shortage in two ways. It set up a number of new agencies to finance and build low-income housing, and it sanctioned government-led land invasions.[8] While never an explicitly stated policy, the latter strategy became evident when two of the mass organizations of the PRI, the Confederación de Trabajadores Mexicanos (CTM) and the Confederación Nacional de Organizaciones Populares (CNOP), began organizing urban land invasions themselves. The objective was for the government to have an administrative presence in the squatter settlements and thereby impede the formation of autonomous urban popular organizations. Allowing its mass organizations to set up land invasions was one way to keep the urban poor linked to the PRI and under its control. Yet neither the CTM nor the CNOP could keep up with the demand for shelter, and neither truly represented the people. The autonomous urban popular movements, therefore, were vying for the same constituency as the official mass organizations. Their success in terms of popular support is an indication that they were indeed filling a gap left by the dominant system.[9]

In Monterrey, Chihuahua, and Durango, after successfully consolidating the first land invasion neighborhoods, the leaders provided support and guidance for new invasions either as expansions of the original invasion or in other parts of the city. In the mid to late 1970s, land invasion neighborhoods in these cities grouped together to form umbrella organizations with memberships in the tens of thousands—the Comité de Defensa Popular in Durango and Chihuahua, and the Frente Popular Tierra y Libertad in Monterrey.[10] Membership included residents of the affiliated land invasion neighborhoods as well as student groups and independent or dissident labor factions.[11] Leaders of these first three urban popular movements were guided by a vision of a socialist Mexico, and they saw the land invasion neighborhoods and the movements themselves as key building blocks of the path to socialism. Thus, at the same time as they struggled to upgrade living conditions in their neighborhoods, they also led reading and discussion groups to form the political and social conscience of the squatters themselves. Their strategy decisions were made with regard not only to short-term benefits but also to their long-term transformative potential.

In the late 1970s and during the 1980s, significant new urban popular movements were created in other Mexican cities including Tijuana, Acapulco, and Mexico City (Ramírez Sais 1986; Tirado Jiménez 1990). While some of the new movements were guided by a totalizing vision of a socialist Mexico, others saw themselves as mediators between their constituents and the government in the struggle to improve living standards in their neighborhoods. In both cases, the movements set themselves up as autonomous organizations, separate from the government or the private sector, and they defended their right to organize. Their immediate goals were issues of housing, land tenure, and public services. Their strategies included direct appropriation, protest, and negotiation with the government.

In 1981, representatives of sixty urban popular movements from fourteen states met in Durango and founded the National Coordinating Committee of Urban Popular Movements (CONAMUP) (Ramírez Sais 1986). At the same time as the urban poor were organizing in the 1970s, independent peasant groups were also being formed, challenging the state-run peasant confederation. In 1979, autonomous peasant groups from across Mexico came together to create the National Plan de Ayala Coordinating Committee (Hernández 1990). Also in 1979, dissatisfied members of Mexico's biggest labor union, the Teachers' Union, formed a dissident union, the National Coordinating Committee of Teachers (Cook 1990). In just a few years, national coordinating committees were in place representing large constituencies, operating in complete autonomy, and consti-tuting powerful alternatives to traditional government and the PRI organizations.

Popular Mobilization in Monterrey

Two issues were at the center of mobilizing efforts by the urban poor in Monterrey during the 1970s and 1980s: housing and water. When Gov-ernor Zorrilla Martínez took office in 1973, Monterrey was a state capital typical of large cities in Mexico. Its population had grown substantially in the previous two decades, but its housing stock and public services had not grown in proportion. In the early 1970s, thousands responded by participating in land invasions.

In July 1971, the first land invasion took place in Monterrey and was repelled by the police within hours. In August, a second attempt suc-ceeded, although the new settlement was surrounded by police for one month. In 1972, three more land invasions occurred, two of which were successful despite violent repression. In 1973, the number of land inva-sions grew, as did their size. Invasions were met with police repression and violence. On March 28, 1973, a group of thirty families invaded bar-ren land on the north side of Monterrey. By 6 p.m. the same day there were eight hundred families, and by the next morning there were fifteen hundred families. They named their new neighborhood Tierra y Libertad (Land and Liberty). The Tierra y Libertad settlement faced extensive po-lice aggression: beatings, shootings, and detentions. In April 1973 another land invasion succeeded with 750 families; and in May, yet another with 600 families. In all cases, the government tried to disband the settlements violently. In the last case the military was called in to mediate. In August of 1973 an explosion in a quarry at the edge of the Tierra y Libertad neigh-borhood injured settlement residents. Residents seized a quarry truck to demand indemnity payments. The police attacked with machine guns. Residents fought the police, took a police car, and set fire to it. Finally, the quarry's owner repudiated the police violence, made indemnity pay-ments, and donated material for a school in the settlement (Pérez Güemes and Garza del Toro 1984).

Successful land invasions continued along Monterrey's western and southern periphery through the first half of the 1970s. In 1976, under the leadership of the Tierra y Libertad settlement, twenty-six land invasion neighborhoods came together to form the Frente Popular Tierra y Libertad. The students who had been the original leaders of the Tierra y Libertad invasion became the leaders of one of the most powerful urban popular movements in Mexico. With its large constituency and strong leadership, the Frente Popular Tierra y Libertad gave squatters in Monterrey a civic presence never before seen in Mexico.

Part of the work of setting up a squatter settlement was obtaining water and electricity. Because land invasions were illegal settlements, the government did not provide them with services. Consequently, at least initially, squatter settlements were left to their own devices. Frequently they were able to directly appropriate both electricity and water. They illegally connected their homes to the nearest electricity line, stringing wires into their community. They also illegally tapped into the nearest water mains, bringing water in through their own pipes and hoses. The use of clandestine water taps was supplemented by water truck deliveries. The Monterrey Water Service estimates that the direct appropriation of water through "clandestine faucets" has consumed at least 10 percent of the city's water supply since the early 1970s.[12] The residents who got water in this fashion paid for the hoses and other supplies necessary to make the connection but they did not pay for the water they consumed. This represented a loss of revenue for the Water Service.[13]

Direct appropriation of water was not always possible; geographic conditions sometimes made illegal tapping difficult, or even too obvious. In those cases, once they consolidated the land invasion, squatters moved on to seeking improvements in their living conditions. Empowered by the successful outcome of the land invasion itself, they continued organizing and demanding services from the government. Twice in September 1972, a large group of squatters from ten land invasions rallied at the governor's palace demanding water services. By the end of the second rally the state government agreed to provide collective faucets and hoses, which the squatters themselves installed (*El Norte,* 9-20-1972, 9-27-1972). In 1973, the number of protests increased. Ten incidents were reported in the newspapers before the end of Governor Farías's term in October. This was the beginning of a protest movement for better water service that would grow throughout the 1970s and 1980s.

The neighborhoods that were the first to organize around water service problems with street demonstrations and other strategies were the neighborhoods with a history of organizing, so the work around water was just one more issue. However, in 1973, 20 percent of the city's population, over three hundred thousand people, did not have in-home water service. Not just squatters, but residents living legally in rented or privately owned homes, were not connected to the water service. While the origin of protest movements over water in Monterrey is found in the politicization of squatters in the early 1970s, the growth of the protests over water occurred in nonsquatter neighborhoods.[14]

Protests Over Water in Monterrey, 1973–1985

The protests over water in Monterrey began in 1972 and grew slowly.[15] During the first seven years of the decade protests over water were insignificant, except for a burst of mobilization in 1973 (see table 4.1 and figure

TABLE 4.1
Incidents of Protest Over Water in Monterrey, 1970–1985

Year	Number of Incidents	Number of Incidents in 2nd Column that Encompass Unspecified Numbers of Other Incidents[a]
1970	0	0
1971	0	0
1972	3	0
1973	12	3
1974	1	1
1975	3	2
1976	3	2
1977	2	2
1978	28	4
1979	23	5
1980	37	3
1981	0	0
1982	25	4
1983	43	5
1984	11	0
1985	10	1

Sources: *El Norte, El Porvenir*, 1970–1985.

[a]For example: "numerous calls to *El Norte*."

4.1). Then, between 1978 and 1980 there was an explosion of activity, with twenty-eight incidents in 1978, twenty-three in 1979, and thirty-seven in 1980. There was a lull in 1981, with no incidents reported in the press. Protests over water exploded once more in 1982 and 1983, then lessened in 1984 and 1985.

One measure of the scope of the protests is the number of neighborhoods that participated in each incident. In most years, the number of neighborhoods participating in the protests was greater than the number of protests (see table 4.2 and figure 4.2).[16] Often, groups of neighborhoods would take action together. For example, in 1976 twenty-eight neighborhoods participated in two incidents, while in 1978 sixty-eight neighborhoods participated in twenty-eight incidents (see table 4.2). Many neighborhoods participated in more than one incident each year. These data indicate that protests over water service encompassed far more of Monterrey's population than might be supposed by looking just at the number of incidents that occurred each year.

One hundred and fifty-six neighborhoods were mentioned by name in the newspaper reports of the protests that took place between 1970 and 1985 (see figure 4.3). Many other neighborhoods that engaged in protest

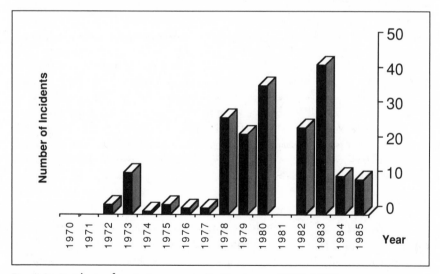

Fig. 4.1. Incidents of protest over water in Monterrey, 1970–1985
Sources: *El Norte, El Porvenir,* 1970–1985.

TABLE 4.2

Number of Neighborhoods Participating in Protests Over Water in Monterrey, 1970–1985

Year	Incidents of Protest	(1) Number of Neighborhoods	(2) General Groupings of Neighborhoods	(3) Total: (1) and (2) plus repeats
1970	0	0	0	0
1971	0	0	0	0
1972	3	11	0	21
1973	12	4	1	12
1974	1	4	1	5
1975	3	6	2	8
1976	3	28	0	28
1977	2	5	1	12
1978	28	68	3	102
1979	23	30	1	62
1980	37	45	2	73
1981	0	0	0	0
1982	25	33	2	45
1983	43	49	2	70
1984	11	10	0	11
1985	10	9	0	13

Sources: El Norte, El Porvenir, 1970–1985.

Note: (1) includes only the neighborhoods listed by name in the newspaper reports about the protests. Column (2) gives the number of general groupings of neighborhoods that participated in the protests each year (i.e., "neighborhoods in the north of the city.") For example, the one general grouping listed for 1972 could include 5, 10, 20, or even more neighborhoods, but there is no way to know. While column (1) counts each neighborhood once regardless of the number of incidents it participated in, column (3) represents the sum of column (2) *plus each* participation of *each* neighborhood included in column (1). For this reason, the total in column (3) may be larger than the simple sum of columns (1) and (2).

were lumped together in newspaper descriptions as the "northwest neighborhoods" or "the downtown area" and thus, for the purposes of this study, their identity is unavailable. Upper-middle and upper-income neighborhoods made up 19.2 percent of the neighborhoods involved in protests, while lower-middle, lower, and marginal-income neighborhoods accounted for more than three-quarters of the neighborhoods that

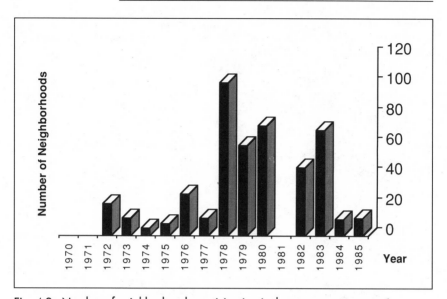

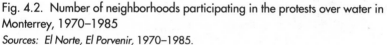

Fig. 4.2. Number of neighborhoods participating in the protests over water in Monterrey, 1970–1985
Sources: El Norte, El Porvenir, 1970–1985.

protested (see table 4.3).[17] Almost half the neighborhoods participated in more than one protest incident related to water services (table 4.4), and all income groups were equally likely to participate more than once (tables 4.5 and 4.6).

The high proportion of lower-income neighborhoods among those participating in protests over water is related to the class structure of Monterrey and to the quality of water services. The breakdown of neighborhood participation in the protests over water by income group reflects income distribution in Monterrey. One study shows the upper-middle and upper-income groups totaling 15.5 percent of the city's population, while the bottom three income groups total 69.1 percent (Pozas 1991: 69).[18] Thus, lower-middle income, lower-income, and marginal-income neighborhoods make up almost three-quarters of Monterrey's population. The proportional representation of these neighborhoods among those that protested is evidence of how widespread inadequate water services were.

Eighty-seven percent of the neighborhoods that protested were connected to the municipal water system, and only 13 percent were neighbor-

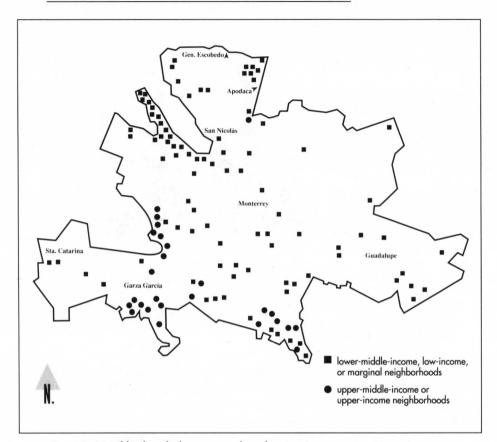

Fig. 4.3. Neighborhoods that protested inadequate water service, Monterrey
Metropolitan Area, 1973–1985
Sources: El Norte, El Porvenir, 1973–1985.

hoods that got their water from collective faucets or water trucks.
Therefore, most of the neighborhoods that protested had been affected
by the citywide water rationing regime imposed by the Water Service in
1978. Once water rationing began, the upper-income population was able
to limit its impact by installing roof or patio cisterns to store water for
use during the periods of rationing. The lower-income groups could not
afford such installations and thus suffered the rationing directly. Because
of this, the real water service for lower-income neighborhoods was worse
than for the upper-income neighborhoods and deteriorated as water rationing increased after 1978.

TABLE 4.3

Neighborhoods Participating in Protests Over Water in Monterrey, 1973–1985, by Income Group

Income Group	Number of Neighborhoods	Percent of Neighborhoods
Upper	10	6.4
Upper middle	20	12.8
Lower middle	46	29.5
Lower	59	37.8
Marginal	13	8.3
Not known	8	5.2
Total	156	100.0

Sources: For data on protests: El Norte, El Porvenir, 1973–1985. For classification of neighborhoods by income level: internal documents of the Secretaría de Asentamientos Humanos y Planificación de Nuevo León and the Departamento de Estadística del Estado de Nuevo León.
Note: Includes only those neighborhoods listed by name in the newspaper reports.

TABLE 4.4

Frequency of Neighborhood Participation in Protests Over Water in Monterrey, 1973–1985

Neighborhood Participation	Number	Percent
Neighborhoods that participated once	84	53.9
Neighborhoods that participated more than once, but within a single year	20	12.8
Neighborhoods that participated in more than one year	52	33.3
Total	156	100.0

Sources: El Norte, El Porvenir, 1973–1985.

STRATEGIES USED IN THE PROTESTS OVER WATER SERVICE

The protests over water in Monterrey used a variety of strategies. Some neighborhoods used one strategy in a single incident, others used a series of strategies, and yet others used the same strategy over and over again in repeated protests. Table 4.7, showing the number of strategy-uses each year compared to the number of incidents, adds flesh to the picture.[19] In every year, the number of strategy-uses exceeded the number of incidents of protest. This reflects both the fact that more than one neighborhood participated in some of the protest incidents, and that

TABLE 4.5

Frequency of Neighborhood Participation in Protests Over Water in Monterrey, 1973–1985, by Income Group

	Frequency of Participation					
	Once		More Than Once in a Single Year		Multiple Years	
Income Group	Number	Percent	Number	Percent	Number	Percent
Upper	6	7.1	0	0	4	7.7
Upper middle	8	9.5	3	15.0	9	17.3
Lower middle	25	29.8	3	15.0	18	34.6
Lower	32	38.1	11	55.0	16	30.8
Marginal	7	8.3	1	5.0	5	9.6
Not known	6	7.1	2	10.0	0	0
Total	84	99.9	20	100.0	52	100.0

Sources: El Norte, El Porvenir, 1973–1985.

TABLE 4.6

Frequency of Neighborhood Participation in Protests Over Water in Monterrey, 1973–1985, by Aggregated Income Groups

	Lower-Income Groups[a]		Upper-Income Groups[b]	
Frequency	Number	Percent	Number	Percent
Multiple years	39	33.1	13	43.3
More than once in a single year	15	12.7	3	10.0
Once	64	54.2	14	46.7
Total	118	100.0	30	100.0

Sources: El Norte, El Porvenir, 1973–1985.

Note: Frequency of participation was unknown for eight neighborhoods. This table reports on 148 neighborhoods.

[a]Lower-Income Groups = Lower middle, Lower, Marginal
[b]Upper-Income Groups = Upper, Upper middle

TABLE 4.7
Number of Strategy-Uses per Incident in Protests Over Water in Monterrey, 1970–1985

Year	Number of Incidents	Number of Strategy-Uses
1970	0	0
1971	0	0
1972	3	21
1973	12	13
1974	1	5
1975	3	9
1976	2	30
1977	2	12
1978	28	213
1979	23	65
1980	37	99
1981	0	0
1982	25	48
1983	43	90
1984	11	12
1985	10	15

Sources: *El Norte, El Porvenir,* 1970–1985.
Note: The number of strategies used in each incident of protest was counted in the following manner. If one neighborhood blocked a street to demand water, that was counted as one strategy-use. If ten neighborhoods blocked the same street together, that one strategy was counted ten times, or as ten strategy-uses, to reflect the decision on the part of each neighborhood to employ that strategy. Thus, the data in the third column reflect the sum total of all strategies used by each neighborhood that participated in each incident.

neighborhoods sometimes used a series of strategies one after the other. The fact that neighborhoods protested together and employed numerous strategies indicates their persistence and their desperate need for water and gives some idea of what the government was facing. The peak years noted earlier, 1978–1980 and 1982–1983, stand out in table 4.7 for the large number of strategy-uses associated with each incident. In addition, there were several years when protest over water seemed insignificant when measured by the number of incidents per year, but those incidents appear more important when the number of neighborhoods that participated and the strategy-uses are taken into consideration. For example, in 1976 there were only two incidents of protest, but twenty-eight neighborhoods participated with thirty strategy-uses (see tables 4.2 and 4.7).

The strategies used in the protests fell into two categories: those that used public space and those that did not. Public space refers to the elements of a city to which citizens have free access: sidewalks and streets, parks and plazas, the foyers and hallways of government buildings, and the parking lots and gardens surrounding government buildings.[20] When people used strategies that involved public space it meant that they had to leave their homes. Nonpublic strategies were those that did not require the use of public space.

There are important differences between the two categories. Public action required group interaction, including communication, coordination, and compromise between neighbors and often between neighborhoods. Nonpublic action was privately carried out by an individual. Consequently, public actions required a greater commitment to the need for change than did nonpublic actions. They also entailed a greater time and energy commitment from the participants than did nonpublic actions. Finally, public actions had risks associated with them that nonpublic actions did not. The use of public space for protest actions could lead to police intervention, public outcry, government reprisals, and so on.

There were two nonpublic strategies and seven public strategies used in Monterrey. The two nonpublic strategies were to telephone the Water Service and the local newspapers. The seven strategies that used public space were to send neighborhood delegations to meet with government officials, to hold mass rallies, to hold neighborhood meetings, to block streets, to seize Water Service vehicles and kidnap Water Service personnel, to threaten to use public space to protest, and to take over government buildings (see the following list of strategies using public space).

DELEGATIONS
    To the Water Service
    To the newspapers
    To the mayor
    To the governor
MASS RALLIES
    At the Water Service
    At Town Hall
    At the governor's office

NEIGHBORHOOD MEETINGS

STREET BLOCKADES

SEIZING WATER SERVICE VEHICLES AND PERSONNEL TO HOLD HOSTAGE WHILE DEMANDING
WATER

THREATS

Not to pay water bills

To block streets

To take over the Water Service building

To look for solutions at a higher level (usually Mexico City)

TAKING OVER THE WATER SERVICE BUILDING

By 1973 there was evidence of the cycle of strategies that would become common in the late 1970s. For example, one neighborhood that had experienced decreased water service with intermittent water cutoffs began by sending a delegation of residents to see the state governor. When that did not work, delegations went to the offices of the Water Service and to the mayor's office. The upshot was a neighborhood meeting held with the mayor and representatives of the Water Service. In the end, when water services did not improve, residents blocked a major avenue near their neighborhood, demanding improvements and threatening not to pay for their water service (*El Norte*, 6-2-1972). This series of incidents demonstrates the use of several public strategies, indicating a hierarchy of strategies. The neighborhood had to have a sense of commitment in order to persevere in sending delegations to talk to public officials. Although they began with public strategies right away, neighborhood residents were clearly willing to explore the possibility of negotiation. When the numerous delegations and the neighborhood meeting brought no result, the neighborhood chose to escalate to a different public strategy that involved a more aggressive use of public space: blocking a major avenue.

Later in 1973, to protest excessively high water bills, hundreds of people from neighborhoods all over the city phoned both the Water Service and the local newspapers. "Disgusted with the Increase in Water Rates" was the newspaper headline, and the text spoke of innumerable complaints (*El Norte*, 10-10-1973). In this case, nonpublic strategies were generally judged to be sufficient, although the intensity of the strategy was enhanced by the volume of individual response.

In reviewing the incidents that used a series of strategies, certain patterns are evident, providing the empirical basis for a hypothesis of strategy escalation. Most incidents started with residents contacting the Water Service, either by telephoning in complaints, by sending neighborhood delegations, or even by taking over the Water Service building—this happened once, in 1984 (*El Norte*, 4-13-1984). Often the initial contact with the Water Service did not produce the desired result. After a period of time ranging from hours to weeks, neighborhood residents tried another tactic. Sometimes the next step was to call the newspapers, report the problem, and denounce the Water Service's lack of response. At least half the time, however, the neighborhoods moved to take action on public space.

In a typical incident, neighborhood residents called the Water Service to report a problem. When the problem continued unabated they held a protest meeting at the governor's office. When that did not achieve results they sent several delegations to meet with officials at the Water Service. Finally, they ran out of patience and seized a Water Service repair truck, demanding water as a condition for the release of the truck and its driver (8-2-1985). In other cases, when the Water Service did not respond to neighborhood complaints, residents took to the streets, forming street blockades by lining up arm in arm across the street with tubs, pails, and buckets in front of them.[21] The strategy of street blockades was used especially by neighborhoods that bordered a major avenue, an industrial artery, or a central downtown area. The steps in strategy escalation are listed below.

STEP 1. Acknowledgment of the Problem.

Neighborhood residents discuss the water service problem informally or formally, i.e., at the collective faucet, in the street, or at a neighborhood meeting.

STEP 2. Negotiation.

A. Neighborhood residents call the Water Service to report the problem and ask for resolution.

B. Neighborhood residents form a committee to meet with, negotiate with, and seek resolution from government officials.

STEP 3. Escalation of Negotiation.

If step 2 does not bring about an acceptable result, the neighborhood committee tries to meet with higher-level government officials, such as the state governor, or they telephone the newspapers to report the lack of response. Both strategies are attempts to increase the pressure on the Water Service to respond to the problem.

STEP 4. Protest.

If all attempts at negotiation fail, neighborhood residents turn to protest, using disruption as a strategy to force government officials to resolve the problem.

From 1974 through 1977, neighborhoods responding to inadequate water services used primarily nonpublic strategies. The incidents reported in the newspapers consisted of phoned-in complaints of water shortages and water cutoffs.[22] There was only one incident reported of a neighborhood choosing a strategy that involved collective action on public space. The neighborhood had lived through a month without water, during which time neighborhood residents had to walk twelve blocks to a public faucet and carry heavy pails of water the twelve blocks back to their neighborhood. Neighborhood children were beginning to have gastrointestinal problems; schoolteachers were complaining of the unsanitary conditions of school bathrooms; and the housewives had been unable to do most of their laundry for four weeks. Driven to desperation, a group of residents called a neighborhood meeting, after which they seized a water truck passing through the streets and held it hostage as they demanded the reinstallation of their water services (*El Norte*, 6-12-1976).

The character of the protests over water changed dramatically in 1978. While in the pre-1978 period nonpublic strategies dominated the response to Monterrey's inadequate water services, starting in 1978 strategies that used public space prevailed (see table 4.8). The total number of strategies used each year was significantly greater, while the type of strategy became more disruptive. The data in table 4.8 underscore that there were two peak phases of protest, 1978–1980 and 1982–1983.

The higher the income group, the less frequently was public space used as a strategy (see table 4.9). The upper-income group relied exclusively on nonpublic strategies, which is to say that they had only one form of response to water service problems—the telephone. Upper-income group response was always individual, never required group coordination, and never took place outside the home. In the upper-middle-

TABLE 4.8
Public versus Nonpublic Protest Strategies Used, 1973–1985

Year	Public Strategies		Nonpublic Strategies	
	Number	Percent	Number	Percent
1973	7	53.9	6	46.2
1974	0	0	5	100.0
1975	0	0	9	100.0
1976	3	10.0	27	90.0
1977	0	0	12	100.0
1978	130	61.0	83	39.0
1979	15	23.0	50	77.0
1980	57	57.6	42	42.4
1981	0	0	0	0
1982	41	85.4	7	14.6
1983	60	66.7	30	33.3
1984	8	66.7	4	33.3
1985	12	80.0	3	20.0

Sources: El Norte, El Porvenir, 1973–1985.

income neighborhoods the tendency to use nonpublic strategies is also striking.

In contrast, for the bottom three income groups public space was a primary element in their struggles for better water service (table 4.9). Ninety-five percent of all public-space-based strategies were carried out by neighborhoods in these income groups. All the kidnappings of Water Service vehicles and personnel were carried out by lower-middle and lower-income neighborhoods. In addition, all but two of the street block-ades were staged by lower-middle and lower-income neighborhoods— two were organized by upper-middle-income neighborhoods (see figure 4.4).

Of all the neighborhoods that blocked streets and kidnapped Water Service personnel, only one was not connected to the water system. Thus these very disruptive strategies were chosen not by neighborhoods de-manding that they be connected up to the water system but by neighbor-hoods that were connected and whose home water service had diminished or even stopped altogether. The combination of hilly terrain, inadequate water storage and pumping facilities, and the absolute deficit

TABLE 4.9
Use of Public versus Nonpublic Protest Strategies, 1973–1985,
by Income Group

Income Group	Neighborhoods That Used Public Strategies		Neighborhoods That Did Not Use Public Strategies	
	Number	Percent	Number	Percent
Upper groups	4	13.3	26	86.7
Upper	0	0	10	100.0
Upper middle	4	20.0	16	80.0
Lower groups	81	68.6	37	31.4
Lower middle	29	63.0	17	37.0
Lower	44	74.6	15	25.4
Marginal	8	61.5	5	38.5
Not known	4	50.0	4	50.0
Total	89		67	

Sources: El Norte, El Porvenir, 1973–1985.
Note: The exact strategies used by eight neighborhoods are unknown. This table reports on 148 neighborhoods.

in the water supply severely reduced water service to certain neighborhoods. Some areas that were connected to the water system were actually forced to rely on water truck deliveries for their water.

One-third of the neighborhoods participated in protests over water in more than one year (see table 4.4). A review of the types of strategies used by these neighborhoods provides further evidence of their increased militancy. In all cases, except for the upper-income group, the tendency to use public space was greater among this subset of neighborhoods (see table 4.10) than among the universe of neighborhoods as a whole (see table 4.9).

There are two explanations for the differing use of public space by different income groups. First, the more water was available to a neighborhood, the less the neighborhood used public space as a strategy. Conversely, the less water was available to a neighborhood, the more their response to the deficient service used public space. Water services in Monterrey's lower-income neighborhoods often were worse than in the upper-income neighborhoods, particularly because low-income residents were unable to offset the water rationing with rooftop storage tanks the way

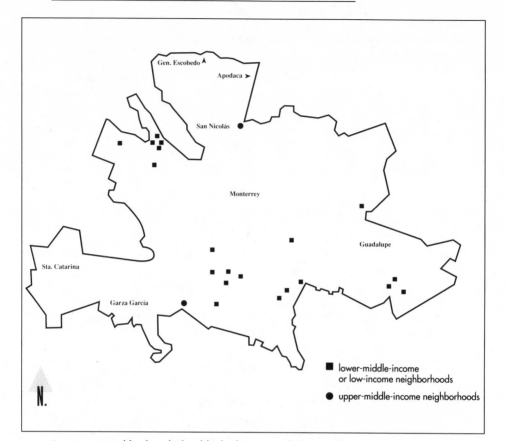

Fig. 4.4. Neighborhoods that blocked streets or kidnapped Water Service personnel and vehicles to protest inadequate water service, Monterrey Metropolitan Area, 1973–1985
Sources: El Norte, El Porvenir, 1973–1985.

wealthier city residents could. Second, the use of public space varied indirectly with income. The greater the income, the less the use of public space. For one thing, when a resident of a high-income neighborhood telephoned to report water service problems, it was likely that the problem would be resolved more quickly than if the call came from a lower-income neighborhood. This meant that higher-income neighborhoods rarely had to move beyond the phone call to get a response to water problems. In addition, private telephones were much less prevalent in low-income neighborhoods, so reporting a problem by phone meant leav-

TABLE 4.10
Use of Public versus Nonpublic Protest Strategies by Neighborhoods
Participating More Than One Year, 1973–1985

Income Group	Neighborhoods That Used Public Stategies		Neighborhoods That Did Not Use Public Strategies	
	Number	Percent	Number	Percent
Upper	0	0	4	100.0
Upper middle	4	44.4	5	55.6
Lower middle	14	77.8	4	22.2
Lower	14	87.5	2	12.5
Marginal	4	80.0	1	20.0
Total	36		16	

Sources: El Norte, El Porvenir, 1973–1985.

ing home and using a public phone. For these reasons, the lower-income neighborhoods had to expand their struggle into the public arena if they wanted to be effective.[23]

Over the years, similar strategies were used again and again as the protests intensified. By 1980, when the Plan Hidráulico was authorized, and by 1984, when Agua Para Todos was planned, the same strategies had swept the city for several summers in a row. Each summer new neighborhoods joined in the protests. For example, of the ninety-nine different neighborhoods that took action in 1978, 1979, or 1980, 20 percent participated in protests over water again in 1982 or 1983. Thus, the majority of neighborhoods that protested in 1982 and 1983 either had never before taken action or had done so before 1978.

WATER POLICY AND THE PROTESTS OVER WATER

Why did protests over water services explode in 1978? First of all, since 1970 there had been no comprehensive water resource development plan for the Monterrey Metropolitan Area. The resignation of Governor Elizondo in 1971 followed by the short interim governorship of Luis M. Farías led to a neglect of the water sector by the state. When Governor Zorrilla took office in 1973, Monterrey's industrial elite still had control of the Water Service and the Water Commission. Governor Zorrilla never formulated a six-year plan for water resource development, so planning remained in the hands of the Grupo Monterrey.

In the mid-1970s Monterrey had three primary sources of water: the Santa Catarina zone with infiltration galleries and deep wells to the west of the city, the Mina zone of deep wells to the north of the city, and the Santiago zone with a dam and infiltration tunnels to the south of the city (see figure 3.1). The three sources sent water to Monterrey via aqueducts. Santa Catarina provided water for west Monterrey, Mina provided water for north and northwest Monterrey, and Santiago provided water for south, central, and east Monterrey. As shown in figure 4.5, within the city the three sources of water were not interconnected, so investment in one zone would only benefit the part of the city receiving water from that zone.

In 1973, 1974, and 1975 over half the investment for water infrastruc-

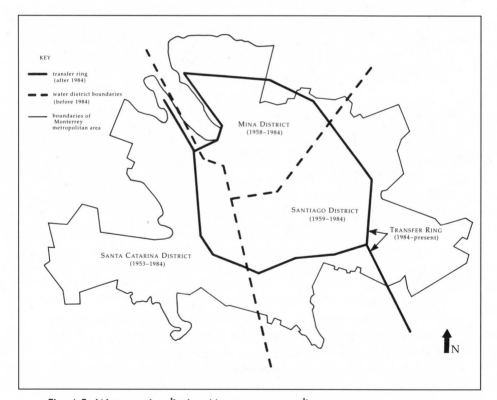

Fig. 4.5. Water service districts, Monterrey metropolitan area

ture development went to the Santa Catarina zone and to improve the distribution service in west Monterrey (Elizondo 1977: cuadro 21). Between 1974 and 1976 all investment for aqueduct extension was made in the west of the city (Comisión 1976b: 18), ten out of thirteen new storage tanks were built in the western part of the city (Laboratorio 1979–1980: II, 65), and six out of nine new pumping stations were constructed in west Monterrey (Servicios 1976a). Almost all the upper-income residential areas in Monterrey were in the part of the city served by the western source at Santa Catarina. Yet that area had experienced less population growth than other parts of the city. While the population in west Monterrey had tripled between 1960 and 1970, the population in east Monterrey had quadrupled, and hardly any investment had been made to increase its water supply since the mid-1960s (Servicios 1971–1976: 15, 21).

After a heavily skewed pattern of investment that favored west Monterrey from 1973 to 1976, in 1977 there was absolutely no spending for water infrastructure or water services in Monterrey at all. At the same time, losses due to leaks, illegal taps of the water mains, and faulty meters increased substantially, so that only 55 percent of the water extracted from the sources could be accounted for at billing time (El Norte, 8-2-1978). While 10 percent of supply was probably mismetered, and another 10 to 15 percent lost to illegal taps, up to 20 percent was being lost due to massive leaks in new polyethylene pipes that had been installed in the late 1960s (Comisión 1976b: 1; Elizondo 1977: 69).

Despite the fact that in real terms the city's water services were deteriorating (population growth had exceeded water service improvements), at the end of 1977 there was a 40 percent increase in water rates (El Norte, 12-15-1977). The increase was purportedly necessary to offset the effect of the 1976 devaluation of the peso on the financial status of the Water Service. The Water Service's costs had also risen in response to inflation, which was 14.3 percent in 1976 and 26.2 percent in 1977.[24] Yet from 1973 to 1977 water rates had increased 252 percent,[25] while the minimum wage in Monterrey had increased only 157 percent (Servicios 1977: 6).

In the spring of 1978, there were warning signals of the impending water crisis. The newspapers ran stories titled "Water Shortages Begin: Crisis Foreseen" (El Norte, 5-4-1978) and "Water Shortages Until 1979, But This Is the Worst Period" (El Porvenir, 6-26-1978). In May, the Water Service paid for a full-page announcement in the newspapers to notify the population that there would be a water deficit during the summer (El

Norte, 5-10-1978). It also announced an emergency program designed to provide some short-term relief ("Actas," 2-20-1978), but even the emergency program could not begin to make up for the deficiencies in Monterrey's water service built up over the previous seven years. In June the first rally was held in front of the governor's office to demand better service (*El Norte,* 6-13-1978). In early July, the Water Service began rationing water, cutting off water service across the city from 10 p.m. to 6 a.m. (*El Porvenir,* 7-2-1978). After night rationing was imposed, service deteriorated further instead of improving. Throughout the summer there were protests held at the governor's office by residents from different groups of neighborhoods, neighborhood delegations met with officials at the Water Service, and Water Service vehicles were seized by frustrated residents who held them hostage as pressure for improvements (*El Norte,* 7-8, 7-9, 7-19, 8-19, 8-20, 8-21, 8-30, 9-4, 9-6-1978; *El Porvenir,* 7-17, 8-20-1978).

One incident from the summer of 1978 provides a good example of the varied use of public space. "Housewives from the western sector of the city protested energetically the lack of water, converting the fountain in front of City Hall into a wash basin and a wading pool for their children" (*El Norte,* 8-29-1978). In this incident, a large group from over eight neighborhoods protested in the plaza at City Hall because they had gone weeks without water. To make their point they washed their dirty laundry in the plaza's fountain and announced that they were going to use the city's public fountains to do their laundry and bathe their children. They threatened to take their problem to higher bureaucratic levels in Mexico City if water was not forthcoming. The director of the Water Service, admitting that the Water Service was unable to provide these neighborhoods with water directly from the municipal water mains, agreed to increase the number of water trucks making deliveries.

The crisis in water services that broke open in Monterrey in 1978 had its roots in the long-term mismanagement of the water system. Solutions could only come about in the long term as well. The type of water infrastructure that was needed at all levels of the system could not be designed, funded, or constructed in a short period of time. As water services failed to improve in the short run the protests continued in 1979 and 1980.

In 1979 the protests began again in the early summer with nonpublic strategies—complaints to the Water Service and to the newspapers (*El Norte,* 6-27-1979). By July residents were out in the streets: blocking streets (7-19-1979) and protesting at the Water Service offices (7-20-1979) and at

Town Hall (7-26-1979). For the first time ever, widespread protests continued into the fall and winter. The headlines read "Discontent Grows Due to Lack of Water" (10-21-1979) and "Despite the Arrival of Fall, Water Shortages Continue" (12-9-1979). Even in December, the newspapers and the Water Service received hundreds of calls complaining of water cutoffs, low pressure, and irregular hours of service (12-21-1979, 12-10-1979).

In July 1979 a new governor was inaugurated in Nuevo León, Alfonso Martínez Domínguez. Martínguez arrived in Monterrey aware that water was the city's most pressing problem. He called 1979 the worst dry year in the decade, attributed the water crisis to lack of rain, and promised that the shortages would disappear once the infrastructure projects begun in 1978 were completed in 1980 (*El Norte*, 12-10-1979, 12-21-1979). While publicly Martínez Domínguez projected confidence that the water shortage was under control, his private actions demonstrated his understanding that Monterrey's water problems had reached a crisis level that even the infrastructure projects begun in 1978 could not alleviate. In the fall of 1979 he wrote to the Secretary of Agriculture and Hydraulic Resources of the urgent need to resolve Monterrey's water problems ("Actas," 10-23-1979). He mentioned a discusssion he had had with President López Portillo in which the president indicated his decision to resolve once and for all Monterrey's water shortages. In the letter he stressed that problems were getting worse each year and that water was Monterrey's priority problem.

In 1980 the popular response to the water crisis grew. For the first time the population mobilized as early as February and March, starting off directly with strategies that used public space (*El Norte*, 2-13-1980). The newspaper noted, "With Street Blockades, Residents Protest Lack of Water" (3-21-1980). There were 60 percent more incidents related to inadequate water service in 1980 than in 1979, and almost four times as many strategies used public space (see table 4.8). In June, the director of the Water Service stated, "We haven't been able to control the water problem. The lack of water during the day is not the result of rationing programmed by the Water Service, it's because the water storage tanks simply run out of water. Monterrey has never been in such a situation before" (6-6-1980).

At the peak of the 1980 protests, residents paralyzed downtown Monterrey for two days by blocking streets to demand water (*El Norte*, 5-23, 5-24, 5-25, 5-26, 11-11-1980; *El Porvenir*, 5-23, 5-24, 5-25-1980). Outraged

and desperate, the protesters lashed out at Governor Martínez Domínguez: "How is it possible that he shows his concern for the people by
brazenly recommending that we boil our water to purify it when we don't
even have any water?" (El Porvenir, 5-23-1980). This strategy was repeated
in other parts of the city (El Norte, 6-7-1980; El Diario, 6-24-1980). Residents also protested at the governor's office (El Norte, 6-6-1980; El Diario,
7-15-1980), and at the Water Service (El Norte, 6-6, 11-11-1980), and seized
water trucks to use as leverage (El Porvenir, 6-7-1980). The city was in a
ferment over water services.

In July 1980, President López Portillo declared Monterrey's water
problems a national priority and appointed a cabinet-level commission to
formulate the plans necessary for a lasting solution (El Porvenir, 7-24-
1980). At the end of August, the Inter-Secretarial Commission turned in
its recommendations, and in early September the president authorized
the Plan Hidráulico de Nuevo León (the Hydraulic Plan of Nuevo León)
(La Tribuna, 8-26-1980). The Plan Hidráulico was a comprehensive water
management program that included the largest dam ever built solely for
residential water consumption in Mexico and the longest aqueduct of its
kind in Latin America. The Plan Hidráulico was expected to provide
Monterrey with sufficient water until the year 2000.

This chapter hypothesizes that the protests over water contributed to
making Monterrey's water needs a national priority. The protests that
surged up in 1978, continuing in 1978 and 1979, had two primary impacts.
One was to call attention to the problem. The other was to threaten the
stability of the city. To begin with, from the point of view of the government and the industrial elite, the status quo in Monterrey was already
threatened by the existence and strength of the militant squatters' organization, the Frente Popular Tierra y Libertad. The protests over water emanated from nonsquatter neighborhoods and used strategies that were
highly visible and disruptive. The protests that used the strategy of blocking traffic on industrial arteries were particularly disruptive, especially
given that "the operative urban layout [in Monterrey] was developed
more as an interconnection of arteries used to feed industry than to
shorten distances—even when they may reduce distances" (Pérez
Güemes and Garza del Toro 1984).

By the late 1970s, then, civil society had made itself an important social actor in Monterrey. Responding to inadequate housing and water services, civil society organized in a variety of ways, creating new voices and

developing strategies to make these voices heard.[26] The Plan Hidráulico responded to a very real crisis situation in Monterrey—water infrastructure of the scope programmed in the Plan Hidráulico was necessary with or without the protests. While the traditionally powerful social actors in Monterrey, the industrial elite and leaders of state government, had direct lines of communication with decision makers in the federal government, civil society in Monterrey had traditionally been the passive recipient of such services as the government provided. The act of protesting and the use of disruption as an overarching tactic intensified the crisis and the search for solutions, although it did not give the new social actors a seat at the planning table.

The Plan Hidráulico had an impact on popular movements over water in 1981. Although the new water infrastructure would not be completed until 1984 and water services continued in crisis, there were no protests over water (according to the newspapers). The government created a massive publicity campaign around the Plan Hidráulico to keep progress on the plan's projects in the public eye and to report on short-term achievements. City residents seemed willing to endure the deficiencies of the Water Service for one more summer, because the publicity campaign promised salvation in the form of water from the new dam by 1982 (*El Porvenir* 9-18-1981).

However, despite the government's promises, the new dam and accompanying infrastructure could not be completed until July 1984. In the meantime, 1982 and 1983 were years of extremes. There was extreme drought; the water shortage was extreme; Mexico's economy, and with it the Water Service's finances, collapsed into crisis; and the protests over water exploded again. By 1982 water rationing was in force all year round throughout the city. During the four years before the completion of the first Plan Hidráulico projects, the city often had a 50 percent deficit in its water supply. The population went back into action in early 1982. While the number of incidents and strategies used in 1982 was lower than in 1978 or 1980, the proportion of strategies using public space was significantly greater (see table 4.10). Eighty-five percent of all actions taken to protest inadequate water services took place outside people's homes, in group action, in public. In 1983 this trend continued.

Cartoons began appearing on the editorial pages of the local newspapers reflecting the crisis. In July 1982 a cartoon showed a street robbery: a man with a gun held up a woman carrying two pails of water. The caption read: "Your water or your life" (see figure 4.6). In April 1983 another cartoon showed a family, sweating and dehydrated, standing with empty buckets in front of a museum display case holding a drop of water. The display's description reads, "Water: liquid with chemical composition H_2O that existed in Monterrey until 1983" (see figure 4.7).

Protests came to a head in April 1983, with more incidents than in any

Fig. 4.6. "Your Water or Your Life," *El Norte* 7-24-1982

Fig. 4.7. "Museum Object: Water, Liquid of Chemical Composition H_2O That Existed in Monterrey Until 1983," *El Norte* 4-22-1983.

other single month in the history of struggles over water in Monterrey. Streets were blocked in several parts of the city, including once again the entire downtown area (*El Sol*, 4-8-1983; *El Norte*, 4-22, 4-23, 4-24-1983; *El Porvenir*, 4-22, 4-23, 4-24, 4-28, 4-29-1983). Residents seized Water Service vehicles, demanding water in their homes and rejecting water truck service (*El Norte*, 4-26-1983; *El Porvenir*, 4-29-1983). Calls came in from all over the city reporting days or weeks without water (*El Porvenir*, 4-2, 4-27-1983; *El Sol*, 4-8-1983; *El Norte*, 4-23, 4-27-1983). Clearly, the pacification effect of the announcement of the Plan Hidráulico had worn off. As the Water Service deteriorated into deeper crisis, the population responded with the strategies that had worked in the past.

After the resurgence of protests in 1982 and 1983 the government authorized a new water infrastructure project, one that was in a way even more significant than the Plan Hidráulico. In March 1984, in his fifth annual report to the people of Nuevo León, Governor Martínez Domínguez announced the Agua Para Todos (Water For All) project (*El Porvenir*, 3-10-1984). Agua Para Todos was a new adjunct to the Plan Hidráulico that would extend Monterrey's water distribution system to the peripheral low-income neighborhoods that depended on collective faucets and water trucks. Agua Para Todos consisted of an urban aqueduct that would circle the city, linking all the city's water sources (see figure 4.5). No longer would water from the Santa Catarina source only reach to the western sector of the city, or water from Mina only serve the north. With the Transfer Ring, as the aqueduct was called, any part of the city could receive water from any source. Most importantly, however, Agua Para Todos included the extension of the water distribution system into all the city's poor neighborhoods, with an in-house connection for every dwelling. Agua Para Todos brought the municipal water system to 157 neighborhoods and an estimated population of 300,000 (see figure 4.8) (Torres López and Santoscoy 1985: 204–08).

Agua Para Todos was significant for two reasons. First, without the Transfer Ring, the Plan Hidráulico would not have improved water service for most of the city's poorest neighborhoods, because water from the new dam would have reached only the southern sector of the city. The low-income neighborhoods that extended to the north of the city would have seen no benefit, and they had been very active in the protests. In addition, neighborhoods that did not have individual house connections in the first place would have received little benefit from the city's increased water supply. Second, large water infrastructure projects in Latin America rarely include extension of the distribution system into the homes of the urban poor. The international banks that fund major infrastructure generally discourage such projects because the costs associated with home connections in poor neighborhoods allegedly are not recoverable.[27] Yet, when the protests over water were renewed with force in 1982 and 1983, the IDB and Mexican government planners decided that Monterrey would become the first city in Mexico to have individual house connections extended into all its poorest neighborhoods. Agua Para Todos and the Plan Hidráulico together constituted a real solution to Monterrey's water crisis. While the Plan Hidráulico alone was an insufficient solution in terms of water service for the lower-income population, Agua Para Todos on its own would have been useless—without the Plan

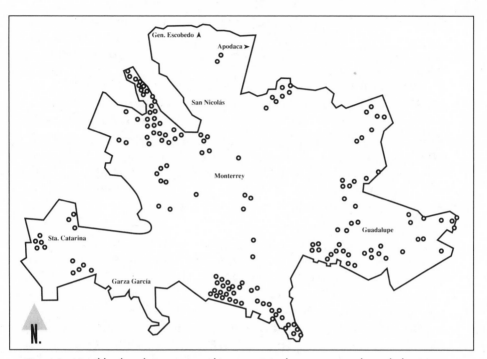

Fig. 4.8. Neighborhoods incorporated into municipal water system through the Agua Para Todos project, Monterrey Metropolitan Area

Source: Enrique Torres López and Mario A. Santoscoy, *La historia del agua en Monterrey desde 1577 hasta 1985* (Monterrey: Ediciones Castillo, 1985), 212–13.

Hidráulico there would not have been enough water to send to the new house connections.

Work began on Agua Para Todos immediately after the program was announced in 1984. As could be expected, therefore, the protests over water decreased in 1984 and 1985. While there were a few incidents in each year, they were more in the nature of isolated neighborhood responses and did not develop citywide. In July 1984 water began arriving from the dam that was the cornerstone of the Plan Hidráulico. By the spring of 1985 water services had improved throughout the city. Infrastructure construction was going on in all neighborhoods that were part of Agua Para Todos. Project completion was set for the summer of 1985 to mesh with the end of Governor Martínez Domínguez's term in office.

CONCLUSION

The protests over water that took place in Monterrey from 1973 to 1985 responded to the deterioration of water services. The protests surged in intensity in two periods, 1978–1980 and 1982–1983. Both periods saw an increase in the number of incidents of protest, in the number of participating neighborhoods, and in the number of strategy-uses. Mobilization is a feature of daily life in urban Latin America. Substandard living conditions combined with the lack of effective institutional mechanisms to process complaints and resolve problems have left the urban poor to develop their own voices and their own channels of communication. They are heard when they protest and when they disrupt the smooth functioning of the city.

The protests in Monterrey were problem oriented and took the form of defensive collective actions (Touraine 1984). The protests responded to a variety of provocations: to the absolute lack of service, to sudden changes in the level of service, to the threat of service disruption (unreliable rationing schedules), to the wearing down caused by constantly inadequate levels of service, and to opposition to government policy (the rationing schedules) (Borja 1975: 18). While the protests in Monterrey did not coalesce into a social movement with an overarching goal of transforming society, the multiplicity of protests across the city had a larger effect than individual defensive collective actions would have had. The whole was greater than its parts. In their geographic spread and volume, the protests became more than individual neighborhoods seeking immediate resolutions to immediate water service problems. The proliferation of protests moved the issue to a new level. Water service became a citywide problem rather than a neighborhood-based need. Once the problem was perceived as citywide it was addressed by massive government-funded infrastructure projects instead of temporary, local, institutionally based fixes such as the Water Service developing new rationing schedules.

Can this be considered planning from below through social mobilization (a form of planning defined by Friedmann [1987: 225–316] and discussed in chapter 2)? On the one hand, through their proliferation the protests made the water problem in Monterrey more visible. If the protests had been isolated, they could have been resolved on a case-by-case basis or even ignored. However, because the protests were widespread, even though they emanated from individual neighborhoods they could no longer effectively be dealt with case by case. The mechanism of protest, employed by a critical mass of neighborhoods, elevated neighborhood problems to city problems and even to national concern. On the other hand, institutional learning, or the redefining of institutional objectives and policies that signals social transformation, did not occur. There was no force either within civil society or within the institutions themselves to promote social change. Nevertheless, part of the government's response to the water crisis in Monterey, the Agua Para Todos project, was an unprecedented step toward equity in water services. The protests in Monterrey, precisely because they were widespread, redefined citizens' rights. By authorizing and financing Agua Para Todos, the government recognized that home water service was a right, not a luxury. Because Agua Para Todos was developed four years after the Plan Hidráulico was designed, and because it came on the heels of forcefully renewed protests over water, it constitutes an example of the integration of planning from below and planning from above. Because of the protests, the range of solutions evaluated and selected by policy makers at the state and national level changed. While falling short of social transformation, the protests in Monterrey went beyond the local community and challenged conventional planning in the water sector.

Protest has become one of the voices of civil society in Latin America. Along with urban popular movements, protests have bypassed government channels for filing complaints because those channels simply do not work. Creating the voice of civil society independently though protests and autonomous organizing does work. The effectiveness of the protests in Monterrey was due to the strategies used, and these in turn, as discussed in chapter 5, were due to the class and gender of the protesters.

5 GENDER, CLASS, AND WATER
The Role of Women in the Protests Over Water

THIS chapter analyzes the role of women in the protests over water in Monterrey, thereby helping to create a historical memory of urban development in which women are protagonists. The protests over water in Monterrey are representative of social activism in contemporary Latin American cities. Research on urban problems in Latin America has documented the rise of protest activity and social movements responding to the dramatic deficiencies of urban infrastructure in the sphere of social reproduction (Watson 1992; Jacobi Neru 1987; Zolezzi and Calderón 1985). Poor urban women are often the protagonists of these protests because infrastructure problems, especially inadequate water services, have an immediate impact on the difficulty of their housekeeping work. At the same time, women's needs are inadequately represented or addressed by formal political institutions such as political parties. As a result, protest has become the public voice of poor urban women. As the data presented here show, the protests over water in Monterrey fit into the Latin American pattern of gendered urban protest.

The theoretical groundwork for understanding women's social activism was laid in the 1970s with the proposition that gender and class oppression are intertwined and, therefore, that the core relations defining women's lives are capitalism and patriarchy (Eisenstein 1979a; Sargent 1981). Power, then, is understood in terms of mutually dependent class origins and patriarchal roots (Eisenstein 1979b: 22). Using a definition of class based on the individual's relationship to the production process, the focus of early research on women in Latin America was on women in the sphere of production. Studies in both the formal and informal sectors of the economy exposed the double exploitation of poor urban women, once by class and once by gender. For example, in the formal sector there was a pattern of wage differentials favoring men, while the right to collective bargaining was often denied to women (Fernández-Kelly 1983; Enloe 1989). As assembly work has shifted out of the formal sector to the informal sector it increasingly has been turned over to women working out of their homes for a piece wage. Frequently, these women are not given protective gear against occupational hazards and do not receive benefits such as health care or social security—amenities that are standard in factories dominated by a male work force (Benería and Roldán 1987). In addition to being disadvantaged in the workplace, women face new struggles at home as their wage income alters the traditional balance of power between spouses based on earnings (Benería and Roldán 1987; Chant 1991; Babb 1989).

Recognizing that class and gender intersect helps to explain not only women's roles in the sphere of production but their activism in the sphere of social reproduction. In a seminal contribution to the study of women's activism, Molyneux (1985) distinguishes between women's practical and strategic gender interests. When women organize from their practical gender interests, they focus on the practical issue at hand and generally do not link their immediate problem (water, finances, childcare, and so on) to the characteristics of patriarchy and social class that structure the unequal relations shaping their lives. Women's actions that stem from their practical gender interests are centered in the sphere of social reproduction—that is to say, in their household and neighborhood, or around household and neighborhood issues, the issues that confront poor urban women on a daily basis. Typical actions include the creation of soup kitchens, block savings associations, and family day-care networks, as well as organizing protests over services that impinge on household work in low-income neighborhoods, such as inadequate water or sewerage and unpaved streets. High female participation in protests over public services in Latin America stems from the gender-biased nature of household work combined with the deficiency of public services in lower-income neighborhoods. The fact that poor urban women do not have interlocutors representing their interests within the formal political structure has forced them to use public protest as a new channel of communication with government decision makers. Thus, the work load of poor urban women now includes public protest, which has become more and more necessary as essential public services deteriorate or are lacking altogether and as Latin American governments reduce social spending.

Beyond women's practical gender interests are their strategic gender interests, which are based on an explicit recognition of the gendered nature of power. Once women understand that their daily lives are structured by gender inequality—in the jobs available to them, the wages they are paid, and their working conditions, in their relationships with husbands, fathers, and male bosses, in the unequal distribution of household work between women and men, and in the inequality of political and economic power—then the focus of organizing changes or expands. At least part of the objective of women's actions becomes the transformation of gender relations.

Sometimes, women participate in a protest action for practical gender interests, but their participation engenders an awareness of their strategic gender interests. For example, numerous studies show that when women become militant, they encounter strong resistance within their households, particularly from husbands who oppose their wives moving into spheres of action beyond their control or beyond the traditional housewifely roles (see Stephen 1989, as well as the case studies in Jelin 1990a). The contact with other women facing the same problems at home can lead to enhanced gender consciousness and to a reevaluation of the scope of their struggle. In another example, women might join together to create a soup kitchen in order to solve immediate budget and time problems. Over time, their collective work leads to the exchange of intimate confidences and the recognition that what they thought were individual problems of domestic violence are in fact problems structured by the inequality of gender relations. In response, women may use the time freed by the soup kitchen to earn money and gain some independence from their husbands.

In short, women may participate in protests, and other collective neighborhood actions, both out of their practical gender need (for better water service, a bus route, or whatever) and out of their strategic gender need to challenge the status quo and to forge a new identity other than that of passive wife and citizen (Caldeira 1990). Even when participation in collective action based on practical gender interests does not lead to an awareness of strategic gender interests, it can lead to an intermediate step that could be called an enhanced sense of citizenship (Massolo 1988: 80–

81). This includes the construction of a panorama of rights, including the right to have basic services. A practical gender need, such as water service, is then transformed into the right of every citizen (Jelin 1990b: 206), challenging government paternalism and the selective nature of government planning.

Collective organizing by women in Latin America has surged in the last two decades, ranging from protests over public services (Jacobi Neru 1987; Watson 1992), to social movements organized by mothers of the disappeared (Navarro 1989; Feijoó 1989), to church-linked women's groups (Alvarez 1990), to popular feminism among peasants and the urban poor (Blondet 1990; Andreas 1985; Cusicanqui 1990; Leon 1990; Barrig 1989), to women's movements that contribute to the transition out of authoritarian rule (Feijoó and Gogna 1990; Chuchryk 1989; Alvarez 1990). Organizing by women in Latin America displays a multiplicity of objectives, including improving neighborhood living conditions, challenging the repressive actions of the state, taking independent action on social welfare issues such as health care and education with the support of Christian activists, establishing new identities based on strategic gender interests, and demanding rights that imply, and contribute to, the toppling of authoritarian regimes. One fundamental characteristic that all these actions have in common is that women are making themselves "the active subjects of social change" (Arizpe 1990); women are taking charge of seeking change in the arenas that affect them.

To a certain extent, organizing by women in Latin America cuts across class lines. While the practical gender interests that lie behind much popular protest are most acutely felt in low-income neighborhoods where public services are most deficient, these neighborhoods are not homogeneous. On the contrary, most low-income neighborhoods are crisscrossed with differentiation in terms of income and education, and even in terms of race, ethnicity, and linkages to a rural past (Schild 1991). Low-income neighborhoods are homogeneous, however, in terms of urban services, and this is what brings together women who may be different in terms of income and race. Other social problems addressed by women are more equalizing even than public service deficiencies. For example, a state policy of "disappearing" suspected opponents to the regime (such as in Argentina, Chile, and El Salvador) crosses class lines by targeting any member of a particular subgroup, such as students, union leaders, political scientists, psychologists, and so on. Mothers who protest such disappearances are not united by class but by gender, by their motherhood. Organizing from strategic gender interests can also cross class lines because gender oppression is common to all women, although women of different classes may experience elements of gender oppression differently.

Social protest, then, should be analyzed in terms of class, gender, and race. Yet, while class, gender, and race may be theoretically distinguishable categories, the experience of these categories by women in everyday life is as an interwoven whole (Bahería and Roldán 1987: 10). As Alvarez (1990: 26) says, "a woman's gendered experience in the world cannot be separated out from her experience as a member of a specific racial-ethnic group or social class." At the same time, women's experience of their class is structured by their gender.

THE INTERSECTION OF CLASS AND GENDER IN THE STRUGGLE FOR BETTER PUBLIC SERVICES

Women are the primary participants in the neighborhood-based struggles for better public services in Latin America, precisely because of the intersection of their gender and class roles.[1] Their gender role makes women the managers of the process of social reproduction.[2] Traditionally, the process of social reproduction has fallen to those family members who are not directly responsible for generating the family's income or the means to acquire whatever the family needs for survival, that is, to women. Women shop and cook, clean house, raise children, do laundry, and care for sick family members.

In the last fifteen years, economic crisis and hardship have forced more and more Latin American women to seek waged labor. Yet women have retained primary responsibility for the household. The result is the double working day, one that is waged and one that is not.[3] The wage-labor part of the double day for urban women may take place away from the home (as domestic servants, market vendors, prostitutes, factory workers, and so forth) or in the home (doing cottage industry or piecework). The unwaged labor part of the day is carried out in the place of residence (the tasks of a housewife and mother).

Women's role as the manager of social reproduction is more difficult under conditions of poverty (one example of the intersection of class and gender). For example, poor women in urban Latin America often live in homes with no running water. Yet water is an essential element in a housewife's daily work. She needs water to cook, clean, wash clothing, and bathe children. Planning meals, keeping children clothed and in school, and caring for the sick are also tasks that are constrained by poverty. Because the income flows within poor households are insufficient and often unreliable (Benería and Roldán 1987), what should be normal purchases of food for a basic diet, minimum clothing, and medicines have to be minutely balanced against each other. Only a handful of studies exist that explore how urban poverty increases the work of social reproduction. Kusnir and Largaespada (1986) detail women's involvement in self-help housing. In Latin America, only the poor live in neighborhoods where they have to build their own homes. In these neighborhoods, women's contributions to the building process run from the financial, to design and planning, physical labor (carrying materials, preparing cement, digging, and detail work), and support work (cooking and cleaning up).

Ortiz Monasterio and Schmink (1986) document women's involvement in testing a low-cost, alternative, waste-recycling technology in two Mexican cities. This alternative technology was only tried in poor neighborhoods because they were not connected to the municipal sewerage system. In the waste-recycling project studied, women were the operators of the new system, again adding to the tasks of their working day. Sara-Lafosse (1986) describes the emergence of cooperative kitchens in Lima, Peru. In response to the rising cost of living, women have joined together to form communal kitchens that allow them to buy food in bulk more cheaply and to reduce some of the daily household work by taking turns cooking. This also frees time for waged labor. For the women who live in poor urban neighborhoods, their experience of their class, which has made them managers of poverty, intersects with their experience of their gender, which makes them managers of the household.

One of the most useful frameworks for understanding class structure in Latin America was developed by Portes (1985). Expanding from the traditional Marxist definition of class as the individual's relationship to the production process, the Portes framework uses three criteria to define class: ownership or control over the means of production, control over the labor power of others, and mode of remuneration. Portes posits five classes: dominant, bureaucratic-technical, formal proletariat, informal petit bourgeoisie, and informal proletariat (see table 5.1).

While gender intersects with class to create different male and female

TABLE 5.1
Latin American Class Structure

Class	Control Over Means of Production	Control Over Labor Power	Mode of Remuneration
Dominant	yes	yes	profits; salaries and bonuses linked to profits
Bureaucratic-technical	no	yes	salaries and fees
Formal proletariat	no	no	protected wages
Informal petit bourgeoisie	yes	yes	irregular profits
Informal proletariat	no	no	casual wages; direct subsistence

Source: Alejandro Portes, "Latin American Class Structures: Their Composition and Change During the Last Decades," *Latin American Research Review* 20, no. 3 (1985): 7–40.

experiences with regard to the three criteria used by Portes, Portes ignores gender in his framework. By doing so, he obscures important gradations that exist within each category. For example, in the dominant class, women find a glass ceiling that prevents equal opportunity for advancement. In all five classes, women are often paid less than men are for the same work performed. Within the formal proletariat, the industrial sectors where women prevail (such as border assembly plants) are less likely to be unionized and fringe benefits are less common. With the growth of the informal sector, more women are joining the waged labor force but their jobs are often in cottage industries with lower pay, no benefits, and no occupational hazard protection. Jobs that used to be held by men working in factories with regulated pay, benefits, and occupational safety controls have been informalized and farmed out to women as piecework (Benería and Roldán 1987). When women work for a wage they are categorized twice: once within one of the five classes described by Portes, and again within the class by gender. Women's place in the class structure can be determined by their direct relation to the production process, or by their indirect relation when they rely solely on wages earned by family members. In the latter case, it is the family member's place in the class structure that determines the dependent woman's class.

Portes (1985: 27–30) emphasizes the importance of the informal proletariat in Latin American class structure. Unlike the experience of the advanced industrialized nations, the informal proletariat in Latin America has not diminished as countries industrialized; rather, it has remained relatively stable. This, in turn, has had an impact on the nature of class struggle in the region. The fact that the informal proletariat constitutes an absolute majority of the work force means, among other things, that a majority of the economically active population is not collectively organized in the workplace. But, as Portes (32) points out, the fact that this large sector of the population rarely organizes around work-related issues does not mean that they never organize. It does mean that when they organize they do not confront the dominant class (as they would if they were workers in the formal sector of the economy) but the bureaucratic-technical class that manages the state agencies which oversee both the regulations governing informal sector work (to the extent that there are any) and those structuring public service provision.

The tendency for conflict to occur between government agencies and lower-income groups over issues of social reproduction is magnified in Latin America by the size of the informal sector (which usually does not live in neighborhoods with fully developed services) and the absolute inadequacies of public services. As a result, issues of social reproduction are territorially based. The need for a bus route may affect one group of neighborhoods and not another, even if they are of the same class. Similarly, the demand to extend a city's water system may be made by a group of neighborhoods in one sector of the city, but it might not make sense for them to ally with neighborhoods in another part of the city even if, again, they are of the same class. In addition, as noted earlier, neighborhoods are not homogeneous with respect to class. When neighborhood demands, protests, or movements over issues of social reproduction bring together members of different classes who happen to live in the same neighborhood(s), such alliances are not class-based but territorially based, as are the demands that emanate from them.

GENDER AND PROTESTS OVER WATER IN MONTERREY

As Latin American cities grew without a concomitant growth in all public services, the government increasingly became the terrain of conflict, and conflict itself increasingly was centered on issues of social reproduction and not only on the standard issues of the sphere of production. The division of labor within the sphere of reproduction meant that women increasingly became the protagonists of these territorially based conflicts.

Women and men are affected differently by residential water problems. Men are expected to be the wage earners. Most men leave their neighborhoods at least five days a week to go to work or to look for work. Women may also be wage earners; however, wage earners or not, women are expected to fulfill their housewifely duties. Because water is a primary element of a housewife's daily work, the water services her neighborhood receives are a crucial determinant of her working conditions. If she does not have water service within her home, the housewife has to keep track of the hours when water is available at the public faucet, she has to make several trips daily to and from the faucet carrying heavy buckets to stock the house with water (sometimes at very inconvenient hours), she has to wait in line at the faucet when there is water, and she has to manage a limited water supply to meet the family's needs. If she does have home water service, when water is rationed the housewife must work around the rationing schedule, filling buckets for when the water is cut off and managing household water use. In contrast, the men of the household usually know little about water service in their neighborhood or about the extra work that an irregular or rationed water supply means to the housewife.

Given that water is a primary tool of women's work as housewives, when residential water supply is consistently irregular or insufficient, women are often the first to do something about it. In 1970, in Monterrey, 282,000 people—almost one-quarter of the city's population—were not connected to the municipal water system (Elizondo 1977: 69). In addition, the supply of water itself was far short of demand. Women in Monterrey began protesting over inadequate water services in 1973, but the protests hit their peak from 1978 to 1980 and again from 1982 to 1984. Table 5.2 shows the number of protests over water in Monterrey in which women were the primary or sole participants from 1973 to 1985.[4] Women were the protagonists of a majority of protests during six out of thirteen years.

Table 5.3 compares women's participation in protests that used public space and protests that did not use public space. The trend here is striking. In eight of the nine years when protests occurred on public space, women were the primary participants in more than half the protests each year. In five of those years, women were the primary participants more than two-thirds of the time. While women often constituted the majority of participants, sometimes they were the sole participants (no men joined them). Some of the protests came out of individual neighborhoods, and some were carried out by groups of neighborhoods. For example, in 1978,

TABLE 5.2
Women as Protagonists of the Protests Over Water in Monterrey

| Year | Incidents of Protest | Incidents in Which Women Were Primary Participants | |
		Number	Percent
1973	12	6	50.0
1974	1	1	100.0
1975	3	1	33.3
1976	2	1	50.0
1977	2	nd[a]	nd
1978	28	8	28.6
1979	23	6	26.1
1980	37	20	54.1
1981	0	0	0.0
1982	25	9	36.0
1983	43	23	53.5
1984	11	3	27.3
1985	10	7	70.0

Sources: El Norte, El Porvenir, 1973–1985.
Note: These data come from newspaper reports of the protests, which did not always identify the gender of the participants. Therefore, the data presented here undercount women's participation in the protests. See the full explanation in chapter 5, note 4.

[a]nd = no data

three of the five protests that used public space and whose participants were primarily women included women from more than one neighborhood. In the first case there were women from seven neighborhoods (*El Norte*, 6-13-1978); in the second case there was a delegation representing forty neighborhoods (7-19-1978); and in the third case there were women from at least ten neighborhoods (8-29-1978). In 1978 women from at least fifty-nine neighborhoods participated in protests over water using public space as a strategy.[5]

Two 1983 cartoons from local Monterrey newspapers address the role of women with respect to water. In Figure 5.1 two women return home from the collective faucet carrying pails of water. The first woman says to the other, "Here we are out blocking streets [to demand water] and my old man won't leave the tub." The second woman exclaims, "But, *comadre*,

TABLE 5.3

Women's Use of Public Space in Protests Over Water in Monterrey

Year	Incidents of Protest	Protests Using Public Space	Protests Using Public Space: Women as Primary Participants		Protests Not Using Public Space: Women as Primary Participants
			Number	Percent	
1973	12	9	6	66.7	nd[a]
1974	1	0	0	0	1
1975	3	0	nd	nd	1
1976	2	1	1	100.0	nd
1977	2	0	nd	nd	nd
1978	28	13	5	38.5	3
1979	23	8	4	50.0	2
1980	37	19	14	77.8	6
1981	0	0	0	0	0
1982	25	15	9	60.0	nd
1983	43	19	16	84.2	7
1984	11	5	3	60.0	nd
1985	10	6	5	83.3	2

Sources: El Norte, El Porvenir, 1973–1985.

Note: These data come from newspaper reports of the protests, which did not always identify the gender of the participants. Therefore, the data presented here severely undercount women's participation in the protests. See the full explanation in chapter 5, note 4.

[a]nd = no data

the tub? There's no water!!'' The first woman responds, "I mean the tub of beer," and the cartoon depicts her husband relaxing on the sofa drinking a beer next to a tin tub full of beer bottles. Figure 5.2 is simply entitled "Scenes of Monterrey." It shows a housewife seated on a stool in front of a large water faucet that has the shape of a cow's udder. She obviously is hard at work yet only a few drops emerge. These two cartoons indicate that not only are women responsible for household water supply, which is a tiring and thankless job, but that protest activity over water had already become a common component of women's work.

THE IMPACT OF WOMEN'S PARTICIPATION ON THE STRATEGIES USED IN THE PROTESTS OVER WATER

Women were major participants in the protests over water in Monterrey because residential water service was an integral part of their work-

Fig. 5.1. "The Lucky Man," *Extra* 4-26-1983

Fig. 5.2. "Scenes of Monterrey," *El Norte* 5-3-1983

ing conditions. When faced with the collective problem of water services, housewives in Monterrey created strategies that would get authorities to resolve the problem, and their selection of strategies was both class and gender based.

When factory workers, teachers, or bus drivers, for example, have work-related complaints, they choose their strategies to have an impact on the relevant authorities. They may ask for changes through their union. They may use sabotage or slowdowns. They may go on strike, shutting down the factory, the schools, or the transportation system. Even in different arenas such as factory work or driving a bus, workers' strategies stem from the same overarching tactics: the disruption or destabilization of the work process, or the threat to do so.

Housewives who live in the same neighborhood usually have the same water service, so when service is deficient they have a common problem. While housewives have a common workplace, their neighborhood, they do not have labor unions to mediate their housework-related problems. At the same time, political parties in Mexico have not functioned as reliable and effective representatives of the population by linking local neighborhood demands to state or national investment projects. Without mediating organizations or representatives to turn to, housewives must deal directly with the institutions and bureaucrats who can resolve their problems. When inadequate water service became intolerable, women in Monterrey responded in their workplace (i.e., their neighborhood) and at the offices of the relevant authorities (at the main offices of the Water Service, at City Hall, and at the governor's office).

When women chose strategies they could carry out within their neighborhood, they had to do something that would be visible outside their neighborhood—otherwise they would not catch the attention of bureaucrats who could respond to their complaints. Two of the strategies that were repeated with great visibility over the years were the blocking of avenues and the kidnapping of Water Service–related vehicles and personnel. Housewives usually chose one of these two strategies when water problems became particularly acute. In neighborhoods that were not connected to the water system, women turned to protest if the weekly water delivery trucks failed to show up when expected. Housewives who depended on collective faucets took action when the hours of water availability at the faucet were too erratic for them to gather water reliably or too brief to service everybody, or when water pressure was so low that it would take a long time to fill each bucket.[6] Housewives who had in-home water service protested when the rationing schedule for their home was unreliable or when service was drastically worse than the rationing schedule they had gotten used to.

By blocking streets and avenues women used public space within their workplace to disrupt the normal flow of life and call attention to their problem. This is similar to workers going on strike and picketing outside a factory, thereby disrupting the normal flow of factory work. The women used tubs, barrels, and their bodies to block streets. They selected the busiest street in or near their neighborhood, paralyzing traffic not only for private citizens but for industry and commerce. They carried signs demanding water and voiced their demands to the police who came to try to unclog traffic and to the reporters who came to cover the incident. Usually the women ignored the entreaties of the police to clear the streets. The police were faced with the dilemma of whether or not to use force to dislodge the women (who frequently had children with them). Although the police were always called in when there was a street blockade in Monterrey, they never actually employed force or violence to remove the women. Rather, they tried to intimidate the women or to negotiate with them. It was not uncommon for a police lineup to string out along the street facing the women, tapping batons and using bullhorns to order the women to move. Women ended the blockades—at least temporarily—when the Water Service provided improved service. Thus, protests that were carried out by women in their neighborhoods (their workplace) had an impact even when the decision makers with regard to water service were located elsewhere.

The second neighborhood-based strategy was for housewives to stop a water-service-related vehicle and then hold both the vehicle and its driver hostage while demanding water. This strategy was possible because the trucks and personnel circulated through residential neighborhoods with regularity. The types of vehicles seized included Water Service maintenance trucks, vehicles used by meter readers, and water tank trucks used to deliver water (including water trucks belonging to the private sector and to different state and city agencies).[7] Once the vehicles and personnel were seized and held hostage they could not continue their work, be it repair, maintenance, reading meters, or other tasks. By seizing these vehicles and drivers the housewives disrupted repair work, meter reading, and water delivery in other neighborhoods, creating a ripple effect.

The drivers were usually sympathetic to the women's plight and smiled for newspaper photographers. Meanwhile, engineers at the Water Service worked frantically to organize improved service to the protesting neighborhood in order to get the truck and driver released as soon as possible. In the summer of 1983, there were days when women in one section of Monterrey would block streets while women in other neighborhoods seized Water Service vehicles. As these protests were reported, the Distribution Section of the Water Service began to resemble a war room. A large city map had pins stuck in it, showing the location of the seized vehicles and blocked avenues.[8] The engineers convened to discuss water management strategies that would allow water to flow to the affected neighborhoods. Usually, getting water to a dry neighborhood meant taking it away from another neighborhood.[9] This was accomplished by opening and shutting valves on water pipes near each neighborhood. Instructions were radioed to Water Service crews throughout the city who carried out the manual valve operations. Then other crews went to the neighborhoods to see if water really arrived. If not, the engineers continued to meet to design new configurations of valve openings and closings. In the worst case, or when a protesting neighborhood was not connected to the city's water system, the Water Service sent out water trucks to deliver water house by house in the protesting neighborhood.

Another set of strategies used in the protests involved leaving the neighborhood to meet with government officials or to hold protest rallies in front of government offices. In Monterrey, the public officials and agencies that were perceived as relevant included the state governor, the mayor, the Water Service, the City Hall water truck delivery office, and so on. The most frequently approached were the state governor and the Water Service.[10] For example, in one 1980 incident, a neighborhood delegation went to the governor's office to complain about severe water rationing. They were attended by the Secretario General de Gobierno, who sent them over to the Water Service (in another part of town) to talk to its director. The day ended with the neighborhood delegation giving the Water Service five days to improve service; otherwise, they would return to the governor's office (*El Norte*, 2-13-1980). In general, the women who organized protests, rallies, and meetings had a clear understanding of Monterrey's power structure with respect to water services, because in fact the Water Service and the governor were the most able to make and carry out the decisions that could resolve neighborhood water problems.

Typically, delegations from a neighborhood, or a large group of residents, would choose a public official who they thought could help. They would go en masse to his office and ask to meet with him. Often they would be told to wait in the lobby or outside the building. In the case of large groups, they would be asked to select representatives who would meet with the official on behalf of the group. Various outcomes were possible. Delaying tactics were often used whereby delegations, and even large groups of residents, were repeatedly instructed to wait, until finally the relevant official had left and gone home for the night. In a 1982 incident, a delegation representing five neighborhoods went to the Water Service to complain about serious service problems. They asked to speak specifically with the director of public relations and were told that she was out. As they left the building they ran into a newspaper reporter and stopped to report their service problem to him. He told them that he had just come from meeting with the director of public relations inside the building, and at that moment, she herself came out of the building. The neighborhood delegation realized they had been lied to, and the reporter described the scene in his newspaper article (*El Norte*, 1-25-1982).

Sometimes after several days of trying, the residents would lose patience and hold a protest rally. Other times, after a long wait, an official would meet with the delegation and promise help. The promises might or might not be kept. If not, the delegation, or group of residents, would return to see the official again, or they might decide to escalate their strategies to a new level by protesting outside the official's office. Sometimes groups from different neighborhoods would meet by accident at the governor's office. As they compared stories and the wait grew longer they would unite to hold a protest. At the peak of the protests, hundreds of residents, primarily women, would rally at the governor's office, bathing their children and doing their laundry in the public fountain.[11]

The Class Composition of Protesting Neighborhoods

The first protests over water in Monterrey emerged in the land invasion neighborhoods formed in the early 1970s. A majority of the families who participated in land invasions came from rural areas. They were part of the intense wave of rural-to-urban migration that took place in the 1950s and 1960s. In many cases, as families migrated they settled in neighborhoods built or created by relatives, friends, or acquaintances. In other cases, groups of families from the same village invaded land together. As a result, there were whole neighborhoods in Monterrey where all the families came from the same rural village or area. This lent a certain unity, facilitated solidarity, and made organizing easier.[12] In addition, the power alignment in rural families gave women a certain authority. When rural families migrated to urban areas the lines of authority remained intact. Thus rural women transplanted to the city were assertive in the face of adversity and were willing to take action.[13] Finally, thousands of families who participated in land invasions developed a social and political consciousness as they lived out the connection between class struggle theory and praxis. This was especially the case for the neighborhoods affiliated with the Tierra y Libertad organization.

At the time the Frente Popular Tierra y Libertad was formed as a grouping of politicized land invasion neighborhoods in 1976, two other organizations were also created to deal with the housing crisis. One was the government's housing agency, Fomerrey (Fomento de la Vivienda en Monterrey), and the other was an informal network of neighborhood unions. Fomerrey built low-income and very low-income subdivisions throughout Monterrey, which were organized with block leaders tied into a rigid vertical network with a neighborhood leader at the top.[14] The neighborhood unions were a response to the rising price of developed land in Monterrey. Residents were permitted to buy unserviced, vacant plots of land and construct their own homes. Because these new neighborhoods had no services, the families organized themselves into neighborhood betterment committees to deal with the problems of water, electricity, paved roads, and so on.[15]

The Frente Popular Tierra y Libertad, Fomerrey, and the neighborhood unions all established patterns of organization within neighborhoods that allowed residents to become accustomed to being able to voice and act on problems. By the late 1970s, many low-income neighborhoods in Monterrey had some sort of internal organization in place that at one time or another had been used successfully to improve living conditions. This had a demonstration effect, so that as water services deteriorated in the 1970s, neighborhoods that had neither a history of organizing, an immediate connection to a rural past, nor the unifying characteristic of all families having shared roots, began protesting. In fact, by 1985, the majority of the neighborhoods that protested during the previous seven years were neighborhoods with no antecedents of popular organizing.

The data in chapter 4 demonstrate that the protests using public space were carried out overwhelmingly by neighborhoods from the three lower-income groups: lower-middle, lower, and marginal. Only four out of the eighty-five incidents of protest on public space came out of upper-middle-income neighborhoods, and none from upper-income neighborhoods. The income groups used in this book can be roughly correlated to the class categories suggested by Portes (see table 5.1). The dominant and bureaucratic-technical classes correspond to the upper and upper-middle income groups. The formal proletariat are lower-middle income or lower income, depending on the number of family members living on the formal worker's wages. The informal petit bourgeoisie belong to the lower-middle, lower, or marginal income group depending on total income. And the informal proletariat are lower income or marginal, depending on the continuity and remuneration of the informal labor.

The Portes class structure allows a more nuanced vision of the heterogeneity of urban neighborhoods than does the income classification system by itself. For example, in a neighborhood classified as lower income, an industrial worker with protected wages and regulated benefits may live next door on one side to an entry-level government bureaucrat, on the other side to a family that operates a small grocery store out of their living room, and across the street from an unemployed family that subsists on odd jobs in the informal sector. Neighborhoods are not only heterogeneous with respect to class but are crosscut by other differentiating factors such as ethnic and regional origin, political and religious preferences, and educational level (Schild 1991; Portes 1985; Logan 1984).

What unites families with different occupations and different incomes living in the same neighborhood are the collective components of daily life: water and sewerage service, electricity, schools, transportation, paved streets, and so on. Whether a family whose sole income is from the father's job as a government bureaucrat earns the same or more than a female-headed family where the mother and three daughters do piecework at home is irrelevant when it comes to public services, because if they live in the same neighborhood they have the same water service, the same bus route, and the same school.

The neighborhoods classified as lower middle, lower, and marginal had worse water service than upper-middle and upper-income neighborhoods. The vast majority of protests were organized in neighborhoods classified in the bottom three income groups. Within those neighborhoods, women from different income groups and with different histories faced similar water service problems and used similar strategies to protest. The repeated use of the same strategies across the city is due to women seeking strategies that were accessible to them. Whether they were destitute, low income, or middle income, whether they were informal proletariat or petit bourgeoisie, women had three choices when it came to getting better water service: make phone calls to ask for water, take militant actions in their neighborhoods, or meet with decision makers in the water sector. Hence, the repeated use of street blockades, vehicle seizures, and mass protests at government offices.

When neighborhoods had an organizational structure in place, that structure could be used as a basis for organizing around water. Thus the block leaders could decide in a meeting to block streets or to protest at the Governor's Palace. Other housewives would be informed through word of mouth of the plans, and they would just show up.[16] Yet, in a survey I carried out in 1983, only 17 percent of the housewives reported that there had been meetings in their neighborhood to discuss water problems—and this was in one of the years when popular movements over water surged.[17] In short, while some neighborhoods had community organizations that planned the protests over water, the existence of such organizations, or even of neighborhood meetings, was not a precondition of the protests. By the 1980s, the same strategies had already been repeated often enough that housewives in different neighborhoods could appropriate them and use them effectively.

CONCLUSION

The fact that women were the prime movers of the protests over water in Monterrey is rooted in the intersection of class and gender in poor urban neighborhoods. Women in Mexico (as elsewhere) continue to be managers of the household in addition to whatever other jobs they have. In short, household work is gender biased. At the same time, urban public services are class biased in Mexico. Urban neighborhoods can generally be divided into two groups, the upper-middle and upper-income neighborhoods that have good public services, and the lower-income and impoverished neighborhoods with deficient public services. In the middle are the middle-income neighborhoods that fall into one of the previous categories: either they have decent public services or they don't. The intersection of gender and class in poor urban neighborhoods means that women have to cope with very inadequate working conditions when it comes to their work as household managers. It also means that women are the first to feel the impact of deficient public services such as water, and therefore are the most likely to seek improvements.

Recent social action or militance by women in Latin America has taken a variety of forms and has had a number of objectives (as discussed earlier in this chapter). The protests in Monterrey fall into several categories of social action. First and foremost, the protests sought to improve neighborhood living conditions and were typical of social action taken for such purposes in many Latin American cities. Second, the protests challenged the distribution of water services organized by the state through the Water Service agency. In order to bring the protests to a halt, the state had to massively upgrade the city's entire water system. It was not enough to provide water temporarily to protesting neighborhoods, because temporary solutions to the water crisis meant ongoing protests.

Lastly, the protests contributed to the formation of new identities for women, as the women of Monterrey made themselves the "active subjects of social change" (Arizpe 1990: xvi) instead of the passive objects of state decisions about public services. While women in Monterrey participated in the protests out of their practical gender need for improved water services, the fact of their participation meant that they were proactive instead of passive. Even if they were not consciously striving to create new gender roles, their participation in the protests contributed to a reformulation of women's identity as citizens that has been going on for some time in Latin America. It is no longer a surprise to see women protesting at government offices, or even to hear about women blockading streets for one purpose or another. It has come to be accepted not only that women's household work includes protest activity, but that women are effective in using the strategy of protest. By constituting themselves as the active subjects of social change, women in Monterrey asserted their right as citizens to have a voice, and at the same time they identified decent water service as the right of all citizens.

The strategies women chose for their protests were also determined by class and gender. Upper-middle and upper-income women relied on making telephone calls to the Water Service or the newspapers. As members of the privileged classes they had private telephones and were accustomed to solving problems on an individual basis. Women from the three lower-income groups were constrained not so much because they did not have private telephones but because of their lesser class power as individuals. They had to turn to collective action in the terrain available to them as poor women: streets, plazas, and government offices. Protesting on public space required collective action because individual action would have passed unnoticed.

The protests over water in Monterrey typify territorially based struggles in urban Latin America. Residents participate together in protests over water, or over any other public service, not necessarily out of class alliances but out of territorial alliances—alliances that stem from living in the same neighborhood and suffering from the same inadequate public services. The targets of such protests are the government officials and agencies that manage public service provision for the state. This has an impact on politics at large in that it signals an increase in conflictual relations between the government and lower-income groups, which will only get worse as the informal sector grows and social spending by governments is reduced.

During the period under study in this book, 1973 to 1985, government investment for water in Monterrey underwent a dramatic change, from negligible to massive. Chapter 6 examines the government's response to Monterrey's water crisis and to the protests over water service.

6 AGUA PARA TODOS
The Government's Response to the Water Crisis

DUE to the highly centralized nature of policy making and resource allocation in Mexico, the public service problems of Mexican cities are the concern not only of municipal governments but also of the state and federal governments. Mexico's centralized system of governance originated during the colonial period,[1] was institutionalized after independence in the nineteenth century, and consolidated after the Revolution, in particular during the presidency of Lázaro Cárdenas in the 1930s (Meyer 1986: 31; Rodríguez 1987: 43). Basing his observations on research conducted in the 1960s, Graham (1971: 3) wrote, "the crucial questions in Mexican local government [do] not revolve around the degree of local autonomy or local initiatives, but around the effectiveness of communications and mobility networks integrating the community with state and national political processes."

Fiscal centralization is such that state and municipal governments depend substantially on transfers, subsidies, and direct investment from the federal government. In 1976, the states received 66 percent of their income from the federal government. Municipalities receive an average of 80 percent of their budgets from state and federal governments (Rodríguez 1987: 219). In 1970, the states received only 12 percent of total tax income in the country, and municipalities received 1.6 percent, leaving 86.4 percent of total tax income for the federal government (Martínez Almazán 1988: 183–85, 258). This means that large public sector expenditures within states or municipalities (such as major water infrastructure) must be authorized and budgeted by the federal government.

According to the 1917 Constitution, municipalities are in charge of urban services including water and sewerage, street lighting, garbage collection, street cleaning, markets, cemeteries, streets, parks, gardens, public security, and traffic control. However, municipal governments were given responsibilities without the means to carry them out (Rodríguez 1987: 115, 120). With virtually no autonomous income, and with their share of state and federal monies highly limited, municipal governments are unable to finance the construction and management of public services legally in their jurisdiction. In consequence, the state and federal governments have assumed responsibility for the service provision and regulation that is supposed to fall to municipal governments. They do this by funding government agencies that operate purely on the municipal level, as well as by funding projects implemented by collaborating municipal, state, and federal government agencies. However, because two-thirds of state budgets emanate from the federal government, policy making has become almost entirely centralized at the federal level. The federal government controls policy formulation and planning, while states are in charge of policy and project implementation (178, 185). Despite the 1984 Municipal Reform Act promulgated by President de la Madrid with the specified intent of increasing the direct income of Mexican municipalities and thereby decentralizing state power, significant decentralization has not occurred.

Extreme fiscal centralization has led to frequent federal and state government involvement even in small budget decisions made at the municipal level. Fagen and Tuohy's (1972: 47–52) classic study of Jalapa, Veracruz, noted the "fiscal and decisional limitations" of the city and, correspondingly, the fact that "all important decisions about public affairs" were made either by the state or the federal government. The authors describe a vicious cycle in which the lack of resources resulted in extremely limited municipal institutions, which in turn were too limited to develop any sort of effective response to the fiscal centralization that faced them (64). In the 1940s, at the initiative of Governor Ruiz Cortines, the state government created Municipal Improvement Committees (Juntas de Mejoramiento Moral, Cívico, y Material) made up of influential members of the private sector. The committees were to identify pressing urban problems and sponsor the public works projects that were necessary, using federal monies. In effect, the Municipal Improvement Committees, led by the private sector, functioned parallel to their municipal governments and actually carried out the public works projects that the municipalities were constitutionally empowered to carry out but were de facto unable to because of fiscal centralization. The committee in Jalapa was particularly successful because when Governor Ruiz Cortines became president of Mexico (1952–1958) he channeled an extraordinary amount of funds to the committee, "actually giving it far more money than the ayuntamiento had in those years" (76). The committee used the money for road and drainage construction projects, for publicizing Jalapa as a tourist destination, and for other community projects. However, only a few years after Ruiz Cortines's presidential term ended, the committee virtually disappeared when the next president cut the major federal subsidies for the committee, and the subsequent governors of Veracruz reduced the committee's institutional autonomy.

Jalapa provides an exceptionally clear example not only of state and federal involvement in municipal-level urban problems but of the impact of municipal-state, state-federal, and municipal-federal relations on public spending at the municipal level. As governor of Veracruz, Ruiz Cortines had a particular interest in Jalapa that contributed to the formation of a local Municipal Improvement Committee with strong ties to the state government. At the same time, of course, the existence in Jalapa of a local bourgeoisie desirous of working with the state government was essential. The relationship between the state and federal levels of government was also strong, because then-President Miguel Alemán was a native of Veracruz. As a result, Governor Ruiz Cortines was able to obtain special funds from the federal government (Fagen and Tuohy 1972: 76). When Ruiz Cortines became president, the municipal-federal relationship (through the committee, not through the actual municipal government) was strengthened at the same time as he favored the state of Veracruz as a whole. Nevertheless, during the Ruiz Cortines presidency, the governor of Veracruz took actions to bring the Municipal Improvement Committees under tighter state control. Thus, whereas the relationship between the Jalapa committee and the executive branch of government was enhanced under President Ruiz Cortines, its relationship with the state government became subject to greater hierarchical exigencies. This state of affairs resulted in unprecedented federal funding for Jalapa from 1952 to 1958 (Ruiz Cortines's term in office), but also led to an abrupt plummeting of the Jalapa committee's fortunes and political standing once President Ruiz Cortines left office.

In a more recent example, Herzog (1990: 203–04) identifies fiscal and policy-making centralization in Mexico as key factors limiting the resolution of border problems in the Tijuana–San Diego transfrontier metropolis. Whereas border problems that affect San Diego can be successfully mediated by San Diego city government officials, the Mexican officials who serve as their counterparts are not located in Tijuana but in Mexicali (the state capital, 120 miles away) or in Mexico City (some 1,800 miles distant). Government bureaucrats in Tijuana have neither the power nor the resources to negotiate solutions to border problems in the San Diego–Tijuana area. Further, Herzog (213) suggests that municipal government bureaucrats in Mexico are constrained from pressuring the state and federal branches of government for the resolution of local problems by the need to maintain harmonious relations with the higher levels of government if they themselves are to move up the political ladder. In short, positive municipal-state and municipal-federal relationships may serve to promote the career paths of municipal bureaucrats rather than to resolve urban problems, although in a sporadic manner they can also lead to exceptional levels of funding as in Jalapa in the 1950s.

Tijuana provides a further example of the effects of centralization in that its development as a city was heavily conditioned by policies developed by the federal government for the border as a whole, instead of being organized around a master plan designed locally (Herzog 1990: 218). From 1965 to 1984, federal funds were available to support industrial growth as well as the development of tourist zones and major commercial centers. Tijuana's growth responded directly to these federal priorities, with the development of major industrial parks for assembly plant manufacturing, the building of a new business and commercial center for the city, and the development of tourist infrastructure (218–19).

> The state makes decisions at the federal level about the type of investment it seeks for Tijuana. Clearly, there is consultation at the local level with regional elites over urban development projects, but ultimately, investment decisions are reached in the national capital, monies are then passed down to state ministry offices, through which development projects are implemented in the city. (Herzog 1990: 221)

Yet the state-level offices of the federal ministries—also called field offices—operate within the same centralized and hierarchical bureaucracy that structures the political system as a whole. The field offices respond directly to their central ministry office in Mexico City and often do not interact with the field offices of other ministries or coordinate their work, even if their functions overlap (Graham 1971).

The recent success of opposition parties in winning office at the municipal level provides another context for examining municipal, state, and federal relations. Until the 1980s, the dominant political party in Mexico, the Partido Revolucionario Institucional (PRI), had held the presidency, all state governorships, and virtually all mayoralties for over sixty years. In 1983, the strongest opposition party, the Partido de Acción Nacional (PAN), won the elections for municipal government in two major cities in northern Mexico, Chihuahua and Ciudad Juárez. From 1983 to 1986, therefore, the municipal governments of those two cities were in the hands of the PAN, while the state and federal governments remained under the control of the PRI. PAN officials allege that state and federal funding for infrastructure and other municipal projects was lower during their years in power than during previous PRI municipal governments (Rodríguez and Ward 1992: 73). While Rodríguez and Ward (70–76) were unable to document open, systematic bias in resource allocation to Chihuahua and Ciudad Juárez by either the state or the federal government during the three years of PAN municipal governance, they did find evidence of the state government using "subtle restraints to shape municipal financial autonomy." For example, the state government engaged in "tortuguismo," the slowdown in processing the transfer of resources from the state to the municipalities (72).

In response to municipal dependence on state and federal transfers, the PAN municipal governments successfully developed alternative sources of funding (Rodríguez and Ward 1992: 74–76). They were able to do so because of the reform of Article 115 of the constitution in 1984, which permitted municipalities to increase their revenues through the collection of property taxes and other fees and charges. However, even with the reform of Article 115, the mayor of Chihuahua had to win the right to collect taxes by bringing a suit against the state government (74). It is highly unlikely, given the paths to power described earlier, that a PRI municipal government would have taken such aggressive steps to increase its autonomy. Nevertheless, the new sources of revenue developed by the PAN municipal governments were sustained by the PRI governments that succeeded them in power. However, even with the new local sources of revenue, the PAN governments had to scale down the municipal problems they could resolve while in office, for two reasons. On the one hand, serious urban problems such as water and sewerage required massive investments and technical expertise that could only come from the federal government.[2] On the other hand, government officials in Ciudad Juárez reported difficulties in coordinating major infrastructure projects with federal agencies such as BANOBRAS and SEDUE (80).[3]

Fiscal centralization lies behind the involvement of the federal and state governments in Monterrey's water sector. Because all the waters of Mexico are by law the property of the nation, water resources are managed by the government (Chávez Padrón 1979). In Monterrey, water service provision involves agencies from all three levels of government.[4] The Water Service, a decentralized government agency operating at the local level, manages the distribution of water within the city and tariff collection. The local Potable Water Commission plans new water and sewerage infrastructure. Both agencies are governed by boards of directors with representatives from the municipal, state, and federal governments as well as from the private sector. The Secretary of Agriculture and Hydraulic Resources (SARH), a federal government ministry, has a state-level office located in Monterrey, but staff from both its state and federal offices are involved in developing and evaluating technical studies for new water infrastructure for Monterrey. The state government, centralized in the person of the governor, plays a key role by presenting Monterrey's urban development needs to the federal government, pressuring for funding of projects he considers priorities, and serving as intermediary between local and federal government agencies.

During the period under study in this book, the Commission and the SARH were the key institutions in the planning and execution of water infrastructure for Monterrey, and the federal government, through the office of the presidency, the Secretary of Planning and Budget (Secretaría de Programación y Presupuesto—SPP), the Treasury (Secretaría de Hacienda y Crédito Público—SHCP), and BANOBRAS, was responsible for financing all new water infrastructure. From 1973 to 1985, the two state governors used their executive powers first to restructure Monterrey's water sector in order to improve the collaboration between local and federal government agencies, and then to help make water infrastructure for Monterrey a priority of the federal government and to keep it a priority during the economic crisis of the 1980s. While improvements in Monterrey's water services required collaboration and coordination between all three levels of government, by controlling finances the federal government had the final say. As demonstrated in chapter 3, there was frequent disagreement between the Commission and the SARH during the 1960s and 1970s over how to prioritize potential water infrastructure projects. During those decades, federal investment for Monterrey's water sector was negligible. As Monterrey's water services deteriorated, city residents engaged in public protests. The response to the protests over water in Monterrey came from all three levels of government, local, state, and federal.

The Government's Response to the Protests, 1973 Through 1977

The protests over water began in the early 1970s (see table 4.1). However, because there were few protests before 1976, it is likely that they passed unnoticed by the government. In fact, the 1973–1977 period was characterized by the continued neglect of water services for the burgeoning lower-income sectors of Monterrey. The only water supply project carried out for Monterrey during those years was a groundwater (deep well) program jointly administered by SARH and the Commission. However, due to the limited capacity of the aqueducts transporting water from the wells to the city, the new supply generated by the project could barely be tapped (Anson 1978; Comisión 1976a; Comisión 1977; *Diario Oficial*, 2-28-1980; Elizondo 1977: 69; Villatoro et al. 1983: app. 7). In 1974, the Mexican development bank, BANOBRAS, authorized the Commission and the Water Service to submit a proposal to the Inter-American Development Bank for a loan to increase aqueduct capacity and to drill new wells ("Actas," 6-14-1974). Although the loan was approved in 1976, the first loan disbursement was not made until 1978 for reasons that will be discussed below.

In addition to the low level of investments from 1973 to 1977, there was a marked skewing of investment that benefited upper-income neighborhoods in particular. Almost 50 percent of total investment in the water sector was directed at the Santa Catarina district, which provided water only for the western sector of the city (see figure 4.1). Ten of the thirteen new storage tanks, six of the nine new pumping stations, and all aqueduct extensions were built in west Monterrey (Comisión 1976b: 18; Laboratorio e Ingeniería 1979–1980: II, 65; Servicios 1976a). The Santa Catarina district not only provided water to a number of new industrial parks, but it serviced the highest proportion of upper-income residents of the three water districts in the Monterrey Metropolitan Area. Monterrey's upper-income neighborhoods were concentrated in the Santa Catarina water district.[5] Thus, while service improved for residents of these neighbor-hoods, it was deteriorating for the rest of the city. Every summer water shortages were felt throughout the city (*El Norte*, 6-5-1974, 6-7-1976; *El Porvenir*, 6-1-1976).

The minutes of the Commission's board meetings in the mid-1970s mention concern over the growing inadequacies of water services for a majority of the city's population ("Actas," 9-2-1975; Servicios 1971–1976: 12). However, the investment pattern did not address those concerns. From 1971 to 1976, the Commission was run by high-ranking members of the Grupo Monterrey—the powerful regional industrial elite. The Commission and SARH repeatedly disagreed on their evaluation of large water projects. Unless the Commission could get approval from the SARH for its projects, or bypass the SARH, it could not get the federal funding that was necessary to build major water infrastructure.

At the same time, the 1976 Inter-American Development Bank loan was postponed by the IDB because of concerns over financial problems at the Water Service (which would have to repay the loan out of the sale of water to local consumers). During the mid-1970s, the financial situation of the Water Service had deteriorated, because 45 percent of the water it supplied was unaccounted for at billing time.[6] In 1976, the Water Service's finances received a serious blow when the peso devaluation implemented by the government doubled the peso value of its foreign debt (and of its foreign currency interest payments). To compensate, the Water Service raised water rates in 1977 ("Actas," 12-3-1974, 8-19-1975; *El Norte*, 8-23-1975, 12-15-1977).[7] In mid-1977, the federal government stepped in with a rescue package that included short-term loans to the Water Service and an agreement to guarantee larger long-term loans, such as the one pend-ing from the IDB (*El Norte*, 7-13-1977; *El Porvenir*, 5-18-1977).

The government's support of the Water Service occurred, and could only have occurred, after a dramatic shift in the alignment of power within Monterrey's water sector. The power shift began in 1976 and was followed by a yearlong battle for control of Monterrey's water agencies, with the state and federal governments allied against the Grupo Monte-rrey. The power struggle began in November 1976, when the governor of Nuevo León, Pedro Zorrilla Martínez, sent a letter to the Water Service's board of directors accepting the resignation of the general director, Leo-bardo Elizondo, who was also the general director of the Commission (*El Porvenir*, 12-3-1976). Elizondo immediately and vociferously denied having submitted his resignation.

Over the following weeks Elizondo was accused of extending water infrastructure to vacant lots owned by large developers at less than cost, of ignoring the needs of the popular classes, of embezzling millions of pesos, of contracting secret loans in the Water Service's name, and of man-aging the daily affairs of the Water Service independently of the board and not reporting fully to it (Comisión 1976c; *El Norte*, 11-27-1976; *El Por-venir*, 12-6-1976; Servicios 1976b). This last accusation was very important because it eventually allowed a transfer of power to take place without causing an even deeper rift in the relationship between the government and the Grupo Monterrey. By claiming that Elizondo acted alone, the government could isolate him and use him as a scapegoat, and thus avoid implicating board members (many of whom were high-ranking members of the Grupo Monterrey) in any wrongdoing. At the time the charges were made against Elizondo in 1976, they were not substantiated. How-ever, two years later the director of the chamber of commerce of Monte-rrey admitted that the Water Service's board had made mistakes and that, in fact, certain large-scale developers had for years not paid the standard fees for water service assessed per square foot of developed land (*El Norte*, 10-20-1979).

The accusations against Elizondo, and the battle over his resignation, were widely reported in the local press and brought the power struggle over Monterrey's water sector into public view. When Elizondo denied having submitted his resignation, the board members split into two fac-tions, with the government representatives supporting the governor, and the representatives of the Grupo Monterrey arguing that the governor did not have the authority to interfere in the internal affairs of the Water Ser-vice (*El Norte*, 11-27-1976, 12-4-1976; *El Porvenir*, 12-3-1976, 12-6-1976). They claimed that because the Water Service was a decentralized state agency, its internal affairs were to be directed solely by its board of direc-tors. If Elizondo wanted to resign he had to present his resignation to the board, which would then decide whether to accept it or not. Nevertheless, Governor Zorrilla took control of the Water Service directly by installing his chief of staff as the general director in November 1976.

For the next two months the battle for the control of the Water Service was a public issue. It was debated in the state legislature, which found Governor Zorrilla's actions to be legal (*El Norte,* 12-3-1976; *El Porvenir,* 12-2-1976). The Congreso de Trabajo, the national umbrella organization of official labor unions, took out a full-page newspaper ad to support the governor (*El Norte,* 12-1-1976). The Grupo Monterrey, through its representatives at the chambers of commerce, industry, and real estate, fought back. They met with the governor, published full-page ads in all the newspapers, and threatened to withdraw from the Water Service's board (11-29-1976, 12-1-1976). The Bar Association of Nuevo León published a legal brief detailing the illegality of Governor Zorrilla's actions (*El Norte,* 12-4-1976; *El Porvenir,* 12-8-1976). Lawyers linked to the Grupo Monterrey asked that the governor be brought to trial (*El Norte,* 12-5-1976, 12-9-1976). Mexico's new president, José López Portillo (inaugurated in December 1976), called for harmony in the Monterrey community (12-4-1976).

This power struggle between the government and the Monterrey bourgeoisie lasted well into 1977. Yet once the conflict moved away from Elizondo's wrongdoings to the question of the governor's authority to intervene in the Water Service's functioning, the shift in control over Monterrey's water sector was, for all intents and purposes, accomplished. By focusing on the legality of the governor's actions a serious investigation of the mismanagement of the Water Service was avoided. While the Grupo Monterrey's ally, Elizondo, lost his job as general director of the Water Service, and the governor suffered the public debate over his actions, that was a smaller net price to pay for the shift in power than laying bare the board of directors' role in the mismanagement of the Water Service—a board that, after all, had representatives from both the government and the Grupo Monterrey. The federal government's commitment to help resolve the Water Service's financial crisis in mid-1977 was an indication that the shift in control over Monterrey's water sector was permanent. The conflicts during the previous fifteen years between the Commission and SARH, and between the Grupo Monterrey and the federal government, would have precluded such support.

However, while the power struggle was over at the Water Service, it had not yet begun at the Commission. After leaving the Water Service, Leobardo Elizondo continued working at the Commission, where he was also general director. The Commission's board of directors had ceased meeting, and work was directed solely by Elizondo and Carlos Maldonado,[8] the latter a powerful member of the Grupo Monterrey who had been on the Commission's board since 1962 and had been its executive director since 1966.[9]

In the fall of 1977 the government moved to gain control of the Commission. A new series of accusations began appearing in the press in which the director of the Water Service's board accused the Commission of the wrongdoings earlier ascribed to itself. The Commission was held responsible for Monterrey's deficient water services (El Norte, 9-2-1977) and was accused of causing the Water Service's financial decline (El Porvenir, 6-9-1977, 10-21-1977). One factor made the power struggle at the Commission different from the power struggle at the Water Service. In creating the Commission in 1954, the president of Mexico had decreed that it had exclusive authority to plan Monterrey's water services. According to the 1954 charter, no other institution or authority had power over the Commission (Diario Oficial, 5-7-1964: 2). The Commission's executive director was thus autonomous. The state governor was powerless to impose change from above, as he had done with the Water Service. The only possibility was the imposition of change through presidential fiat. In September 1977, President López Portillo decreed the reorganization of the Commission's board of directors, mandating the addition of three members. The new members were to be representatives of federal ministries, and the president of the board would be the representative from the Secretary of Housing and Public Works (SAHOP). With three new members, the government had majority representation on the board as well as veto power through the president of the board.

This time there was no public outcry in response to the realignment of power. The private sector representatives to the Commission's board did not put up a fight. There are two possible explanations for the ease with which the transfer of power within the Commission occurred. First, it is likely that the members of the Commission's board took the power shift at the Water Service as a warning and expected the changes, because after all, it was the Commission and not the Water Service that was responsible for planning Monterrey's water system. Second, President López Portillo was striving for a spirit of cooperation between the federal government and the Grupo Monterrey in the sphere of production and economic growth. In early 1977, López Portillo had met with leaders of the Grupo Monterrey to coordinate an agreement whereby the Grupo Monterrey would jointly invest one hundred billion pesos (almost 4.5 billion U.S. dollars) with the federal government to restructure production in Mexico (*Proceso* 4-2-1977: 20).

The shift in the relationship between the Grupo Monterrey and the federal government was reflected at the Commission. The private sector representatives to the Commission's board were high-level members of the Grupo Monterrey. They had more to gain by withdrawing peacefully from the water sector and collaborating with the government on economic development than from fighting to preserve their power over Monterrey's Potable Water Commission. The restructured board of directors, created by President López Portillo, was made up almost entirely of new representatives. While all the old representatives of the Grupo Monterrey remained nominally on the board, none of them attended a board meeting again, and eventually they were replaced. Elizondo, the general director, was left isolated.[10] After the autumn of 1977, the Commission was directed almost solely by the government.[11]

In one year, from the autumn of 1976 to the autumn of 1977, the power structure of Monterrey's water services was completely altered. During that year no new projects were carried out in the water sector itself. The board of directors of the Water Service did not meet between November 1976 and May 1977, while the board of the Commission stopped meeting for fourteen months, between September 1976 and November 1977. It is notable that these events took place in the last month of President Echeverría's term in office, and over the course of the first year of López Portillo's presidency. During the last twenty years, there have not been two presidents in Mexico more different in their style and objectives than Echeverría and López Portillo. Echeverría's presidency (1970–1976) was marked by a democratic opening and wide-ranging attempts to bring about social reform funded through fiscal reform. His reform project collapsed in the face of angry opposition from Mexico's private sector, which responded by scaling back production and investment in both industry and agriculture. The Grupo Monterrey stood in strong opposition to Echeverría as well as to the governor he appointed to run the Nuevo León state government, Pedro Zorrilla Martínez. In contrast, López Portillo's presidency (1976–1982) was characterized by a state–private sector alliance for economic growth, financed through foreign debt. López Portillo deliberately set aside social reform as a goal of the federal government. Focusing on promoting growth through an industrial development plan to produce for export as well as for the internal market, he offered guarantees to domestic capitalists who returned capital from abroad and offered a series of tax incentives to domestic investors. The private sector responded positively to López Portillo's economic program, and Mexico's economy saw a quick recovery during the first two years of his term.

There are several possible explanations for why both the Echeverría and López Portillo administrations were involved in the process of taking back Monterrey's water sector from the Grupo Monterrey. The initial move, "creating the resignation" of the Water Service's general director, was carried out in November 1976 by Governor Zorrilla Martínez, an ally of President Echeverría. President López Portillo's actions to achieve full government control over Monterrey's water sector during his first year in office are consistent with Governor Zorrilla's and President Echeverría's actions. However, although the actions of the two presidents were consistent, they each may have had different motives for pursuing them. Despite the fact that the last few months of the presidential term in Mexico are lame duck months in an extreme sense (because the next president has already been elected), Echeverría's last months in office were far from typical. Instead of remaining in the shadows, he remained visibly in command (Smith 1979: 296). Echeverría may have sought one last confrontation with the Grupo Monterrey that he could win. Relations between the executive branch of government and leaders of the Grupo Monterrey had reached all-time lows during the Echeverría administration. Already in hostile opposition to Echeverría's reform policies, the Grupo Monterrey bitterly blamed the government for losing control of the nation when a guerrilla group assassinated their patriarch, Eugenio Garza Sada, in 1973. While Echeverría was able to effect a rapprochement with the Grupo Monterrey when he began to abandon his reform policies in 1974, relations soured once again in response to his Law of Human Settlements, which the high bourgeoisie interpreted as threat to property rights and a constraint on real estate development (Martínez Nava 1984: 197–203). However, once the law was passed in May 1976, another rapprochement occurred.

In his last few months in office, Echeverría took several actions that once again alienated Mexico's economic elite, including the Grupo Monterrey: he decreed the expropriation of land in Sonora, and he devalued the peso. It was in that context of renewed hostility, and with the full support of the president, that Governor Zorrilla initiated actions to take over the Water Service. On the other hand, Governor Zorrilla's actions were consistent with efforts made in Echeverría's last year in office to rationalize urban planning with the passage of the Law of Human Settlements (Herzog 1990: 216). Camp (1989: 26) suggests that Echeverría was not aiming so much to improve social welfare but to "revive the state's role as arbiter among competing groups . . . and to restore . . . the vitality of the state." Insofar as these goals challenged the power of increasingly important economic groups, they would provoke a hostile response.

President López Portillo inherited the new urban planning bureaucracy from Echeverría and continued executive support for it by creating a new ministry, the Secretariat of Housing and Public Works (Secretaría de Asentamientos Humanos y Obras Públicas—SAHOP). SAHOP was one of three ministries created by López Portillo early in his presidential term as part of a new National System of Planning (Palacios 1989: 88).[12] His actions to support the government's takeover of Monterrey's water sector were part of an effort, therefore, to rationalize urban infrastructure planning in general, and had the effect of bringing planning for Monterrey's water sector into the mainstream of planning by the federal government. In 1977, he even appointed as president of the Commission's board the SAHOP representative.

The key difference between López Portillo and Echeverría was that López Portillo's primary goal was to forge a new, mutually beneficial working relationship between the government and Mexico's economic elites. Major infrastructure development in northern Mexico was necessary to support López Portillo's industrial development plan. Despite the fact that President López Portillo continued the takeover of Monterrey's water sector initiated by President Echeverría, he did so within a context of developing a far more important alliance with the Grupo Monterrey in the economic arena.[13] While the Grupo Monterrey screamed bloody murder at Zorrilla, Echeverría, and López Portillo during the first months of the takeover battle, by the end of 1977 they had ceded control of the Commission and the Water Service to the government and had signed on to the Alliance for Production with López Portillo.

In the summer of 1977 Monterrey suffered extreme water shortages (*El Norte*, 6-6-1977; *El Porvenir*, 7-7-1977). When the Commission's new board of directors met in November 1977 the primary topic was the need to get new waterworks projects under way rapidly. In addition, if the first disbursement of the IDB loan that had been approved in April 1976 was not made by January 1978 the loan would be canceled. The board agreed to proceed with a series of projects approved by the IDB that would increase the city's water supply, expand aqueduct capacity, and extend the distribution network and sewage system. Concurrently, the Water Service finally embarked on a leak reduction program that planned to reduce water losses from 45 to 20 percent of total supply ("Actas," 11-28-1977).

In reviewing government activity in Monterrey's water sector during the 1973–1977 cycle of struggle, two trends emerge. The first is neglect. As long as the Grupo Monterrey was in charge of the water sector, the government provided only very low levels of funding for Monterrey's water system, and water service for the lower-income neighborhoods in particular was neglected. The second trend was the government's determination to gain control of Monterrey's water sector in 1976 and 1977. By the time that protests over inadequate water service exploded in Monterrey in 1978, the federal government through its representatives on the Commission's board of directors was firmly in control of Monterrey's water sector.

THE GOVERNMENT'S RESPONSE TO THE PROTESTS, 1978–1985

The beginning of the second cycle of protests over water in 1978 coincided with the first year of government control of the water sector. In 1978, Governor Zorrilla had one and a half years left in office. Not only was he a lame duck governor, but his last two years in office coincided with the first two years of the López Portillo presidency. In Mexico, incoming governors install their own teams in key government positions, and each governor enters office with a widely publicized agenda that is meant to differentiate him from his predecessor. The lame duck period is especially difficult in terms of initiating new state-directed or state-funded activity, because new projects must generally be finished when the governor who authorized them leaves office. In addition, when the lame duck period of a governorship coincides with the first two years of a presidential term, as happened in Nuevo León in 1978 and 1979, authorization of new programs is even less likely, for two reasons. First, the president is in the transition and consolidation phase, during which he sets the policy guidelines that will shape decision making and investments during his term in office. Typically, large new projects are not initiated during this phase but are more common in the middle two years of the presidential term (Bailey 1988). Second, the president is likely to want to initiate new projects only after the inauguration of the next governor, whom he will appoint. For these reasons, it was practically impossible for significant new water infrastructure to be built in Monterrey during 1978 and 1979.

In 1978, protests over water exploded in Monterrey—twenty-eight protests were reported in the local newspapers, with sixty-eight neighborhoods participating. The legacy of the previous years of insufficient spending on water infrastructure was felt with a vengeance. In the summer of 1978 the real water supply for Monterrey was only 58 percent of demand (*El Norte*, 8-2-1978). The government's takeover of the water sector itself might have contributed to the explosion of protests. Because the struggle over control of the water sector and its outcome were highly publicized in the local press, city residents might have received a new impetus to protest in a public manner: now that the government was in charge of planning the city's water services it was worthwhile protesting, because protest could bring about real change.[14]

The government's newly established control over the water sector meant that the pending IDB loan could be released. However, while bidding on the loan projects began in the fall of 1978, the projects themselves were not completed until 1980 ("Actas," 11-13-1978). The projects built with this loan might have constituted a useful intermediary step in the early seventies, but by the late 1970s the magnitude of the deficiencies of Monterrey's water services required projects on a much larger scale. In the last year and a half of Governor Zorrilla's term the most that could be done was of a short-term nature, and thus insufficient. In July 1978, the Water Service announced that water would be cut off throughout the city between 10 p.m. and 6 a.m. (*El Porvenir*, 7-2-1978). As the summer progressed, water services deteriorated even further.

In 1979 protests continued, but with the inauguration of the new governor, Alfonso Martínez Domínguez, the government was empowered to respond. Martínez Domínguez had been the regent of the Federal District under President Echeverría from December 1970 until June 1971. In June 1971, he was forced to resign after being held responsible for the handling of a student protest in which eleven students were killed. While he was still regent, Martínez Domínguez had been designated by the PRI as the precandidate for governor of Nuevo León for the term beginning in 1973 (Camp 1982: 190). He had already made an initial visit to Monterrey, where a support committee had been formed.[15] After the massacre in Mexico City he not only lost his job as regent but his position as precandidate as well. As a result, in 1973 Pedro Zorrilla Martínez became governor of Nuevo León. The governorship of Nuevo León in 1979 was Martínez Domínguez's return to political life.

In order to make a successful political comeback Martínez Domínguez had to shake his reputation as a violent strongman. In selecting Martínez Domínguez, President López Portillo found the ideal man for the governorship of Nuevo León in 1979—a man who he could be reasonably certain would not use violent repression and yet whose past would send a warning to opposition or protest movements. After all, Monterrey had one of the largest organized popular movements in Mexico, the Frente Popular Tierra y Libertad. Martínez Domínguez's political experience and his own political agenda made him the forceful governor needed by the federal government to manage Monterrey in the 1980s.[16] In 1979 and 1980 the needs of the Monterrey population in general and the needs of the new governor converged. By the time Martínez Domínguez took office he was well aware that water was Monterrey's priority problem ("Actas," 10-23-1979). While protests demanding better water services continued unabated, Martínez Domínguez made improving Monterrey's water services the centerpiece of his political comeback.

During 1979 and 1980 the new IDB loan projects were completed but barely made a difference in the by-then critical status of Monterrey's water services. By 1980 water shortages were so acute that over half of the city was rationed year-round (*El Porvenir*, 2-17-1980). In both 1978 and 1979, Monterrey's growing water crisis was news even in Mexico City, where the major national newspapers reported, "More Thirst in Monterrey Due to Public Works Delay: 50% Deficit [in water supply]" (*Excelsior*, 9-1-1978: 4), and "Monterrey Suffers the Worst Shortage of Water of the Last Ten Years" (6-12-1979: 5), and "In Monterrey, 30% of the Population Lacks Potable Water" (*El Universal*, 10-28-1979).

Meanwhile, for the third summer in a row, protests over the water shortages were erupting onto public space. The protests reached a national audience when reported by the press in Mexico City: "Women and Children Protest in Monterrey Over Lack of Water" (*Excelsior*, 3-22-1980: 12), "Housewives Block Streets in Monterrey: No Water for Fifteen Days" (*Novedades*, 5-24-1980: 1), and "Protests Continue Over Lack of Water in Monterrey" (5-25-1980: 1). The latter two reports were front-page stories.

Signaling the executive branch's awareness of the magnitude of the water crisis in Monterrey, in July 1980 President López Portillo appointed a cabinet-level commission to develop a major waterworks project to solve the city's water problems. Two months later, the president authorized financing for the projects recommended by the Commission, which were known together as the Plan Hidráulico de Nuevo León (the Hydraulic Plan of Nuevo León) (*El Norte*, 9-3-1980; *El Porvenir*, 8-28-1980). The Plan Hidráulico reflected the federal government's new relationship with Monterrey. By directing substantial resources toward water infrastructure in Monterrey, the federal government affirmed both its new level of cooperation with the northern city and the central place that Monterrey held in the López Portillo economic program. Initial cost estimates for the Plan Hidráulico were six billion pesos, which included construction of the Cerro Prieto dam—the largest dam for urban water supply in Mexico—and a 150-kilometer aqueduct connecting the dam to Monterrey, the longest aqueduct of its kind in Latin America.[17]

The Cerro Prieto dam and aqueduct would not be ready until 1984. In the meantime, Monterrey had to survive with its existing water supply and infrastructure. Nevertheless, the protests over water that had swept Monterrey in 1978, 1979, and 1980 subsided in 1981. After announcing the Plan Hidráulico with great fanfare in 1980, the government built a publicity campaign around the new water infrastructure projects. News bulletins were issued frequently on the dam's progress, and completion was targeted for 1982, sending the message that relief was in sight. In addition, 1981 was a cooler and rainier year than normal. The publicity campaign worked in 1981, but in 1982 the government had to admit that the dam would not be finished that year. Protests over water surged up with renewed vigor.

While the construction crews worked on the Cerro Prieto dam and related waterworks, the Commission and the Water Service began designing the Anillo de Transferencia (the Transfer Ring), a pipeline that would encircle Monterrey, finally interconnecting all the city's sources of water (Servicios 1980: 11). To finance the Transfer Ring the government again turned to the Inter-American Development Bank. However, shortly after submitting the loan proposal to the IDB in 1982, Mexico's economy collapsed and the government had to temporarily withdraw the proposal (Villatoro et al. 1983: 1).

Without the Transfer Ring the water from the Plan Hidráulico would only improve water services for the southern part of the city, the sector that could be connected to the new aqueduct. The other sectors of the city would be left with the old sources of water at Mina and Santa Catarina, both of which were experiencing unusually low production levels due to an ongoing drought. The protests over water in 1982 made it clear that the Plan Hidráulico could not be finished a moment too soon, and the Transfer Ring was an essential factor in the plan's success.

President López Portillo's term in office came to a close in 1982, and his hand-picked successor, Miguel de la Madrid Hurtado, was inaugurated in December of that year. De la Madrid had been the secretary of budget and planning in the López Portillo administration and was therefore intimately acquainted with the problems in Monterrey and with the details of the Plan Hidráulico. Thus, in 1983, even in the midst of the economic crisis, the federal government authorized the resubmission of the IDB loan proposal (Villatoro et al. 1983: 1).

However, by 1983, the Water Service was once again in serious financial trouble. And, once more, before authorizing another loan, the IDB required that the Water Service recover its financial equilibrium (Villatoro et al. 1983: 77). Two steps were taken, one by the state government and one by the federal government. First, in early 1983, Governor Martínez Domínguez authorized a 75 percent increase in water rates that would be followed by a 2 percent monthly increase as long as inflation remained high (*El Porvenir*, 1-18-1983). A cartoonist summed up public reaction to the increase by depicting a hand opening a faucet, but instead of water coming out, the water bill emerges from the pipe (see figure 6.1). Strategically, the governor instituted the rate increase in the winter when the water shortages were not as critical as in the summer.

Second, in May 1983, President de la Madrid authorized the Secretary of the Treasury and Public Credit to absorb all of the Water Service's foreign currency debt and to restructure its peso debt (a total of fifty-one million in 1983 U.S. dollars—see chapter 3 for more detail). In addition, he authorized 2.662 billion pesos (sixteen million in 1983 U.S. dollars) more for the Plan Hidráulico, the Transfer Ring, and for an Emergency Water Plan (*El Norte*, 5-24-1983; *El Porvenir*, 5-24-1983, 6-27-1983). The bailout of the Water Service reflects the federal government's continued commitment to helping Monterrey.[18] Further evidence that Monterrey's water crisis was a national priority came in de la Madrid's first state-of-the-nation speech, in September 1983, when, in a new section on water

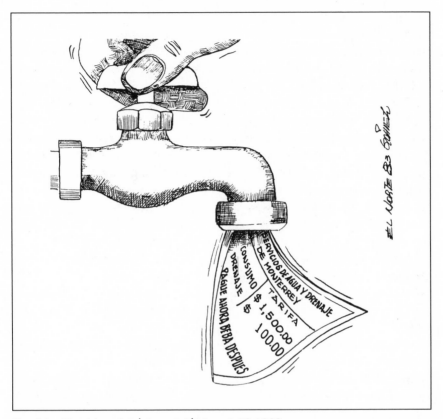

Fig. 6.1. "Pay Now, Drink Later," *El Norte* 1-23-1983

infrastructure, two out of four major projects mentioned by the president were for Monterrey (Presidencia 1988: 294).

In June 1983, the IDB authorized its third loan (for sixty-one million dollars) to Monterrey to build the Transfer Ring and complementary infrastructure. The federal government assumed the foreign exchange risk of the loan, which, given the disastrous decline in the value of the peso over the following years, saved the Water Service from bankruptcy (Villatoro et al. 1983: 1–2).

In 1982 and 1983, the deficiencies in Monterrey's water services became even more extreme. A report on water problems in Monterrey by the federal Ministry of Planning and Budget (Secretaría de Programación y Presupuesto 1985: 108) stated, "In April 1983, the supply of potable water in Monterrey reached its lowest point. There were civic protests, housewives blocked streets and avenues with pails; they kidnapped water trucks and, for the first time, the demands of industrialists, merchants, unions, residents, and students came together. . . . Water was the problem with the greatest impact in Monterrey, and the lack of a solution had exacerbated more than any other factor, the effects of the [economic] crisis." This report provides direct evidence that the executive branch of the federal government knew about the protests over water in Monterrey.

The government developed new responses to the crisis. In the summer of 1982 Governor Martínez Domínguez named a high-level state commission to work out options for the summer as the water shortages became more acute. Their solution was the Programa Emergente Verano 82 (the Summer 1982 Emergency Program), which consisted of drilling new wells in a number of underserved neighborhoods (*El Norte*, 7-22-1982). In the summers of 1982 and 1983 the governor had to ask the Grupo Monterrey to help by contributing water from their private wells. The construction industry responded by lending water trucks, while a number of industries agreed to donate small amounts of water in the short term (7-24-1982).

Toward the end of 1982, the state government initiated a publicity campaign aimed at creating a new collective mentality that would reduce participation in the protests. The campaign had two main messages. One was to emphasize the natural (versus man-made) origin of the problem by depicting Monterrey as a city within a desert. The second was to urge the population not to waste water. Government representations of past and present through the creative use of images (the desert) and symbolism (the each-drop-counts campaign) sought to alter popular response to the water crisis. By re-creating the crisis as an inevitable natural phenomenon made worse by the carelessness of the population, the government shifted blame for the crisis from itself to the environment and drew the population into sharing responsibility for resolving the crisis. Instead of protesting at government offices or in the streets, residents were to cooperate with the government by finding ways to save water within their homes. By the summer of 1983, a survey I carried out in twenty neighborhoods indicated the success of this publicity campaign. When asked what they thought were the causes of the water crisis, a majority of those sampled responded "natural causes" or "wasteful use of water." The publicity campaign continued with different forms through 1984.

Simultaneously, the Water Service contributed its own response to the protests by trying to develop a better system for rationing water. By April 1983, the city had a 50 percent deficit in its water supply (Servicios 1983). Sanitary engineers were not trained to manage water systems under such conditions, so Monterrey's water service became an experimental field as the engineers at the Water Service tried out different systems for rationing water. Their goal was to stabilize hours of service within each neighborhood, so that even if the hours of service were short they could be relied upon. To do this required setting up work teams to open and close valves all over the city all day long. By controlling valves at the neighborhood level the Water Service aimed for precision in directing the flow of water. Unfortunately, despite their best intentions, the engineers' first attempt at regularizing rationing did not work. By May 1983 there were over twenty different water service schedules operative within the city simultaneously. The result was chaos. Neighborhoods that had water only in the evening every other day were contiguous to neighborhoods that had water in the morning every day. Instead of being reassured by reliable service the population was bewildered and frustrated by the inconsistency of service across neighborhoods. Consequently, while the idea of addressing the technical dimensions of the water crisis was valid, the immediate result was to contribute to increased protest instead of reducing it.

Through the summer of 1983 the engineers at the Water Service continued trying to develop a workable rationing system. During the summers of 1982 and 1983 there were calls all day long reporting the lack of service or that a Water Service vehicle had been seized or a repairman kidnapped by irate residents. Meanwhile, the engineers did the best they could with an extremely limited system. Many worked overtime all summer long trying to improve water services neighborhood by neighborhood, but the shortages and insufficient distribution system were greater than their best intentions. And good intentions meant nothing to the hundreds of thousands of residents who faced the summer heat with no water.

By October 1983, the Water Service engineers had managed to reduce the number of different schedules operative within the city to eight— three primary ones covering most of the city, and five others in isolated neighborhoods. It had become clear that as a pacification strategy it was better to set up water rationing schedules based on the lowest common denominator. It was more effective to give as many neighborhoods as possible the same hours of service than to try to give the most hours possible to each neighborhood on an individual basis. Even if the Water Service knew it could give certain neighborhoods more hours of service, it had to choose not to in order to avoid public reaction to service disparities. Trial by fire taught the Water Service engineers how to effectively ration water. The protests, by informing the Water Service of which neighborhoods had no water, actually contributed to finding the best technical solution.

While the Water Service worked on the technical dimensions of the crisis, and the publicity campaign was in full swing, the state government continued implementing short-term projects to carry the city through the period until the Cerro Prieto dam was completed. In 1983, the state and federal governments together funded the Programa Colateral al Plan Hidráulico (the Collateral Program of the Hydraulic Plan)—another short-term summer project (Torres López and Santoscoy 1985: 128). In May 1983, the director of the Water Service announced that anyone who blocked streets, seized Water Service vehicles, or kidnapped Water Service personnel would be arrested and turned over to the appropriate authorities (*El Norte*, 5-4-1983). Despite the promise of water from Cerro Prieto, the publicity campaign, President de la Madrid's highly visible visit to Monterrey to announce the federal government's absorbing of the Water Service's foreign debt, the various emergency programs, and threats of prosecution, protests over water continued aggressively during the summer of 1983.

A turning point for water services in Monterrey was reached in 1984 when the government announced an adjunct program to the Plan Hidráulico, called Agua Para Todos (Water For All) (*El Porvenir*, 3-10-1984). Announced publicly by Governor Martínez Domínguez as if it were his project, Water For All was to extend the water distribution system to all the low-income neighborhoods that depended on collective faucets and water trucks, reaching an estimated three hundred thousand people. Without the Water For All project, the water from the Cerro Prieto dam would have provided negligible benefits, if any, to the lowest-income neighborhoods. At best, there would have been more hours of service at the collective faucets, but women still would have had to wait in line and carry heavy buckets home. Water truck service still would have been constrained by the limited number of trucks available to make the rounds. In short, without the new pipelines extended into their neighborhoods by the Water For All program, city residents who were not connected to the municipal water system could not have participated substantially in the improved water service that would result from the Cerro Prieto dam.

Water For All was unprecedented in the history of residential water service in Mexico. The Mexican government had never extended individual home water service into all poor neighborhoods of a city at one time. In general, planners at agencies such as the IDB, the World Bank, and government ministries are guided by the perception that the costs of bringing in-home water service to poor neighborhoods are not recoverable and that, therefore, the urban poor should be serviced with the cheapest, most limited water infrastructure. In fact, however, the poorest of the poor in Monterrey paid ten times more for water delivered from water trucks than families paid for regular city service through home faucets. The vastly higher price paid for water from water trucks by the urban poor has been documented in cities throughout the Third World. This challenges entrenched notions of the nonrecuperability of costs associated with providing services to the urban poor. Not only would the urban poor be able to pay off new neighborhood water infrastructure over time, they are already paying exorbitant prices for far worse service.

In Monterrey, the neighborhoods that participated in the Water For All project (see figure 4.6) signed a contract with the Water Service agreeing to one of three payment plans: full payment within thirty days, six monthly payments, or thirty-six monthly payments. The full cost of the Water For All project was recovered through user payments, because not only did 95 percent of users pay according to their contract, but a small interest charge was levied to cover delinquent accounts. The experience with Water For All in Monterrey proves that home water service *can* be extended into the poorest neighborhoods, that the poor *will* pay for service improvements, and that project costs *can* be recovered.

In his speech announcing Water For All the governor said, "It would be antisocial and incongruent with the principles of equality and justice of the Mexican Revolution for the residents of low-income neighborhoods to see daily work proceeding on the Plan Hidráulico while they do not even have a water faucet in their homes" (*El Norte,* 10-11-1984; *Nota informativa* 1984). Yet the IDB's evaluation of the Water Service's loan proposal, written in August 1983, did not include a project such as Water For All (Villatoro et al. 1983). In the fall of 1983, the director of the Water Service mentioned to me in an interview that they were working on plans that would benefit the poorest neighborhoods. Thus, the Water For All project was developed between August 1983 and March 1984, after "the supply of water for Monterrey had reached its lowest point [April 1983] . . . and there had been civic protests, housewives had blocked streets . . . and kidnapped water trucks," according to a federal government publication (Secretaría de Programación y Presupuesto 1985: 108). The timing suggests that Water For All was in part a response by the government to the continued intensity of the protests over water.[19]

During 1984 and 1985 there was construction of water infrastructure all over Monterrey. The Plan Hidráulico and Water For All had to be completed by the time Governor Martínez Domínguez left office in the summer of 1985.[20] The aqueduct from Cerro Prieto to Monterrey was being laid at a record pace; work was going on along several sections of the Transfer Ring simultaneously; trenches were being dug and pipes laid in low-income neighborhoods. Throughout the city, streets were being torn up to place pipes—one could not live in Monterrey without being aware of the new water infrastructure.

While work proceeded at a feverish pace, water services were still in crisis. The persistent drought had affected aquifer levels, so the city had a 40 percent deficit in its water supply. Finally, in July 1984 the Cerro Prieto dam began sending water to Monterrey. Water services slowly began improving throughout the city. By the spring of 1985, 60 percent of neighborhoods no longer had their water rationed (*El Norte*, 5-4-1985). The Water Service forecasted that, by summer, one hundred percent of the population connected to the municipal system would have water twenty-four hours a day (4-2-1985).

In June 1985 Martínez Domínguez gave his last report as governor of Nuevo León. In the section on water he proclaimed, "We have won the great battle." But he warned that the fight was not over, that planning for water must go hand in hand with a reasoned plan, for future urban and demographic growth. His last words were, "The Plan Hidráulico and Water For All confirm the great capacity that the Mexican political system has to respond to great problems. It is great undertakings that make the Mexican Revolution" (*El Norte*, 6-15-1985). With thirty-six billion pesos for the Plan Hidráulico and 4.5 billion for Water For All, waterworks under Martínez Domínguez were indeed grand undertakings.[21] But as he himself said, these public works were a response, a response by the Mexican government to grand problems. Helping to make the water problems of Monterrey grand enough to merit a revolutionary-sized response were the protests over water so vigorously waged by those most affected by the problem, low-income housewives.

GOVERNMENT INVESTMENT FOR WATER INFRASTRUCTURE IN MONTERREY AFTER 1985

Starting when the Cerro Prieto dam came on line in July 1984 until Governor Martínez Domínguez left office in July 1985, most residents of Monterrey had water at least twelve hours per day, and many had water around the clock. However, at the end of September 1985, the Water Service announced that it was resuming rationing throughout the city (*El Norte*, 9-20-1985). First of all, even with the Cerro Prieto water, there was still a 15 percent deficit in the water supply, assuming maximum exploitation of all water sources (9-20-1985).[22] However, all the other sources of water for Monterrey had been severely overexploited during the previous seven years, both because of the long-lasting drought and because once the Plan Hidráulico was approved the Water Service continued overexploitation of the sources in anticipation of allowing them to replenish after the Cerro Prieto dam was completed.

Starting at the end of 1985, therefore, the Water Service used the water from Cerro Prieto to carry out a more rational, integrated management of all the sources of water for Monterrey. Sources whose water level dropped too low could be allowed to replenish while the city drew its water from Cerro Prieto. In essence, water from the Cerro Prieto dam substituted for water that had until then been drawn from other sources, instead of complementing continued extraction of water from the other sources. As a result, the total water supply for Monterrey did not leap up once the Cerro Prieto dam opened but increased by only about 15 percent. Due to the system of integrated water management, and the necessity of reducing water extraction from many of the wells, infiltration galleries, and springs that provided water for Monterrey, the average yearly water supply stayed fairly steady, and by 1991 was still virtually identical to 1985 (Servicios 1985–1991). Since 1985, despite the end of the drought, water has continued to be rationed in Monterrey, although hours of service are much more reliable than they were from 1980 to 1985.[23] Most homes in the city receive water from six in the morning until two in the afternoon. There have been no more protest actions over water service, presumably because the hours of service are uniform across the city (Chávez Gutiérrez 1992).

When it was designed in 1980, the Plan Hidráulico was a three-phase program, beginning with the Cerro Prieto dam and continuing with a smaller dam also south of the Monterrey Metropolitan Area. After the Cerro Prieto dam was completed in 1984, attention turned to phase two. However, fierce opposition to the next dam by citrus fruit growers in the region, who worried that their irrigation waters would disappear, led to the eventual abandonment of the remaining Plan Hidráulico projects. In any case, since the water from the Cerro Prieto dam was in great measure substituting for other, depleted sources of water, and had not therefore served to significantly increase Monterrey's total water supply, the city still needed another major new source of water. None of the other Plan Hidráulico dams, which were far smaller than Cerro Prieto, could have filled the order, even if their construction had been possible.

The next big water infrastructure project for Monterrey had to await the election of Mexico's next president, Carlos Salinas de Gortari, in 1988. Within the first year of his presidency, the Mexican government sought financing from the Inter-American Development Bank for another massive waterworks project, giving it a high priority within its overall development programs, according to the IDB report (Villatoro et al. 1990: 3). In 1990, the Proyecto de Agua Potable y Alcantarillado—Monterrey IV (the Potable Water and Sewerage Project—Monterrey IV) was authorized by President Salinas, a program of water infrastructure for Monterrey that was even bigger than the Plan Hidráulico.[24]

The context for this project differs radically from the context in which the Plan Hidráulico was approved ten years earlier. The Plan Hidráulico came at the very beginning of a new relationship between the Grupo Monterrey and the government. After years of distance or conflict, culminating in a particularly acrimonious period (1970–1978) when the Grupo Monterrey simultaneously battled the president (Echeverría) and the state governor (Zorrilla Martínez), President López Portillo sought a rapprochement and an alliance to further Mexico's economic growth. The Plan Hidráulico was authorized by López Portillo in the context of the new alliance with Monterrey's industrial elite, the budgetary flexibility created by the petroleum boom, the government's recent reappropriation of the Commission and the Water Service in Monterrey, the street protests over inadequate water service, and the very real deficiencies of Monterrey's water system.

In contrast, the El Cuchillo dam was approved during a period of major economic transformation in Mexico aimed at pulling the country out of the economic crisis of the 1980s. In order to stimulate economic growth, both the de la Madrid and Salinas administrations pursued an agenda of liberalizing Mexico's trade regulations and privatizing state enterprises. Monterrey was targeted as the major development pole of Mexico under the new rules of trade liberalization and in anticipation of the Free Trade Agreement with the United States and Canada. The Grupo Monterrey has taken the lead in industrial transformation and in the transnationalization of production and distribution. As the Mexican government opens the country to direct foreign investment, it risks losing control over the direction that economic growth will take. In such a situation, the only allies it can have are domestic producers. Financing major infrastructure, such as the El Cuchillo dam, not only supports economic growth but contributes to the relationship of collaboration between the federal government and the Grupo Monterrey.

The cornerstone of the new project is the massive El Cuchillo dam being constructed 102 kilometers west of the city, with a capacity more than three times the size of the Cerro Prieto dam.[25] In order to transport the water from El Cuchillo, two aqueducts are needed. The dam and the first aqueduct were completed by the end of 1993, and by early 1994 were sending an initial three cubic meters of water per second to Monterrey. Rainfall permitting, the first aqueduct has the capacity to send five cubic meters per second, almost equal to the total amount of water available to the city from all sources combined in 1985, after deducting losses in the system. The second aqueduct, of similar size, is scheduled to undergo construction beginning in 1996. In addition to the size of the investment, the El Cuchillo dam project represents a complex negotiation between the states of Nuevo León and Tamaulipas. The river that will feed the El Cuchillo dam currently feeds the Marte R. Gómez dam in Tamaulipas, which provides water essential for irrigation in that state. As part of the new project, therefore, Monterrey has agreed to return treated city wastewater to the riverbed to compensate for the clean water it will extract through the new dam. This is the first contract of its kind in Mexico between two states and two categories of water users, urban and agricultural.

Given that the Water Service has successfully developed a sustainable, integrated water management program using all of its current sources of water, the water from El Cuchillo will augment significantly the total water supply for Monterrey.[26] Even the initial five cubic meters per second available in the first phase of the project will mean a 60 percent increase in the city's water supply relative to average supply between 1985 and 1991. The IDB project evaluation for the El Cuchillo venture estimated demand for water in 1990 to be twelve cubic meters per second (Villatoro et al. 1990: 3). Upon completion of the first phase of El Cuchillo, total water supply will be approximately thirteen cubic meters per second. The second phase, which will provide an additional five cubic meters per second, will clearly create an ample margin for Monterrey's growth at least over the next decade.

While the Plan Hidráulico was billed as the "public work of the century for Monterrey" and was guaranteed to solve Monterrey's water needs forever, it was the combination of the Plan Hidráulico and El Cuchillo that lifted Monterrey out of the profound water crisis created during the 1960s and 1970s. Nevertheless, it is clear that the Plan Hidráulico was authorized by the federal government not a moment too soon. Given that the Water Service was forced by the lack of new water infrastructure construction during the 1960s and 1970s to drastically overexploit Monterrey's sources of water in order for the water supply to reach even 50 percent of demand, and given that most of those sources were severely depleted by the early 1980s, the conditions were present for a potential and unprecedented disaster to unfold. Further overexploitation of the city's sources of water could not have continued for long without having to shut them down to allow replenishment. With no alternative sources of supply, the city quickly would have had only 40 or even 30 percent of the water it needed. Would this have led to a partial evacuation of the city? That scenario was presented to me in an interview with a high-level official at the Water Service—but only after the Cerro Prieto dam had begun sending water to Monterrey and the scare was over.

CONCLUSION

Just as there were two cycles of protests, from 1973 to 1977 and from 1978 to 1985, there were two cycles of government response to Monterrey's water sector needs. The government began the first cycle by continuing an already established practice of not funding or barely funding water infrastructure for Monterrey. Until 1976, the government allowed representatives from Monterrey's industrial elite to control the water sector. This policy changed in mid-1976 when the state governor, with the support of the president of Mexico, challenged the private sector for control of the Commission and the Water Service. By the end of 1977, the government had taken over both of the water sector agencies, and leadership was in the hands of the federal government. This change of policy on the part of the government, from neglect to aggressive action, paved the way for massive state investments during the second cycle. When the protests over water exploded in 1978 and 1979, the government was at least in a position to respond, because by then it had control over Monterrey's water sector agencies. The fact that the government took over the Commission and the Water Service in 1977 suggests that it was planning to finance new water infrastructure for Monterrey even before the protests accelerated. On the other hand, the protests themselves may have gained momentum in part from popular recognition that finally the government was committed to improving water services. From 1977 through 1980, during the first half of President López Portillo's term in office, major infrastructure projects of all sorts were financed throughout the country using earnings from the petroleum boom. The president's authorization of the multibillion-peso Plan Hidráulico in 1980 occurred in the context of expanded public spending in general. However, the protests that swept Monterrey from 1978 to 1980, which were reported in the national press, added urgency to the decision making.

From 1980 to 1984, the continued protests over inadequate water service brought about a variety of responses from the government. The emergency summer projects to increase water supply, the technical reorganization of the water rationing system, and the publicity campaigns were immediate responses to the protests as the city waited for the Cerro Prieto dam to be completed. At the same time, the government continued on with other new and large investments to correct problems that had developed from the lack of funding in the 1960s and 1970s, when the Grupo Monterrey controlled the water sector. The Transfer Ring, the restructuring of the Water Service's massive debt, and Agua Para Todos are evidence of the government's new support for improving water services in Monterrey.

Agua Para Todos stands out from all the other projects. First, it was the only large project designed just to benefit Monterrey's lowest-income neighborhoods. Second, it was the only project of its kind ever implemented in Mexico. And third, it was approved during the worst moments of Mexico's economic crisis. The Mexican government agreed to take on new foreign currency debt during the debt crisis to finance Agua Para Todos, a project directed solely at the urban poor. Just before Martínez Domínguez left office in 1985, the World Health Organization stated that Monterrey had the best water services of any Latin American city (*El Norte*, 6-15-1985). Again, the fact that a Ministry of Planning and Budget report (Secretaría de Programación y Presupuesto 1985) gave prominent play to the protests over water in Monterrey suggests that the scale of urban protest contributed to shaping the scale of government response.

The discussion in this chapter of the government's involvement in Monterrey's water sector illustrates two salient characteristics of the Mexican political system: the power of the presidency and the impact of presidential cycles on program development. Mexico has a presidentialist system of governance. The president has control over the legislative and judicial branches and can personally select the candidates for public office at any level of government (Bailey 1988; Cornelius and Craig 1991). The president sets the priorities that will guide government activity during his six-year term in office. Policy making and budget decisions are first shaped according to criteria determined by the president. No policy shift or large budgeting decision can occur without presidential support. The impact of presidential priorities is felt in all government agencies, at all levels of the system. Individual government agencies may take slightly different approaches, but drastic deviation from presidential policy is very unlikely (Rodríguez 1987: 171).

The six-year presidential terms in Mexico proceed according to predictable cycles (Bailey 1988). Years one and two are the period of transition and consolidation, during which the president defines his priorities and assesses projects. Program implementation occurs with vigor during years three and four. The last two years of the presidency, years five and six, are the lame-duck years, when concern about the succession to the presidency takes over. During the last two years, projects are finished but new programs are rarely begun.

Similar cycles prevail during the six-year terms of state governors, although each phase of a governor's term is severely constrained by whatever phase the presidential term is in. In Nuevo León, the governor's term does not coincide with the president's term. Years one and two of the gubernatorial term coincide with years four and five of the presidential term. This means that each incoming governor of Nuevo León gets an immediate jump start because his first year in office coincides with the peak year of program implementation at the federal level (and he himself has been selected to be governor by the current president). However, in year four of the governor's term, a new president enters office. Because years four and five of the governor's term coincide with years one and two of the new president's term, the governor can have difficulty meeting his own agenda unless he has a prior working relationship with the president or his priorities coincide with the new president's priorities.

Because Mexico has a presidential system of governance, the cycles within both the presidential and gubernatorial terms influenced the evolution of water services in Monterrey. During the first two years of President Echeverría's term, 1970 and 1971, no new projects were authorized for Monterrey's water sector, and the only work that was carried out was the end of a project that had been authorized under the previous president, Gustavo Díaz Ordaz (during his fourth year in office). In 1970 and 1971, the governor of Nuevo León, Eduardo Elizondo, was in his third and fourth years in office. However, he and President Echeverría had a conflictive relationship, which culminated with the governor's resignation from office in June 1971 (see chapter 3). The interim governor had only two years and four months in office to finish out Elizondo's term, and that did not leave time to develop and implement significant water infrastructure projects. It wasn't until 1973, with the election of Zorrilla Martínez, that President Echeverría had an ally in the Nuevo León governorship.

In the fourth year of Echeverría's term, 1974, the Water Service was authorized to submit a loan proposal to the Inter-American Development Bank for new water infrastructure. During the last two years of the presidential term, 1975 and 1976, no new projects were authorized. The government takeover of the Commission and the Water Service in 1976 and 1977, the most significant action in Monterrey's water sector during the 1970s, began in the last months of President Echeverría's term and continued throughout the first year of President López Portillo's term. However, that takeover was carried out directly by the state governor, Zorrilla Martínez, who at the time was in his third and fourth years in office. Zorrilla Martínez received strong support from both presidents Echeverría and

López Portillo for his actions with regard to Monterrey's two water agencies. This indicates that his actions served the political agendas or priorities of both presidents (although that does not mean the agendas and priorities of the two presidents were the same).

Under President López Portillo, no new funding for Monterrey's water sector was allocated during the first two years of his term, 1977 and 1978, although in the first year he supported the restructuring of the water sector agencies by decreeing the creation of a new board of directors for the Commission, which gave control to the federal government. The Plan Hidráulico was authorized in year four (1980, which was year one for the new governor, who had been personally selected by López Portillo), with budget increases approved in years five and six of López Portillo's term (years two and three of the governor's term). In year six (1982), the Water Service was authorized to submit a new loan proposal to the IDB but was then asked to withdraw the proposal at the outbreak of the economic crisis.

During the first year of President de la Madrid's term (1983), the Water Service was authorized to resubmit the loan proposal to the IDB, and the president himself flew to Monterrey to announce that the federal government was absorbing all of the Water Service's foreign currency debt and restructuring its peso debt with more favorable terms. In year two (1984), the Agua Para Todos project was approved. President de la Madrid's actions during his first two years in office appear to be out of line with the Bailey framework. However, two factors explain the apparent anomaly of immediate presidential action during the first two years of the term. First, President de la Madrid was secretary of planning and budget under López Portillo, which meant that he had been involved at the highest levels of policy making and budgeting for Monterrey's water sector since 1977. In the case of Monterrey, de la Madrid did not need lead time to formulate policy because his actions were the continuation of policy he had already formulated. Second, from 1979 to 1985, the governor of Nuevo León, Martínez Domínguez, played a very strong role in implementing and even shaping water sector policy for Monterrey. A career politician, Martínez Domínguez had been president of the PRI and mayor of the Federal District prior to his governorship in Nuevo León. He was a seasoned veteran of Mexico's political system, with good contacts and with support from the top of the system. Years one and two of de la Madrid's term (1983 and 1984) coincided with the fourth and fifth years of his governorship, and Martínez Domínguez played a positive role in achieving continuity for Monterrey's water sector between the López Portillo presidency and the de la Madrid presidency.

Within Mexico's presidentialist political system, with its predictable cycles in each president's and each governor's term, there are three factors of overarching importance that explain federal government investment at the municipal level. The first is extreme fiscal centralization, as a result of which the federal government is the decision maker on policy and investment for municipal services. The second is the political and economic context in which the investment decision is made. The third is the relationship between political actors, including the president, the state governor, the directors of local government agencies, leaders of the local bourgeoisie, and the citizenry. The case of Monterrey, like the cases of Jalapa, Ciudad Juárez, and Chihuahua discussed in the first section of this chapter, demonstrates that the political and economic contexts along with the relationships between political actors shaped the possibilities for federal financing of urban infrastructure.

The Plan Hidráulico, Agua Para Todos, and the El Cuchillo dam were approved under very different political and economic circumstances, but in each case it was the particular political and economic circumstances combined with the relationships between key political actors that made the projects possible and even necessary. For the Plan Hidráulico, the political context was that President López Portillo, in order to combat the political crisis left by his predecessor (Echeverría), was trying to establish or reestablish good working relationships with leaders of Mexico's private sector through an alliance for production. The Plan Hidráulico was authorized by López Portillo in 1980, when the presidency and the Grupo Monterrey had the most harmonious and collaborative relationship they had had in decades. At the same time, Governor Martínez Domínguez of Nuevo León also had a good working relationship with López Portillo and a relationship of mutual respect with leaders of the Grupo Monterrey. In the economic sphere, the Plan Hidráulico was developed and funded during Mexico's petroleum boom, when López Portillo was authorizing large, government-funded infrastructure projects all over Mexico. The very real crisis in Monterrey's water services, kept visible by the protests described in chapters 4 and 5, made new water infrastructure necessary; the improved relationship between the government and the Grupo Monterrey (including the government's takeover of the Water Service and the Commission), and the availability of funds generated by the petroleum boom, made it possible.

Agua Para Todos was approved in 1984 under very different circumstances. By the end of López Portillo's term, Mexico was in a deep economic crisis and the closer relationship between the government and the private sector had come undone. The wild overspending and corruption of the López Portillo administration had come to light in 1982, when the president declared that Mexico was unable to make the interest payments on its foreign debt. The private sector, also in serious financial trouble due to over-borrowing on the international credit markets, was bitter about the scale of government mismanagement of the budget and about López Portillo's nationalization of the banks in his last months in office. Thus when President de la Madrid was inaugurated in 1982, he had neither the confidence of Mexico's private sector, nor sufficient government revenue, a growing economy, or the support of the international banking community. Despite these severe limitations, or maybe because of them, de la Madrid sought an improved relationship with the private sector. Using mechanisms such as preferential exchange rates, he extended government help to financially weakened regional economic leaders including the Grupo Monterrey. In addition, because de la Madrid had been the minister of planning and budget under López Portillo, he had participated in making Monterrey's water problems a priority of the federal government, and he had a good relationship with Governor Martínez Domínguez of Nuevo León.

De la Madrid's presidential support of the Plan Hidráulico and Agua Para Todos was the continuation, therefore, of policies he had established under different political and economic circumstances. But it was also a response to the political and economic crisis that defined his presidency, insofar as it sent a message to the private sector that the president supported Monterrey's economic recovery and its continued preeminence as the economic motor of northern Mexico, and another message to the citizenry that the presidency could be responsive to citizen's demands.

The El Cuchillo dam was approved by President Salinas, who had been elected in 1988 by the smallest margin of any president. Despite the fact that his political party, the PRI, was in crisis, Salinas actually had a stronger relationship with the Grupo Monterrey than the former presidents did. This was due in great measure to the significant overlap in their economic vision. By 1988, Mexico was beginning to emerge from its economic crisis. The Grupo Monterrey in particular had recovered earlier than other industrial groups. Both the new president and the leaders of the Grupo Monterrey embraced trade liberalization and a model of economic growth based on exports, which made them natural allies in the economic arena. As explained earlier, a major new dam was essential for Monterrey once it became clear that the water from the Plan Hidráulico had not provided a net increase in total water supply for the city. The El Cuchillo dam, an essential component in the consolidation of Monterrey as a center of international trade and as a development pole for modern Mexico, was the result of the strong alliance between President Salinas and the Grupo Monterrey. It was also evidence of the government's commitment to that alliance.

The period reviewed in this chapter encompasses the full range of government–private sector relations, from hostility and open conflict to cooperation and collaboration. Until 1976, while leaders of the Grupo Monterrey controlled the Water Service and the Commission, the Commission and the federal government were unable to agree on how to prioritize government investment in water infrastructure. As a result, the major waterworks that were necessary were not constructed, city water service deteriorated, and dramatic water shortages led to years of city-wide protests from the late 1970s to the mid 1980s. By 1992, however, the government had completed one major water infrastructure project for Monterrey, costing close to one billion dollars, and was embarked on a second project of even greater dimensions.

Two key relationships changed during the fifteen years from 1977 to 1992. First, through protests that used strategies of disruption, low-income residents of Monterrey constituted themselves as a political actor, created new channels of communication with the government, and held the government responsible for providing dependable water service. Second, during three presidencies the government worked to establish an alliance with the Grupo Monterrey. By 1992, the hostility that had been the hallmark of the relationship through almost five decades had been replaced by open collaboration. One would like to think that major investment decisions are made according to technical criteria. However, the case of Monterrey's water services shows that major investment decisions by the federal government were shaped by the political context, the economic context, and the relationship between key political actors. It was only when the political-economic context and key relationships were in place that the government authorized investment in waterworks, and only then were the technical dimensions decided upon.

7 CONCLUSION
The Politics of Water

THE research presented in this book exposes the social and political relationships that underlie the provision of water to the city of Monterrey, and therefore permits conclusions in three areas. First, the exploration of Monterrey's water service development contributes to a deeper understanding of relations of power in Mexican society and in its political system. Second, the history of protests over water in Monterrey suggests that protest has an impact on planning and portrays the impact of gender on protest. Third, the history of water service development in Monterrey provides data for the ongoing debate about the benefits of government versus private sector provision of public services.

RELATIONS OF POWER

The development of Monterrey's water system after 1954 demonstrates the constraints on effective planning that arise from two key aspects of Mexico's political system: the centralization of policy making and budgetary decisions, and the power of the presidency.

As discussed in chapter 6, Mexico has a highly centralized political system with power concentrated in the presidency (Cornelius and Craig 1991). Centralization has resulted in tremendous imbalances of power between federal, state, and local governments, as well as in distortions within the planning and budgeting process. To begin with, despite the fact that planning is highly centralized, until 1970 there was no formal regional development policy with national scope (Palacios 1989: 62). Regional development consisted primarily of large river-basin management projects designed to support agricultural modernization in different regions, not in order to promote regional development as a goal in and of itself but to stimulate agricultural export trade in order to generate the foreign currency earnings necessary to support import substitution industrialization (ISI) (Palerm 1972). As a result, true regional development, understood as the redistribution of wealth and rising standards of living across the board, did not occur (Palacios 1989).

During the 1960s, federal investment was concentrated in just a few states and was carried out according to centrally developed sectoral strategies designed to support the ISI development model. The Federal District, Tamaulipas, and Veracruz together received an average of 37 percent of total federal investment per year between 1959 and 1964, and an average of 44 percent between 1965 and 1970 (Palacios 1989: 162–63).[1] Sectorally, during the same period, industrial investment garnered almost 40 percent of total federal investment (161).

After 1970, a marked break with the past occurred in terms of stated policy for regional development. Presidents Echeverría and López Portillo both presented comprehensive regional development plans with the goal of reorienting geographic patterns of development in Mexico (Palacios 1989: 62). Echeverría made an unprecedented commitment to the redistribution of wealth and of population across the nation and created the Comisión Nacional de Desarrollo Regional to coordinate regional planning. For his part, López Portillo further systematized regional planning by creating the Sistema Nacional de Planeación, which operated through three new ministries.[2] While regional development under Echeverría was mostly oriented to rural zones, under López Portillo there was a primarily urban focus, within which *low* priority was assigned to the most developed urban centers of the country and higher priority was given on paper to small- and medium-sized cities.

Despite the unprecedented commitments to regional development on paper after 1970, in practice the geographic distribution of federal spending remained concentrated in the same states as before 1970 (Palacios 1989: 170–72). From 1971 to 1976 (President Echeverría), 43 percent of federal investment went to the Federal District, Veracruz, Tamaulipas, and Tabasco; while from 1977 to 1982 (President López Portillo), almost 50 percent went to the same four states (170–71).[3] In general, under both presidents, public spending was positively correlated with the existing level of development, state by state.

Under Echeverría, the industrial sector continued to receive an average of close to 40 percent a year of total federal investment, which rose under López Portillo to an average of 47 percent per year (Palacios 1989: 166, 168). The major change in the 1977–1982 period was a decrease in federal spending on social and economic infrastructure.[4] From a high of an average of 24 percent per year from 1965 to 1970, spending on social infrastructure dropped to an average of 20 percent per year from 1971 to 1976, and further to 14 percent per year from 1977 to 1982. Spending on economic infrastructure dropped from an average of 22 percent per year from 1965 to 1970, to an average of 20 percent per year from 1971 to 1976, to an average of 14 percent per year from 1977 to 1982 (161, 166, 168). In short, under Presidents Echeverría and López Portillo, federal investment continued to be assigned according to sectoral criteria rather than to the goals of regional development.

At the same time as federal investment was skewed toward industrialization, and favored a small number of states, fiscal centralization meant that state and municipal governments depended heavily on transfers, subsidies, and direct investment from the federal government and did not have sufficient independent income to carry out development in their own region if they were not among the states favored by the federal government. The fact that more than half of state budgets emanated from the federal government reinforced the centralization of policy making. The federal government controlled policy formulation and planning, while states were in charge of policy and project implementation (Rodríguez 1987: 178, 185).

Under these circumstances, networks that cut across the three levels of government have become extremely important. Influencing policy making at the center and achieving the needed budget allocations has become, to a great extent, a matter of municipal and state bureaucrats and politicians belonging to networks with the right contacts in the federal government. Project design, approval, and financing for the water sector in Monterrey were affected not only by centralization, and by the cycles of the presidential term as discussed in chapter 6, but also by the impact of networking on policy making and budgeting.

The Mexican government has a very large bureaucracy with no career service (Bailey 1988: 75–77).[5] As a result, stability and upward mobility in government employment are based on connections and networks within and across levels of government. The building block of the bureaucracy is the *camarilla*, or team.[6] Each *camarilla* has a leader, who also holds the highest level of office among team members. As *camarilla* leaders move up through the bureaucracy, their teams go with them. Likewise, as team leaders move horizontally in the bureaucracy, from one sector to another, their teams move with them. Job tenure depends more on loyalty to the team leader than it does on skill or on knowledge of a particular sector. Thus, a *camarilla* may be in the Secretary of the Interior with its leader as general director under one president, and may find itself at the Secretary of Health and Welfare with its leader as subsecretary under the next president. Individual bureaucrats usually belong to more than one *camarilla*, as do *camarilla* leaders themselves. In fact, Cornelius and Craig (1991: 39) characterize the Mexican government system as "interlocking chains of patron-client relationships," where the *camarilla* leader is the patron and the team members are the clients.

Interlocking *camarillas* provide linkages between municipal, state, and federal government and between sectors of the government apparatus. This system of linkages has positive and negative impacts on governance. On the positive side, the linkages oil the process of policy making and implementation. On the negative side, tenure based on loyalty to the team leader instead of merit means that specialized personnel often end up in sectors unrelated to their training (Bailey 1988: 77). In addition, this system discourages policy making from below since team members seek to demonstrate loyalty by following the guidance of their leader (Cornelius and Craig 1991: 42). Planning at the lower levels of government is made difficult by the fact that planning means taking a stand on policy, and lower-level *camarilla* members are reluctant to make decisions that may land them on the wrong side of their *camarilla* leader (Rodríguez 1987: 172). Even bureaucrats at the top of the system tend not to formulate long-term goals beyond the six-year presidential term because they are not likely to be in place to implement policy under the next president (178).[7] Policy making depends first and foremost on the priorities of the Mexican president, which are then fleshed out in each sector by the highest government officials.

Centralization and the *camarilla* system worked to Monterrey's disadvantage before 1976, when the Grupo Monterrey had a leadership role in the city's water sector. The patron-client system extends beyond the government bureaucracy to the public at large, so that getting things done often depends on who you know in the bureaucracy and on who owes you a favor. While the Commission and the Water Service were local institutions mandated with providing water for the Monterrey Metropolitan

Area, they depended totally on funding from the federal government.[8] From its creation in 1954 until 1977, the board of directors of the Commission had one representative from the municipal government, one from the state government, two representatives from the low-income neighborhoods, three from the private sector, and three from the federal government.[9] The low power of municipal government was reflected in the fact that of the five municipalities constituting the Monterrey Metropolitan Area, only one (Monterrey) had a representative on the Commission's board.[10] The power of the private sector in Monterrey over the state government also was reflected in the uneven board membership (three representatives from the private sector, one from the state government). To make matters worse, the representative of the municipal government quit in 1956, and the representative of the state government died in 1954. Neither was replaced until 1977, when the state and federal governments took back control of the Commission from the Grupo Monterrey. As a result, for over twenty years decision making for Monterrey's water sector was in the hands of two groups, the private sector representatives and the federal government. Given this context of highly centralized decision making and budgeting that was guided by policy set forth by the executive branch and carried out by teams of bureaucrats operating on the basis of networks, the expansion of Monterrey's water system depended on the Grupo Monterrey working smoothly with government networks and fitting into the constraints imposed by centralization.

However, Monterrey's private sector, dominated and controlled by the group of families known as the Grupo Monterrey, did not have a good working relationship with the Mexican government, especially at the federal level. The independence that the Grupo Monterrey sought from government intervention in the economic sphere characterized the group's relationship with the government in other spheres. Thus, for example, in the 1950s the Grupo Monterrey vehemently opposed the institutionalization of standardized textbooks across Mexico. And in the water sector, the representatives of the Grupo Monterrey on the board of directors of the Potable Water Commission formed a block that repeatedly was in opposition to the Secretaría de Recursos Hidráulicos (Secretary of Water Resources, the cabinet-level ministry in charge of studying and authorizing water sector projects). The government representatives to the Commission's board of directors stopped attending meetings early on, or attended only sporadically, leaving local decision making in the hands of the representatives from Monterrey's private sector.[11] Year after year, the SRH project teams and the private sector representatives to the Commission reached different conclusions about which infrastructure projects to approve. The result was that no major projects and only one medium-sized project (the La Boca dam) were approved over a twenty-five-year period (1954–1979).[12]

Given that the government had purchased Monterrey's water service from its private owners in 1945, precisely because the service was already vastly deficient, and had created the Potable Water Commission in 1954 to provide the kind of comprehensive planning needed to expand the city's water system, the virtual moratorium on major infrastructure construction over the next twenty-five years could only lead to crisis, as it did by the late 1970s. This demonstrates the severe limitations of centralized policy and decision making that can arise when regional power groups thwart centralized control on the local level. Centralization works for those who can work well with high levels of the central bureaucracy.

In Mexico, centralization is exacerbated by the power of the presidency (see chapter 6). Yet there are contradictions within Mexico's presidentialist system. To wit, despite the president's power, the relationship that he has with state governors and with regional private sector elites can constrain policy making and budgeting and therefore can impinge upon regional development. For example, the relationship between the president of Mexico and the governor of the state of Nuevo León affected the disbursement of funds for Monterrey's water sector. Governors serve six-year terms, but their terms rarely coincide with presidential terms. As a result, governors are chosen by one president but then have to finish out their term in office under the succeeding president.[13] In Nuevo León, Governor Zorrilla Martínez was selected by President Echeverría in 1973, but the last two and a half years of his term coincided with the presidency of López Portillo. Despite the fact that Monterrey's water services were nearing crisis when López Portillo took office in 1976 and there was urgent need for federal intervention, he did not authorize any projects or funding for water infrastructure until "his" governor, Alfonso Martínez Domínguez, had assumed office in 1979.[14] Then, and only then, did President López Portillo act, and he did so on a massive scale, authorizing the six-billion-peso Plan Hidráulico.

Because of the power of the presidency, the conflictive relationship between the Grupo Monterrey and the president also constrained federal spending for water services in Monterrey. Hostility between the Grupo Monterrey and the executive was particularly severe during the presidencies of López Mateos (1958–1964) and Echeverría (1970–1976). It is notable that, during the six-year term of President López Mateos, there was no construction of water infrastructure at all for three years, extremely minor construction in the next two years, and only in the fifth year of his term was money allocated for a medium-sized project: treating the water of the La Boca dam to convert it from industrial to residential use. Under Presidents López Mateos, Díaz Ordaz (1964–1970), and Echeverría, the private sector representatives to the Commission's board were slowly allowed to take over leadership of the board. The federal government, through the mechanism of centralized policy making and budgeting, retained de facto veto power without ever having to attend a board meeting. Because all major water infrastructure projects for Monterrey had to be approved by the SARH and funded by the federal government, the Commission's board and the SARH had to reach agreement or project development was stymied. As shown in chapter 3, failure to reach agreement did prevent infrastructure development and led to Monterrey's water crisis.

Centralization, combined with the failure of Monterrey's private sector to play according to the rules of networking with the highest levels of the federal government, exacted a heavy price on the residents of Monterrey who live with deficient water service. At the same time, the federal government and the executive let their relationship with the Grupo Monterrey prevail over their responsibility to provide water services for the city's population. Despite an unprecedented commitment to improving social welfare, and despite the lack of water infrastructure construction in the previous twenty years, during Echeverría's term Nuevo León ranked sixteenth (out of thirty-two states) in terms of federal investment allocated to social infrastructure (Palacios 1989: 175). This is all the more striking given Palacios's conclusion that public spending under Echeverría was concentrated in the states that contributed most heavily to the GDP, among which Nuevo León ranked fifth throughout the 1970s (123, 188).[15]

This analysis demonstrates that how a problem is solved during one period of time shapes the possible or necessary responses in the next period. The failure of prior administrations to address the growing water service problem in Monterrey meant that President López Portillo had to address it even though Monterrey (and Nuevo León in general) was listed as a low-priority area for government investment in his regional development plan. As a result, under López Portillo, Nuevo León ranked sixth among the thirty-two states in terms of federal investment for social infrastructure (Palacios 1989: 177).

Did the hostility and noncooperation between the Grupo Monterrey and the federal government serve a larger purpose in terms of relations of power in Mexico? In the short run, for the Grupo Monterrey it was one more instance of independence, reinforcing their autonomy from the central government. For the government, the conflicts with the Grupo Monterrey served to underline, if not exacerbate, divisions within the private sector in Mexico as a whole. As cited by Camp (1989: 244), "The secret of the [Mexican] government's relationship to the business community is to divide it, a policy they have been very successful in implementing." During the 1960s and 1970s, the benefits to the government of a divided private sector converged with the Grupo Monterrey's insistence on preserving its autonomy. This engendered a severe crisis in water services for Monterrey.

In the long run, however, once the government shifted policy and addressed the water crisis in Monterrey, the context of conflict and division also changed. The 1980s and 1990s have been characterized by collaboration between the government and the Grupo Monterrey, with both working toward a shared goal of promoting Monterrey's role in the international economy. In this new context, massive government investment for water infrastructure in Nuevo León not only supports economic growth in the region but enhances the new relationship of cooperation between the government and the private sector.

The Impact of Protest on Planning in the Water Sector

Water service deficiencies were so severe in Monterrey by the late 1970s that the low-income residents of the city, who normally have no say in policy making or government investment decisions, constituted themselves as a social actor and used protest and other tactics of disruption as a mechanism to communicate their needs to the government. The protests over water in Monterrey were typical of protests arising in urban neighborhoods across Latin America in response to dramatically inadequate urban infrastructure. As discussed in chapter 4, militant actions by the urban poor in Latin America have tended to bypass electoral politics to take the form of grassroots protests or of longer-lasting social movements. The strategies of disruption that are used by these protests and social movements call attention to urgent needs that are otherwise ignored by the formal political system. As stated by Tarrow (1989: 6), "The power of the protest is in its power to disrupt the lives of others, and this it does through its drama, its symbolism, and the uncertainty it creates." Water service is a particular focus of urban protest because water is essential for human survival and irreplaceable for a myriad of daily tasks. There have been large-scale protests over water service in other Latin American cities, including São Paulo, Brazil, and Lima, Peru, where protests resulted in significantly improved water service (Jacobi Neru 1987; Watson 1992; Zolezzi and Calderón 1985).

The protests in Monterrey were highly focused, concerning themselves with one problem only: water. They did not expand over time to embrace other causes. They were initiated and carried out by residents of discrete neighborhoods. Thus, even when they moved out onto public space, such as with street blockades, they did not turn into mass protests attracting the participation of residents from different neighborhoods. The protests were not organized by identifiable institutions, there was no coordination of the protests across the city as a whole, and there was no leader or set of leaders identified with the protests.[16]

The characteristics of the protests were in great part due to the intersection of class and gender that shaped the strategies used: the majority of participants were low-income women. The highly focused nature of the protests is partially expanded by the central role of water for women's tasks in the sphere of social reproduction, and partially by the fact that the women were protesting based on their practical gender interests. They did not link their immediate, practical need for water with the larger context of gendered relations of power. Doing so would have been to act out of their strategic as well as their practical gender interests (see chapter 5) and would have enabled them to see commonalities between their immediate water problems and those of women in other neighborhoods, leading perhaps to cross-neighborhood coalitions or movements.

Because women acted primarily out of their practical gender interests, the protests remained based in individual neighborhoods or groups of adjacent neighborhoods instead of turning into mass protests citywide. While water service was uniformly worse in low-income and impoverished neighborhoods, unless the housewives in these neighborhoods moved from complaining about their own service to seeing water service problems as a feminist issue and a class issue, they had no mechanism to link them with housewives from other neighborhoods. Without that mechanism, they remained concerned only with their own problems instead of becoming connected to others through similar living conditions imposed by the intersection of class and gender. For the same reason, while some of the protests in individual neighborhoods may have had local leaders, these leaders did not link up with each other or try to expand their local protests into mass protests across the city or into a more lasting social movement addressing a range of gender-based problems in the sphere of reproduction.

However, that the protests did not coalesce into a social movement served two important purposes. First, the time commitment required for short-term protests is less than for a social movement. Women who might not have had time to devote to a social movement could participate in the more focused and limited protests. Housewives in the neighborhoods with the worst water service are women whose domestic chores are significantly more arduous and time-consuming because they have few of the amenities of modern life (reliable water supply, hot water heaters, washing machines, dryers, dishwashers, blenders, and so on). In many cases, in addition to the hours of household work, these women participate in the labor force, as domestic servants, doing piecework at home, or running a small retail business out of their home. They are also responsible for taking care of pre-school-age children and for the after-school care of older children. Participating in protests means having to postpone household work, possibly facing an angry husband, finding someone to take care of the children, even giving up income-earning activities. But if the protest action is bounded both in terms of its objective (more water right now) and in terms of its time commitment, when the particular service problem becomes serious enough, as the research presented here shows, women are willing to take action (Jelin 1990a: 8; Jelin 1990b: 186).[17]

The fact that the protests in Monterrey did not have citywide leaders, strategies, or organizational structure served a second purpose. It made it difficult for the government to respond with co-optation or repression. For co-optation to work there have to be leaders who can be co-opted, because it is difficult to co-opt all the participants in a protest.[18] Similarly, repression works best when it is used either against leaders or on occasion against a whole neighborhood as a means of intimidating other neighborhoods. The government faced three obstacles in using repression. First, it wanted to protect Monterrey's image as a stable city for economic investment. Violence against citizens in highly visible areas such as Monterrey would have tarnished that image. Second, there were no leaders with citywide visibility, and thus no one leader, set of leaders, or organization could be repressed to stop the protests at the mass level. Third, women constituted the majority of participants in the protests. The political culture of Mexico in the late 1970s and early 1980s constrained physical repression against groups of protesting women. Unlike in other Latin American countries, in Mexico it is uncommon for violent repression to be used against women in public. Even during the peak years of protest in Monterrey, when women blockaded streets and kidnapped Water Service vehicles and the police were sent in to confront them, the police did not move against the women, and the women always stood their ground.[19] If the protesters had been men, it is certainly possible that the police might have used force. In 1983, the Monterrey Water Service announced that it was criminalizing protests over water service, meaning that during a protest it could arrest protesters and remove them from the scene. This circumvented the problems of using violent repression against groups of protesting women. However, women continued protesting en masse, and the government never enforced its threat of arresting the protesters.

The government's primary response to the protests was to improve water service. In 1980, President López Portillo authorized the Plan Hidráulico. Five factors explain the timing and the magnitude of the government's project. First, there really was a critical water shortage in Monterrey. Second, Alfonso Martínez Domínguez, President López Portillo's choice for governor of Nuevo León, had been inaugurated in 1979, providing the link between the federal and the state government that was necessary to coordinate a massive public works project. Third, the president had established a better working relationship between the executive branch of the federal government and the Grupo Monterrey, after the extreme hostility present during the Echeverría administration. The high level of government investment in the water sector was evidence of government support for Monterrey's continued growth as an industrial center under the leadership of the Grupo Monterrey. Fourth, the petroleum boom during the first four years of the López Portillo administration provided resources for large infrastructure projects. And fifth, preceding the president's announcement of the Plan Hidráulico there were three summers of protest over inadequate water services, protests of a dimension and form never before seen in Monterrey. Citywide protests over water occurred in 1978, 1979, and 1980, coinciding with the peak years of the squatter's movement in Monterrey (the Frente Popular Tierra y Libertad). The Frente itself did not lead or in any way interact with the protests, most of which did not emanate from land invasion neighborhoods. However, the protests over water, coming on the heels of the formation of Mexico's biggest urban popular movement, urged a real solution to the water crisis.

In 1984, when President de la Madrid authorized the Agua Para Todos project, four of the five factors that explained the Plan Hidráulico remained to explain Agua Para Todos. First, while the Plan Hidráulico was going to resolve the water supply problem for Monterrey, it did not address the corollary problem of getting the water to the people who needed it most. Agua Para Todos did so by extending water service into all of Monterrey's poorest neighborhoods and by connecting all of Monterrey's water sources to a large transfer pipe circumnavigating the city. Thus, Agua Para Todos responded to a critical need.

Second, the good relationship between the executive branches of the state and federal governments continued when de la Madrid became president. When President de la Madrid took office in 1982, the governor of Nuevo León was still Martínez Domínguez, who had been chosen by President López Portillo. Because the Plan Hidráulico had been designed and approved while de la Madrid was the secretary of planning and budget under President López Portillo, de la Madrid had an ongoing working relationship with Governor Martínez Domínguez.

Third, the improved working relationship between the executive and the Grupo Monterrey continued with President de la Madrid. Despite the nationalization of the banks and the near collapse of the Mexican economy in 1982, the Grupo Monterrey did not use the crisis to turn on the federal government or on the executive branch. The biggest industrial groups in Monterrey (Alfa, Cydsa, Visa, and Vitro) entered a period of extreme financial crisis in the early 1980s and received help from the federal government (through preferential exchange rates, for example). The hostile and critical voices from the north, which could have characterized the worst years of Mexico's economic crash, were noticeably absent. Continued funding for the Plan Hidráulico, for Agua Para Todos, and to absorb the Water Service's foreign currency debt not only addressed the protests and led to civic stability but contributed to the process of bringing Monterrey's urban infrastructure up to par with the industrial development spearheaded by the Grupo Monterrey.

Fourth, the incidence of protest was as significant as it was before the authorization of the Plan Hidráulico. After a lull in 1981, the protests picked up in 1982 with as much fervor as in the late 1970s. In 1982 and 1983, there were protests across the city, with the same tactics as in earlier years: street blockades, taking hostage Water Service employees, and protests at government offices. While most cities in Latin America have ongoing programs to improve water service to poor neighborhoods and extend rudimentary services into new neighborhoods, in no other Mexican city has piped water service been extended into all poor neighborhoods at once.[20] Ward (1986) found that in Mexico City it was often the neighborhoods with the strongest links to local government or those that were the best organized that received better services. Service improvements were decided case by case, often as a form of patronage. One reason that is commonly given for this is that funding agencies do not consider the costs associated with installing in-home water service to poor neighborhoods recoverable. Yet, in Monterrey more than one hundred poor neighborhoods received improved service at one time—and not the stepwise improvements of installing collective faucets in neighborhoods that had received only water truck deliveries, or increasing the number of collective faucets in neighborhoods that already had the collective faucet pipeline. Agua Para Todos brought in-house, metered service to every home in almost every poor neighborhood of Monterrey.

The fifth factor that made the Plan Hidráulico possible was the economic resources available to the government thanks to the discovery of massive oil reserves in the 1970s. This critical factor is the one that was not present as President de la Madrid continued to fund water infrastructure projects for Monterrey. The drop in oil prices in the early 1980s led to a dramatic drop in revenue for the Mexican government. The loss of revenue combined with large interest payments due to overborrowing during the late 1970s led to economic crisis in 1982. President de la Madrid authorized Agua Para Todos, a project targeted at the urban poor, and all the other outlays for Monterrey's water sector at a time when the federal government was implementing austerity programs and slashing social spending.

This suggests that urban protests of the form that occurred in Monterrey between 1978 and 1984 can have an impact on government planning and investment at the local, state, and federal levels. The protests had three results in the short run. First, residents who carried out the most disruptive protests usually received immediate improvements in their water service, albeit often only temporarily. Second, the protests helped the Water Service perfect its water rationing program because they provided up-to-the-minute information on actual water services in residential neighborhoods. Operating a city's water system with less than 50 percent of the water needed is a complex technical and engineering feat. The Water Service's initial water rationing system had the goal of delivering as much water as possible to each individual neighborhood. The rationing was accomplished by work crews who manually opened and closed neighborhood water pipe valves, allowing water into some neighborhoods and bypassing (rationing) others. That system resulted in widespread dissatisfaction when adjacent neighborhoods had wildly differing hours of service. In addition, sometimes a configuration of valve openings and closings was designed but did not yield the desired result; that is, the water did not flow into the neighborhoods the Water Service had targeted. Despite remarkable efforts at managing an intricate rationing system, the Water Service did not always know where there was water and where there was none in the city. Although the Water Service did not actively want street blockades, personnel kidnappings, or protest rallies, these did serve to inform the Water Service—protesting neighborhoods were those without water. In response, the Water Service was able to redesign and simplify the rationing system, placing as many neighborhoods as possible on the same schedule, even if that meant reducing the hours of service to certain sectors of the city.

Paradoxically, while challenging both local and state government institutions and disrupting the stability of the city, the protests in Monterrey also taught the water authority how to better manage the water system under crisis conditions. In other words, the water authority gained expertise in how to administer a water system for a major urban area with only half the water it needed. This in turn allowed the water authority to return Monterrey to more stable and peaceful daily life. A decision to channel water to a protesting neighborhood was a decision based on achieving social control more than a decision to improve water service.[21] This is evident because unless the overall supply of water in-

creased, the water authority could only provide a protesting neighborhood with water by taking water away from another neighborhood (and
hoping that the other neighborhood would not then erupt in protest).

In the long run, the protests helped shape investment by the federal
government for large water infrastructure. Protest can influence the topic
of debate, it can make debate more urgent, and it can influence the willingness of decision makers to see alternatives (Pinch 1985). The timing of
the protests over water in Monterrey (1978–1980, 1982–1983) compared
to the timing of the two big water infrastructure projects (1980, 1984), and
the specific targeting of poor neighborhoods by Agua Para Todos, suggest
that in the 1970s the protests made the debate over resolving Monterrey's
water crisis more urgent, while in the 1980s the protests influenced the
topic of debate as well as encouraged government officials to develop
more creative and far-reaching solutions to the crisis.

These results led to the following reflections on our theoretical understanding of collective action. Touraine (1984) suggests three categories for
collective action. The first consists of defensive collective actions that he
terms conflictual actions. The second category, social struggle, consists of
actions that "modify decisions or whole systems of decision-making"
(cited in Slater 1985b: 19). The third, social movement, consists of collective actions that are explicitly intended to change relations of power in
key areas of society. Castells (1982), like Touraine, considers collective
actions to be social movements only if they seek social transformation.
Yet the research on protests in Monterrey suggests that collective actions
without such an explicit goal might become transformative by their proliferation.[22]

In the Monterrey case, if there had been just a few neighborhood protests over water they could rightly have been called conflictual actions.
The proliferation of protests, however, led to the series of results described above, which required the modification of "decisions or even of
whole systems of decision-making." Therefore, the protests must at the
least be considered social struggle. Yet if the decision by the government
to extend water service into the homes of all of Monterrey's poor residents through the Agua Para Todos program implied a recognition that
home water service was a right of all citizens, even of the very poorest,
then social transformation had occurred. In fact, however, while the Agua
Para Todos program redefined citizens' rights in Monterrey in 1984 and
1985, the government did not adopt a general guideline that all Mexican

citizens should have potable water in their homes, and similar programs were not carried out in other cities.

On the one hand, through their protest activity, low-income women in Monterrey altered relations of power because they were able to insert their own voice and new demands into a process that had until then considered the voices of only two actors, the government and the Grupo Monterrey. On the other hand, low-income women were never included in the formal decision-making process for water infrastructure extension in Monterrey, a process that continues to be controlled by the government and leaders of the private sector. In conclusion, because of their impact, the protests over water in Monterrey transcend the category of conflictual action, and must at least be labeled social struggle. In addition, the intensity and range of government response to the protests (see chapter 6) means that there were at least temporary alterations in the relations of power in Monterrey, which in turn force us to expand our understanding of the accomplishments that are possible by neighborhood-based, demand-oriented protests that use strategies of disruption.

Public Versus Private Management of Municipal Water Services

In response to the economic crisis that engulfed many Third World nations during the 1980s, governments were obliged to cut back social sector spending, even for services that urgently had required increased investments before the crisis. This prompted international lending agencies along with national governments to consider privatizing public services, allowing private sector resources to mitigate the negative effects of decreased public spending. Economists suggest four scenarios in which outright privatization of public services might *not* lead to the most efficient service, or in which the private sector might not want to be involved. First, when the characteristics of the service create a natural monopoly, this allows the private sector to charge monopoly prices. Similarly, if the service can support the presence of only a few firms, a situation of oligopoly power can develop. Second, the public service may create negative externalities that the private sector may ignore. Third, efficiency suffers when the service cannot be charged for on an individual basis (street lighting, for example). Fourth, the service may be considered to have special merit but might not be provided adequately by the private sector or purchased in adequate quantities by the poor population. Health, education, and school lunches are examples of merit goods (Roth 1987: 7–10).

When municipal water service is considered in light of the above scenarios, it turns out that it is not a public service well suited for complete privatization. Economies of scale exist in most of the steps of water provision, from extraction and purification to transport and distribution. As a result, monopoly would be the most efficient form of private production, leading to the problems occasioned by monopoly ownership. Water has substantial positive externalities; it is necessary for human survival, essential for good health, and critical to the production process. It also has two serious negative externalities; standing water can lead to the spread of disease, and reckless extraction of water can lead to the depletion of sources. Supporters of privatization argue that private ownership would lead to greater efficiency as water would go to its priority uses, emphasizing the positive externalities. Critics contend that water rates determined by a monopoly market would exclude low-end buyers, thus creating the added negative externality of ill health. This leads to scenario three: because water is necessary for human survival and for good health it is not possible to exclude nonpayers from service. Finally, water is a merit good. The government should guarantee water to all because low-income sectors of the population usually do not know all the health benefits of an adequate water supply and may not choose to purchase enough water. For these reasons, urban water systems have not usually been considered the first candidate for privatization of public services (Roth 1987: 231–43).

However, privatization does not have to mean full private sector ownership and management of public services. It can also mean private sector involvement with government regulation. Typically, there are four methods of private sector involvement outside of full private ownership. First, the private sector can be involved through contracting, while the public sector continues to provide work specifications and financing. Second, when a public service is most efficiently handled by one company, then the government may authorize the private sector to operate a monopoly franchise according to standards provided by the government. Third, a private sector firm may be hired to manage a public service, while the government retains full responsibility for the service and its financing. Fourth, the government may allow competing private sector firms to supply a public service but retains the ability to subsidize specific customers through a voucher system, whereby certain population groups receive government vouchers to exchange for the service provided by the private sector (Roth 1987: 2–3). Because municipal water services consist of a series of steps, starting with the extraction of water at a source and ending with delivery of the water to the consumer, it may be possible to include the private sector in one or more of the intermediate steps through direct ownership, franchising, or management contracts, without necessarily having to privatize the whole service.

Empirical evidence shows that in many cases privately owned firms are more cost-effective than public firms (Hanke 1987b: 78–83). Supporters of privatization believe that by shrinking the size of government, privatization will improve the quality of services still in government hands. They also suggest that the profit-seeking nature of private firms will make the service more responsive to customer satisfaction. Critics maintain that precisely due to profit-seeking motives, private sector practices may make public services inaccessible to the poor, both in terms of price and location. Supporters view government provision of public services as one more example of the unnecessary involvement of government in private life. Critics of privatization point out that the efficient provision of services is but one objective of public services, yet it is the one stressed by the private sector; another equally important objective is distributive justice, and that cannot be left to market forces (Goodman and Loveman 1991: 26–28).

The question driving the debate over the merits of privatization of public services is whether development can be enhanced if some of the responsibility for public service provision is shifted to the private sector. Goodman and Loveman (1991: 28) suggest recasting the debate over privatization: "Privatization involves the displacement of one set of managers entrusted by the shareholders—the citizens—with another set of managers who may answer to a very different set of shareholders. . . . Managerial accountability to the public's interest is what counts most, not the form of ownership." The debate then is no longer over private versus public sector ownership but over managerial accountability, a central issue under either public or private ownership. Goodman and Loveman draw three conclusions. First, that neither public nor private sector managers always work to the best interest of the consumer. Therefore, both need incentives or regulations to ensure the best service. Second, privatization of public services will work best in a competitive environment. Third, if a competitive market is not possible, government regulation of the privatized service will be necessary. One possibility is for the government to privatize pieces of a public service and, as part of the contract with the private provider, to define certain levels of service that must be attained or maintained.

Up to now in Mexico, no city has privatized its municipal water service, but several have contemplated doing so.[23] Article 27 of the Mexican Constitution and the Federal Water Law of 1971 establish that all surface and groundwater found on Mexican territory, as well as all coastal waters within the limits defined by international law, are property of the nation (Chávez Padrón 1979). This sets the legal basis for the government regulation and provision of water services. In urban areas, the government finances and manages the supply, purification, transport, and distribution of water. Private extraction of water is allowed only by permits granted by the government, and metering of all private extraction is obligatory.[24] Privatization of urban water services in Mexico could take a variety of forms; however, in all cases the water itself would continue to belong to the nation. For example, the purification system for each of a city's sources could be sold to the private sector, or the distribution system for given sectors of the city could be franchised out to the highest bidder.

The history of Monterrey's water service is instructive because it illustrates two forms of private sector involvement, ownership versus management. In the early 1900s, when the state government of Nuevo León decided to construct the first municipal water system for Monterrey, it was common in Mexico to turn to a foreign company for construction, ownership, and management. Thus, Monterrey's water system was owned and operated until 1945 by a private firm, Mackenzie, Mann, and Company, of Toronto, Canada. The operation and expansion of the waterworks were guided by regulations developed by the state government. The contract signed by Mackenzie and the state government gave Monterrey's water service to the private firm for one hundred years, from 1909 to 2008. However, by 1940, only half of Monterrey's population received water from the municipal system. This was due to two flaws in the state's contract with Mackenzie. First, water supply per capita had been determined in 1909, and there was no mechanism to change the amount even though per capita needs had more than doubled by 1940.[25] Second, Mackenzie, Mann, and Company had not adhered to the clauses in the contract that stipulated increasing service in proportion to the city's growth, nor to its own internal regulations on standards for the distribution system. Unfortunately, the contract did not include any effective mechanisms for the state to use to force Mackenzie to comply with the contract.

By the 1940s, Monterrey was in a water crisis. In 1943, the state government broke its contract with Mackenzie by confiscating customer payments and provoking the firm to enter a legal battle. The conflict eventually reached the Supreme Court of Mexico, which ruled in favor of the state government. In 1945, the state government purchased the water company from Mackenzie, Mann, and Company using a loan from the financing arm of the federal government.

This example of private ownership of a municipal water service illustrates two fundamental issues. First, despite signing a contract intended to protect the public interest (extension of the water system to match population growth), a private firm does not necessarily have the public interest as its objective. If the contract is not explicit about how to protect the public interest, such protection may not occur. Therefore, private sector involvement in the provision of public services must be guided by detailed government regulation. Second, an unenforceable contract is a useless contract. Good intentions and goodwill at the time the contract is signed mean nothing. The contract must include provisions for the enforcement of each clause. In addition, the government must have the will to enforce contracts with private providers of public services. Otherwise, civil society will find itself without an advocate if the government does not enforce the private firm's contractual obligation to provide adequate services. As living conditions in most Mexican cities demonstrate, the government does not always have the public interest in mind, either. The choice, therefore, may not be between outstanding public services offered by the public sector and potentially inadequate services offered by the private sector. Rather, it might be between inadequate public services offered by the public sector versus inadequate services offered by a private firm that is inadequately regulated by the government.

After the state government of Nuevo León bought the water company in 1945, it took eleven years for the final administrative form of the water service to develop. By 1956, Monterrey's water system was run by two agencies: the Potable Water Commission, which was mandated to study, design, and find financing for water infrastructure, and the Water Service, charged with managing the distribution of water within the city and with collecting customer payments. Given that at least half of the city's population was not connected to the city's water system at the time it was transferred from private to state ownership, the Potable Water Commission had an urgent and critical job ahead of it. The Commission had a board of directors empowered to recommend infrastructure projects and to seek funding from the federal government. The future of Monterrey's water service was therefore in the hands of the Commission's board of directors and the federal government bureaucrats who decided on funding. As described in chapters 3 and 6, while the board of directors consisted of members drawn almost equally from Monterrey's private sector and from the government, over time the government representatives stopped attending meetings, and the members of the board who represented the private sector came to dominate board decisions.[26] Overall, this had negative consequences for Monterrey's water services.

The members of the Commission's board of directors who represented Monterrey's private sector not only came from the Grupo Monterrey, they came from the most elite families within the Grupo Monterrey and were themselves major industrialists or real estate developers. This study has shown that the conflictual relationship between the Grupo Monterrey and the executive branch of the federal government contributed to the inability to reach agreement on which infrastructure projects to fund. As a result, no definitive water supply project was built for Monterrey during the entire time that the private sector representatives were active members or leaders of the Commission's board, from 1954 to 1976.[27]

Meanwhile, of course, many small projects were funded, intended to serve as emergency measures, as stopgaps, or as pieces of a larger system that never got funded. The minutes of the Commission's board meetings show that board members were aware of the need to expand the water system into the rapidly growing poor neighborhoods of the city. They also were concerned that the water supply itself was too limited to provide water to all neighborhoods, even if the piped water lines were extended. However, their actions did not match their concerns.[28] As shown in chapter 4, after 1971, when the Commission's board was fully in the hands of the private sector, water infrastructure projects were heavily skewed to the western portion of the city, which housed the majority of upper-income neighborhoods in Monterrey. The northern and eastern sectors of the metropolitan area, which had experienced the greatest population growth, had the majority of low-income neighborhoods, and had the most deficient water infrastructure, experienced relatively little investment to improve their water services.

The Water Service was the sole supplier of water for all water users in the city. That included not only residential customers but commercial establishments (such as laundries, beauty salons, car washes, and *tortillerías*), government buildings (such as schools and hospitals), and industrial enterprises (factories). During the years of the "Mexican Miracle," 1940 to 1970, Monterrey had become one of two major industrial zones in Mexico. Highly diversified, its industrial base included almost every heavy water-using industry possible, from iron foundries to breweries to glassworks to paper products. Some of the early industries, such as the brewery (Cervecería Cuauhtémoc), built their own wells and pipelines before legislation existed regulating the private extraction of water. Others began building their own water systems during the 1940s when the municipal water system was already inadequate. By 1980, numerous factories had private wells on their grounds or private pipelines from remote water sources. In that year, it was estimated that industrial water use from private wells equaled the total amount of water supplied by the Water Service to all other users (residential, commercial, government, and small industrial) (Laboratorio 1979–1980).

Yet all government efforts to have the industries comply with the regulation of private wells had failed. The industries did not allow government inspectors to install meters and keep records of their water use. Nor did they provide any data of their own to the government on their extraction of water through the private wells. The seriousness of the situation derived not only from the quantity of water the industries used, but from the fact that they drew their water from one of the same aquifers used by the Water Service, the Monterrey aquifer. Aquifer management requires that there be centralized data kept on the total amount of water extracted over time. There is no other way to prevent aquifer depletion than to balance the extraction and replenishment of water. Given that the industrial owners of the Grupo Monterrey refused to comply with government regulations, the Water Service could not carry out proper aquifer management and had to be extremely conservative in its use of the Monterrey aquifer—this, during years of extreme water shortages and during the period when the Potable Water Commission's board was being run by members of the Grupo Monterrey elite.[29]

This segment of Monterrey's water service history provides an example of private sector management of a public service. In this case, the government did not make an objective decision to turn management over to the private sector, there was no bidding or awarding of a management contract, and no stipulation of standards and guidelines to be followed by the private sector managers. Rather, the private sector members of the Commission's board slowly gained control of decision making through persistence and hard work. Out of fifty meetings between 1965 and 1971, the representatives of the chamber of industries and of the developers missed no more than seven sessions, while the representatives of the municipal and state governments did not attend a single meeting. Between 1971 and 1976, there were forty board meetings. The representative of the developers missed one; the representative of the chamber of industries missed ten (primarily due to illness); the representative of the Secretary of Hydraulic Resources missed thirty; the representatives of the municipal and state governments declined to participate ("Actas," 1954–1976). In short, the representatives of the private sector came most regularly to meetings, and as they gained more power within the board, the government representatives stopped attending altogether.

There were two checks on the decision making of the Commission's board, one of which worked and one that did not. The first check was to include a wide range of government representatives on the board. This check did not work because there was no mechanism to enforce attendance by board members, or to make voting on new projects dependent on a quorum of members from both the public and the private sector. The second check was that funding for water infrastructure, and authorization of new projects, came from the federal government. If the federal bureaucracy or the president did not agree with the priorities of the board, funding would not be available. This check often came into play in the 1960s and 1970s (until 1976), as the Commission's board and the Secretary of Hydraulic Resources were rarely able to agree on the prioritizing of new projects.[30]

The government is as much at fault as the private sector for the growing water crisis in Monterrey. The city was in crisis when the state government purchased the water system in 1945, and until 1976 no state governor and no president took the steps necessary to resolve Monterrey's water problems—either by intervening in the management of the Potable Water Commission or by authorizing projects big enough to make a significant difference. Left on its own, the private sector did not act in the best interests of the population at large.

This study of Monterrey indicates that water services, whether they are publicly or privately owned or managed, need to be systematically regulated by the government. Standards of service need to be set for each subgroup of consumers.[31] There must be systematic supervision and review to prevent the accumulation of problems and the development of crisis. Contracts with the private sector must be closely monitored and include sanctions or other mechanisms that can be used to enforce regulations. This is the case no matter whether the entire water system is sold to the private sector or whether only one piece is contracted out for private management.[32] The involvement of the private sector must be both politically and financially viable, allowing the timely development and execution of long-term projects. The bottom line is that the government must have the will to serve the public interest, even if services for the public are being provided or managed by the private sector.[33] Otherwise, in the case of a public service as critical as urban water supply, ineffective management, whether it be public or private, can accentuate disparities in service provision and lead to an urban crisis whereby ordinary citizens take to the streets to get the government to do its job of safeguarding the public interest.

CONCLUSION

The history of Monterrey's water services is a political history. It provides a lens through which to view relationships between political actors in Mexico, changes in those relationships over time, and the interplay between relations of power and the planning of public services. Three political actors—top government leaders, the regional private sector elite, and low-income women in Monterrey—were central to the evolution of the city's water system. Among these political actors, two relationships were critical: between the Grupo Monterrey and the government, and between low-income residents and the government. As Walton (1992: 1) states,

> It is a paradox of modern democratic societies that the state is considered both the cause and the cure of injustice. The state is believed to foster social ills directly by conferring privilege on certain powerful constituents and indirectly by failing to serve the less coherent public interest. To ensure justice, citizens must then confront authority as outsiders, either by mobilizing protest or withdrawing their approval from the state.

There is no question that Walton's statement holds true for Mexico, whether or not Mexico is a "modern democratic society." As shown in previous chapters, the Mexican government is the provider of major urban infrastructure, and as such is considered the "cure of injustice." However, insofar as the government fails to provide essential services to all citizens, it is also the "cause of injustice." Because of this paradox, the state has become the terrain of struggle. Political actors, including the private sector elite and the urban poor, confront or negotiate with the state in order to influence policy making and budget decisions. Powerful political actors, such as the Grupo Monterrey, can interact with the top levels of the Mexican government directly as individuals, or they can communicate through their leadership, or even through civil organizations that represent their interests. Political actors who are less powerful as individuals, such as the urban poor in Monterrey, have neither direct contacts with key government officials, nor the leadership, nor representative organizations with such contacts. These actors gain influence only by constituting themselves as a collectivity. Because these groups are outsiders—there are no formal political groups or organizations that effectively represent their interests—they use protest and other strategies of disruption to communicate with other political actors. When it comes to issues of social reproduction such as residential water service, protest is directed at the state as the "cure of injustice."

However, the state is not monolithic. As illustrated in chapter 6, business-state relations changed in Monterrey as government leadership changed. From 1970 to 1993, the relationship between the Grupo Monterrey and the government evolved from outright antagonism to close collaboration. The key factors in the changing relationship were the president of Mexico himself, the government's economic policy, and often, the governor of Nuevo León. The Grupo Monterrey was more consistent than the government, sustaining an ideology that strongly favored as little government intervention in the economy as possible; the closer that presidential ideology moved to the Grupo Monterrey's vision, the closer the relationship between the two groups. Given that, for decades, leaders of the Grupo Monterrey and top federal government officials controlled the decision-making process for the expansion of Monterrey's water system, the fluctuating relationship between the government and the Grupo Monterrey sometimes served as an obstacle to water system development, while at other times it was a help.

The state's response to the protests over water in Monterrey was also multifaceted and changed over time. From publicity campaigns aimed at manipulating public opinion (so that the public would not blame the state, "the cause of injustice," for the water crisis), to stopgap measures designed to quell urban protests temporarily, to grand infrastructure projects that addressed the protests by finally providing the city with reliable (albeit limited) water service, the state acted in its capacity as the "cure of injustice." While the government experimented with a wide range of responses to the protests and to the water crisis, the low-income residents who protested used the same four or five strategies over and over again. Nevertheless, the protesters came from different neighborhoods, chose different strategies from among four or five at different times, and got different results. For example, one group of protesters may have gotten as far as having an appointment with the state governor but still would not get its demands met, while another got results without ever leaving its neighborhood (for example, by kidnapping Water Service vehicles and personnel). The impact of the protests came not from each individual protest and the immediate response it received, but from the cumulative effect of many protests over several years using tactics of disruption to exert pressure on the government to assume its responsibilities as the "cure of injustice." The large infrastructure projects financed by the government were not presented to the public as responses to the protests, yet archival research shows that both local and national newspapers carried prominent stories on the protests, and that government publications themselves referred to the protests when addressing Monterrey's water crisis. Both the Plan Hidráulico and Agua Para Todos came on the heels of the most severe protests over water that Monterrey had ever seen.

Further research is needed to document the link between the activities of social movements or urban protests in Latin America and decisions by governments to improve public services (Watson 1992: 9). Clearly, not all public works projects are responses to public protests or to citizens' demands. However, sometimes they are. Watson's study of São Paulo and this one of Monterrey point in the same direction: in both cities, catastrophically inadequate water services provoked massive public protests, which were followed by far-reaching government investment in infrastructure to vastly improve service. Future studies might concentrate on exploring government decision making about public service infrastructure during periods of intensive public protest.

Another fruitful line of inquiry that emerges from this book is to take research on popular organizing beyond the easily identifiable consolidated social movements to the seemingly more spontaneous type of protests that occurred in Monterrey, São Paulo, and other Latin American cities. Little is known about how these protests are organized. The Monterrey experience is typical in that there was no overarching organization that managed the protests, nor was there an identifiable set of leaders that emerged to organize the protests citywide. Instead, decision making took place in each neighborhood separately, or among certain individuals within separate neighborhoods. As a result, future researchers, instead of focusing on social movement leaders and organizational structures, would have to work closely with residents of underserviced neighborhoods over periods of time long enough to observe the natural development of protest as a response to inadequate public services.

As Wolf (1982: 3) says, "The world is a manifold, a totality of interconnected processes." We have separated those processes and analyzed them individually. Yet many of the processes we have explored occurred simultaneously. For example, the rapprochement between the Grupo Monterrey and the government under President López Portillo occurred at the same time as the urban poor in Monterrey began to protest. The protests reached their peak just when the Mexican economy was at its weakest. Simultaneity does not imply cause and effect; it does remind us that political and economic contexts shape and constrain possibilities for action for all political actors. In the end, Monterrey's water services improved because relations of power changed between the Grupo Monterrey and the president of Mexico, and because through their protests poor women in Monterrey made national news out of the city's water crisis, contributing thereby to the government's decision to prioritize Monterrey and provide water for all.

APPENDIX
NOTES
BIBLIOGRAPHY
INDEX

APPENDIX:
FIELD RESEARCH

This book is based on research I carried out in Monterrey, Mexico, between 1980 and 1986. I lived in Monterrey from 1982 through 1985, and made many trips to the city in 1980, 1981, and 1986, returning again in 1988 and 1991. Anyone who has done in-depth research in public institutions knows the systematic detective work and good luck needed to uncover the information that will help piece together the answers to one's research questions. When I arrived in Monterrey I did not have any contacts at any of the government institutions in the water sector. After several months of carrying out background research at local university libraries and in the state archives, I was referred by an assistant at the archives to a local accountant who was renowned for his hobby of tracking the history of Monterrey's water services. This turned out to be my lucky break, because this person immediately opened the doors for me at the highest levels of the two government agencies in charge of planning and providing water services for the metropolitan area.

Once the doors were open, I was very fortunate to be able to establish long-term working relationships with the top administrators and engineers at both the Servicios de Agua y Drenaje de Monterrey (the Water Service) and at the Comisión de Agua Potable de Monterrey (the Commission). For two years I had weekly meetings with one of the high-level officials at the Water Service, who facilitated my research by providing material from the Water Service's archives and setting up interviews with engineers and other professionals in charge of different departments of the Water Service. For example, ongoing interviews over three years with the engineer in charge of the Water Distribution Section served as a crash course in hydraulic engineering and helped me understand the complexities and goals of the Water Service's water rationing program after 1980. For three years I also had office space at the Potable Water Commission, which enabled me not only to work my way through extensive documents but to have innumerable clarifying conversations with the Commission's administrators and engineers on technical, political, and historical matters.

Chapters 3 and 6 are based on extensive reviews of internal documents of the Water Service and the Commission and on the interviews described above. In addition to being given access to a wide range of internal reports, I was able to read the minutes of all of the meetings of the board of directors of the Commission from its inception in 1954 through 1979. Sections of both chapters that discuss the power structure of Monterrey's water sector are based in great part on those minutes, which detailed who came to meetings, who said what, and how decisions were made. I also carried out interviews with officials in other government and private sector offices (for example, at the Monterrey office of the Secretaría de Agricultura y Recursos Hidráulicos, at the Cámara de Industrias de la Transformación, at the Laboratorio e Ingeniería de la Calidad del Agua, and so on).

Chapters 4 and 5 are based on extensive archival work with Monterrey's two most important newspapers, *El Norte* and *El Porvenir*, and on surveys and numerous interviews in the community. Every issue of both newspapers was reviewed for a fifteen-year period, 1970 through 1985, in order to track coverage of all aspects of water service in Monterrey. The outcome of the archival review was not only extensive documentation of protests over water, but ancillary material that complemented my research at the Water Service and the Commission.

For six months in 1983 I carried out a survey in twenty neighborhoods across Monterrey. The neighborhoods were selected by stratified random sampling, with the neighborhoods classified according to prevailing income group. The purpose of the survey was to confirm the data on rationing schedules given to me by the Water Service, to document the different types of water service available to different neighborhoods, and to explore residents' understanding of and attitudes toward the water crisis and its causes and possible solutions. The newspaper coverage, the surveys, and in-depth interviews with selected families confirmed the widespread participation of women in the protests.

During my years in Monterrey I also benefited from collegial relationships with academics at a number of institutions, including the Universidad Autónoma de Nuevo León, the Universidad de Monterrey, the Universidad Regiomontana, and the Oficina de Información y Difusión del Movimiento Obrero. In general, I found a great willingness to share information, analysis, and opinion. Monterrey was an extraordinarily hospitable place for me as a foreign researcher—because of that I was able to approach this research from many different angles and receive the cooperation of government officials, scholars, city residents, and friends from many walks of life.

NOTES

1. INTRODUCTION

1. See, for example, Vargas González (1991) on the case of Pachuca, Hidalgo. Also, the city of Aguascalientes turned the management of its water services over to a private sector firm in 1989.

2. Nevertheless, because of high rates of population growth, although the proportion of rural inhabitants declined, their actual number increased, implying a continuous increase of rural unemployment. By 1980, two to six million Mexicans resided illegally in the United States in any given year, and a million more left the rural areas yearly for Mexican cities (Hellman 1983: 110, 115).

3. Preliminary data from the 1990 census gives population totals for Mexico City, Guadalajara, and Monterrey that are way below what common sense and common consensus dictate. Total population for the Mexico City Metropolitan Area is given as 14,028,639; for the Guadalajara Metropolitan Area as 2,884,052; and for the Monterrey Metropolitan Area as 2,562,547 (Instituto Nacional de Estadística, Geografía, e Informática 1990). In contrast, for example, the Mexico City Metropolitan Area is popularly thought to have a population of between 18 million and 20 million.

4. Vizcaya Canales 1971: 72.

Average rainfall annually:

Monterrey	640 mm
San Luis Potosí	361 mm
Saltillo	393 mm
Monclova	230 mm
Torreón	242 mm
Durango	484 mm
Chihuahua	394 mm
Zacatecas	367 mm

5. Capital accumulation in Monterrey received a big boost during the U.S. Civil War, when Monterrey served as a conduit for Confederate cotton exports and for the resupply of merchandise and equipment to the Confederate states. However, as Cerutti (1983: 32–34, 79) indicates, the mercantile activities in Monterrey related to the U.S. Civil War were less important in and of themselves than in how they demonstrate the significance to Monterrey of its proximity to the U.S. border.

6. The Grupo Monterrey controlled two of the important employer confederations, Coparmex (Confederación Patronal de la República Mexicana) and Concamin (Confederación de Cámaras Industriales). Vellinga 1988: 68–69.

2. URBAN WATER SERVICES: THEORY AND PLANNING

1. It is primarily the upper-income groups who are able to take advantage of using water for pleasure. For them, water has usefulness beyond health and hygiene to keep lawns green, to fill swimming pools, to run through decorative fountains, and to wash cars.

2. A common assumption is that individual home water connections constitute the best water service. This is an assumption derived from the characteristics of water service in advanced industrialized nations. Recent concern with sustainable development raises the question of whether the most convenient and reliable water service combined with the best use of both infrastructure material and water itself is obtained with individual home faucets. Further research on this topic is necessary.

3. For example, a survey I carried out in twenty Monterrey neighborhoods from May through September 1983 demonstrated that the poor who used water-truck water paid eleven times more for every two hundred liters of water (about forty-five gallons) than did families who had in-house water faucets.

4. As a result of the economic crisis of the 1980s in Mexico, the government developed new strategies to reduce the burden of providing the means of collective consumption. The building of new superhighways, for example, has been turned over to private sector firms who are allowed to charge tolls for highway usage over as many years as are needed to recover their costs plus profit. The new highways are therefore so expensive to use that only the upper-income population will be able to afford them, while the increased cost of transportation for commerce and industry will be passed along to the consumer through higher product prices. Another example of the privatization of the means of collective consumption is the debate in some Mexican cities over the merits of turning the management of their water systems over to private firms.

5. See chapter 7 for a discussion of private versus public ownership and management of public services.

6. The slow upgrading of water services means that firms involved in water infrastructure construction may receive multiple contracts for the same neighborhood (as opposed to building the best water service right away).

7. Nevertheless, most water authorities in Latin American cities do not run at a financial surplus and water services end up being subsidized by the government.

8. Even when water is not scarce, the status of water services, especially in the Third World, can reflect sectoral interests. These can change over time, so social dynamics must be studied over time (Coing 1991).

9. For an expanded exploration of the terms top-down and bottom-up as applied to planning, see the essays in Stohr and Taylor (1981), which apply the terms to different interpretations of development and to models of planning, leading to concepts such as top-down development or bottom-up planning. Also, Portes and Walton (1976) analyzed the politics of urban poverty using the twin perspectives of "politics from above" and "politics from below," searching for the interface of the two.

3. BUILDUP OF A CRISIS: THE EVOLUTION OF MONTERREY'S WATER SERVICE, 1909–1985

1. In Mexico, water is measured in liters and cubic meters. There are one thousand liters of water in one cubic meter. The unit of measurement for the extraction and delivery of water is *liters per second* (lps). The recommended daily usage for each household is measured in *liters per day per person* (see the List of Acronyms at the front of the book for definitions of these terms). In 1980, the recommended consumption of water per person in Monterrey was 200 liters per day. This is the equivalent of 52.8 gallons (U.S.) per day. Compare this to San Diego's 1991 recommended daily allowance for a family of three (under drought conditions) of 280 gallons per day; the 1980 Monterrey per capita allowance is just slightly more than half the 1991 San Diego per capita allowance. The 1909 criterion mentioned in the text above, 200 liters per day per capita, was a different measure. Instead of

being the recommended allowance *per person* for daily home use, it was a measure of total city need (commercial, industrial, public, and residential) divided by the city's total population to achieve a per capita figure. Therefore, only a part of the 200 liters per person per day suggested in 1909 actually went to residential water use, whereas in 1980 all of the recommended 200 liters per person per day was for residential use. Thus the 1909 Monterrey criterion assumes a much smaller per person daily use than the 1980 Monterrey figure does, which is already one-half that suggested for U.S. residential users.

2. Two hundred liters per day per person for a population of 212,000 is the equivalent of 490 liters per second (lps). Monterrey's water supply in 1940 was actually 673 liters per second; however, 40 percent was lost in leaks, leaving a real supply of 404 lps—or 164 liters per day for a population of 212,000 (Cámara Nacional de Comercio de Monterrey 1946: 12). Saldaña (1965) shows 400 lps of water consumption in 1945 with the following breakdown: domestic use, 276 lps; industrial use, 69 lps; electrical use, 33 lps; Railroads of Mexico, 16 lps; city and state government offices, 6 lps.

3. Traditionally, Mexican municipalities are very weak; they have a very limited tax base and receive limited funds from the state and federal governments. Consequently, it is common practice for the state and federal government in Mexico to become deeply involved in municipal public services, as has been the case with the water system in Monterrey. For more on the relationship between municipal, state, and federal governments in Mexico, see Rodríguez 1987.

4. All the information on the contract and ensuing disputes between the government of Nuevo León and the water company described on the following two pages comes from Cabrera and Molina Font 1944.

5. The real supply of water is to be distinguished from the total supply. For the water authority, real supply means the total liters billable by the water service at the end of a given period of time. Liters billable represents the total supply extracted from all sources minus water lost through leaks, illegal taps into the water mains, and faulty metering. Note that water lost through leaks in the pipelines is truly lost, while water that is consumed through illegal taps into the water mains, or that is consumed but not registered by faulty meters, is simply unbillable, not truly lost. In other words, the Water Service only collects fees on water registered by its meters. Illegal taps are not metered, and faulty meters may under- or overrepresent consumption. However, while not billable, water consumed illegally or incorrectly metered still constitutes a social good and should count in estimates of the city's total water supply. In this text, therefore, real water supply refers to total water supply extracted from all sources minus leaks. As Monterrey's water system aged, leaks constituted the biggest cause of water loss.

6. Migration was important for continued economic development because it provided part of the labor force.

7. "Actas de la Comisión de Agua Potable de Monterrey 1954–1979." These are the handwritten minutes of the meetings of the Comisión de Agua Potable de Monterrey. Future references to the minutes of the Commission's meetings will abbreviate the reference by citing the date of the meeting in the following form, for example: "Actas," 4-21-1955.

8. The Mexican term is *institución pública descentralizada*.

9. Because of devaluations of the Mexican peso, the U.S. dollar value of the 150,000 pesos earned annually by the Water Service dropped from 30,927 U.S. dollars in 1945 to 12,000 U.S. dollars in 1956.

10. According to the Mexican census, Monterrey's population in 1950 was 377,106 persons, and in 1960 it was 710,223 persons. Total water supply in 1950 was 800 lps, and real supply was 640 lps (Torres López and Santoscoy 1985: 101). In 1960, total supply was 1,885

lps and real supply was 1,508 lps (Comisión 1977). I assume water lost through leaks to be 40 percent in both years, which is a conservative estimate.

11. While the thirty-four-million-peso loan was approved in 1963, the La Boca water treatment project did not actually begin until 1964. Therefore, in tables 3.2 and 3.3 the disbursement of the loan is counted as 1964 spending instead of 1963.

12. A secondary method for industries to bypass the city's water system was to construct wastewater treatment plants. However, only the largest industries could afford this option. Four treatment plants were constructed between 1956 and 1963, three by major industries and one by the Federal Electricity Commission: Cydsa, opened in 1965, capacity of 140 lps; Aceros Planos, S.A., opened in 1961, capacity of 162 lps; Papelera Maldonado, opened 1963, capacity 50 lps; Comisión Federal de Electricidad, opened 1963, capacity 160 lps. A consortium of large industries opened a wastewater treatment plant in 1966 with a capacity of 300 lps (Villatoro et al. 1983: 21).

13. The 1971 Ley Federal de Aguas (Federal Water Law), guided by Article 27 of the 1917 Mexican Constitution, confirms that all of the waters of Mexico (rivers, lakes, streams, groundwater, and coastal waters) belong to the nation. Consequently, all private use of the nation's waters is regulated by the Secretary of Agriculture and Hydraulic Resources with a system of permits, meters, and payments for water extracted (Chávez Padrón 1979.) The Monterrey industrialists do not have permits for the private wells from which they extract groundwater for industrial processes, nor do they report or pay for the water extracted.

14. In a speech given in Monterrey in 1983 on the past, present, and future of Monterrey's water supply, José Hernández Terán, who was secretary of hydraulic resources under President Díaz Ordaz, stated that he had "instructions to build the Cerro Prieto dam" but could not, due to opposition in Monterrey (Hernández Terán 1983: 7).

15. In 1961, after meetings in Mexico City, the manager of the Commission reported that he had "discovered that the SRH had a bad impression of the [Commission]." While the SRH thought that the Commission's "technical work was good, its management did not allow SRH any control" ("Actas," 10–30–1961).

16. As noted in chapter 1, the Grupo Monterrey has historically been opposed to the expansion of state policy into economic and social arenas. As a result, it had an often conflictive relationship with Mexico's presidents, with various branches of the federal government, and even with the governors of the state of Nuevo León. Chapter 6 provides detail on how these conflicts eventually came to a head within the Commission and the Water Service in the mid-1970s.

17. The dam projects proposed by the SRH and by the Commission both had technical merit. This is evidenced by the fact that one of the three dams favored by the SRH in its 1965 and 1966 reports, the Cerro Prieto dam, was built by the federal government in the early 1980s—the first major dam project for the city of Monterrey. However, the El Cuchillo dam, heavily favored by the Commission in 1965, was built by the federal government in the early 1990s. Thus, one of the dams prioritized by the Commission and one prioritized by the SRH ended up being built years after the conflict between the two institutions was over. This indicates that both the SRH and the Commission were producing technically competent and viable proposals. In addition, before 1985 the federal government did not charge municipal water authorities for the water they used from dams, wells, or other sources. Therefore, the potential cost of water from a new dam was not a factor in the SRH-CAPM disagreements over dam projects.

18. Population growth was only one element of increased demand for water. The continued growth of industry and commerce also contributed to the need for a larger supply of water for Monterrey.

19. The minutes of the Commission's board meetings indicate that, starting in 1968, bidding on Commission projects was not open. Instead, the board invited specific firms to bid and selected from among them ("Actas," 1968). One interpretation of this is that it allowed the representatives of Monterrey's private sector, who by then controlled the Commission's board, to determine who profited from the Commission's construction projects.

20. Interview, Ing. Aguirre, Jefatura del Programa Hidráulico, Sección Técnica, Secretaría de Recursos Hidráulicos, Monterrey, Mexico, November 25, 1983.

21. The significant inadequacies of Monterrey's water system in the early 1970s were not unique in the Third World. Other Latin American cities also had experienced rapid industrial and population growth unmatched by an equal growth of infrastructure. International development banks and foundations, including the World Bank, the Inter-American Development Bank, and the Ford Foundation, had working groups studying the water and sewerage problems of Third World cities. What is notable about the case of Monterrey is that two highly qualified technical groups, the SRH and the Commission, had already spent more than fifteen years studying the region's water resources and designing complex water infrastructure, almost none of which had been built. In addition, the federal government was committed to a model of development based on import substitution industrialization, and federal public investment was being channeled to other Mexican states to support their industrialization efforts. Throughout the 1960s and 1970s, despite the size of its industrial sector and its population, and despite its need for infrastructure development, Nuevo León received a disproportionately low share of federal public investment (Scott 1982: 112–15; Secretaría 1980: 151).

22. When President Echeverría began his term in office in 1970 he had the reputation of being a repressive strongman because of his role in the 1968 massacre of students in Tlatelolco. To combat that reputation he began his presidency with a "democratic opening" designed to create new spaces for political participation and dialogue. His support of the university autonomy movement, which was taking place at many state universities, was a strategy to repair the government's relationship with the student sector (Schmidt 1991: 93–96). The sphere of higher education was important for two reasons. First, the population of Mexico was proportionately very young, with half the country under sixteen years of age. Therefore, issues pertaining to education, especially in a period of "democratic opening," were critical. Second, outside of Mexico City, the rectorship of a state university was often the jumping-off point for the state governorship. For these two reasons, it was strategically very effective for President Echeverría to support the university autonomy movement.

23. The city's total water supply was 4,884 lps, but losses from leaks alone were estimated to be 20 percent of supply, leaving a real supply of 3,175 lps. Another 15 percent of the water supply was incorrectly metered or unmetered, resulting in a total of 35 percent of the water supply not being paid for by consumers (Elizondo 1977: 6; Anson 1978: 47). This represented a significant loss of revenue for the Water Service.

24. By way of comparison, in 1970 the state of Veracruz had the third largest population of the Mexican states and ranked fourth in terms of population employed in manufacturing (Scott 1982: 220–22). However, for seven of the ten years from 1969 through 1978 it ranked among the top six states in terms of federal public investment received for the social welfare sector (Secretaría 1980: 154–55).

25. During this period, the Commission also obtained several very small, short-term loans from local Monterrey banks for the water sector.

26. Centro de Investigaciones Económicas, Universidad Autónoma de Nuevo León, *Boletín Trimestral* no. 87 (junio 1977), as quoted by Servicios 1977: 3–4.

27. SADM paid 8 percent interest to the IDB and 1 percent to BANOBRAS. While it

seems unusual that SADM had to pay interest on a loan that was not being disbursed, that is what is reported by the local Monterrey press.

28. The average of the figures given in Comisión 1976d: 1; and Comisión 1977: 15.

29. The real increase in the water supply from 1973 to 1977 was calculated using data on the total increase in supply from Elizondo (1977: 69) and Villatoro et al. (1983: appendix 7) and data on water lost through leaks from "Actas," 11-28-1977; Comisión 1976b: 1; Elizondo (1977: 69); and from an interview with Ing. Francisco Cantú Ramos, head of the Distribution Department, Servicios de Agua y Drenaje de Monterrey, April 6, 1983. In 1979, 25 percent of the total water supply was lost through leaks.

30. The initial budget for the Plan Hidráulico was 6,000,000,000 pesos, roughly 260,000,000 in 1980 U.S. dollars.

31. The Cerro Prieto dam had been originally suggested by the SRH in 1965 but was opposed by the Commission's board.

32. Servicios 1983: 1. Also, according to the director of the Water Service, the deficit for 1980 itself was estimated to be 40 percent of demand (*El Porvenir*, 12-5-1980).

33. According to figures quoted in *El Porvenir* (5-24-1983), at the end of 1982 the Water Service's foreign currency debt was the equivalent of 5,416,000,000 pesos (36 million dollars) and its peso debt was 2,300,000,000 pesos (15 million dollars).

34. Typically in Mexico, infrastructure projects of this magnitude, or at least key phases of them, are completed during the term in office of the high government official responsible for them, so he can inaugurate them and receive direct credit for them.

4. THE VOICE OF THE PEOPLE: PROTESTS OVER WATER SERVICE IN MONTERREY BETWEEN 1973 AND 1985

1. Government land was preferred for two reasons. First, because government land was not owned by a specific individual the response to the land invasion would not be motivated by personal injury (the loss of one's property) but by the upholding of a principle (the sanctity of private property). The response would come not from an affected individual but from a representative of government. Second, the government was widely seen as responsible for providing housing for the low-income population. In addition, because part of the government's job was to maintain stability, governments often tacitly accepted the existence of land invasion neighborhoods because the loss of government property was a smaller price to pay than the potential loss of stability derived from the constant battle to evict squatters who had nowhere else to live.

2. In some cases, land invasions were guided by radicalized students who decided to leave the university and work directly with the poor. The students provided models of community organization, which might have included features such as block leaders, block meetings, communitywide assemblies, neighborhood committees, and communitywide building days. Often, the students also tried to integrate the squatters' experiences with political teachings (Bennett 1992a).

3. President Salinas de Gortari, elected in 1988, set up a new mechanism to link urban popular movements directly to the office of the presidency, the *convenios de concertación* (cooperation agreements). The *convenios* were contracts between the government and a given popular movement for the shared execution of projects requested by the movement. The movement shared in the project's cost by contributing time, labor, money, material, supervision, and so on. Some movements saw the *convenios* as a victory and signed on; others saw them as co-optation by the government and refused to participate. President Salinas also inaugurated a large antipoverty program, the Programa Nacional de Solidaridad (Pronasol). Pronasol operates through neighborhood committees structured to give the

average citizen a voice in infrastructure decisions affecting his or her neighborhood. Prona-sol addresses the basic public service needs made visible by the mobilizing of urban popular movements over the last two decades. For more on the *convenios de concertación* see Haber 1992; for more on Pronasol see Dresser 1991.

4. An urban popular movement is an organization among the urban poor, created outside of state or private-sector-controlled institutions, that seeks to maintain autonomy from those institutions. The word "popular" implies a precariousness of daily life due to income, land tenure, living conditions, or job security. Urban popular movements seek to resolve the immediate problems of their members, while framing their understanding of the problems caused by poverty in a social analysis. Some urban popular movements have a primary goal of effecting social transformation, while others take the role of mediators between their poor constituencies and the government. Urban protest refers to protests over individual issues that do not coalesce into lasting organizations such as urban popular movements.

5. For data on overcrowding of dwellings in urban Mexico, see Scott 1982: 198-203.

6. The mass organizations are the Confederación de Trabajadores Mexicanos (CTM), the workers' federation; the Confederación Nacional Campesina (CNC), the peasants' feder-ation; and the Confederación Nacional de Organizaciones Populares (CNOP), the federation of popular organizations.

7. The student movement in Mexico disintegrated after government troops and police fired on a peaceful rally on October 2, 1968, killing over two hundred students and injuring more than a thousand. In the aftermath of the repression many socially committed students decided to leave the university setting and work directly with the poor, with peasants in the countryside, and with impoverished urban dwellers. For more on the 1968 student move-ment, see Zermeño 1985; Hellman 1983; and Stevens 1974. For more on the students' shift from university organizing to popular organizing among the poor, see Bennett 1992a. For more on the importance of popular organizing in Mexico in general, see Craig 1990.

8. New agencies included the Instituto Nacional para el Desarrollo de la Comunidad y de la Vivienda (INDECO, founded in 1970), the Instituto del Fondo Nacional de la Vivienda para los Trabajadores (INFONAVIT, founded in 1972), and the Fondo de Vivienda para los Trabajadores del Estado (FOVISSSTE, founded in 1972) (Garza and Schteingart 1978).

9. Paul Haber's insights on how UPMs challenge the mass organizations of the PRI were helpful here.

10. On the Comité de Defensa Popular de Durango, see Haber 1992. On the Comité de Defensa Popular de Chihuahua, see Lau and Quintana Silveyra 1991. On the Frente Popular Tierra y Libertad, see Pérez Güemes and Garza del Toro 1984 and Pozas Garza 1990.

11. For more on the evolution of urban popular movements in Mexico between 1968 and 1988, see Bennett 1992b.

12. Interview with Ingeniero Francisco Cantú Ramos, director of distribution, Servicios de Agua y Drenaje de Monterrey, December 8, 1982; and interview with Ingeniero Rogelio González Rodríguez, director of operations, Servicios de Agua y Drenaje de Monterrey, November 8, 1983.

13. Not all the clandestine faucets are in land invasion neighborhoods. It is suspected that other poor residents of legal neighborhoods have copied this method of obtaining free water from the city.

14. Word of mouth, and the experience of witnessing protests over water, contributed to the spread of protests throughout the city in nonsquatter neighborhoods. Interview, Li-

cenciada María de los Angeles Pozas Garza, director, Post-Graduate Program in Sociology, Universidad Autónoma de Nuevo León, Monterrey, November 21, 1985.

15. The data in the tables and figures presented in this chapter are based on what was reported in Monterrey's two leading newspapers, *El Norte* and *El Porvenir*, from 1970 to 1985. A complete search of both newspapers for the sixteen-year period provided information not only on incidents of protest but on strategies used and location of participating neighborhoods. However, it is likely that not all of the protests that occurred in Monterrey were reported by the press, especially during periods of widespread mobilization. Thus, the incidence of popular mobilizing over water discussed in this chapter, which in some years is quite heavy, can be considered the minimum that occurred.

16. The figures given for the number of neighborhoods involved in protests over water are conservative for two reasons. First, they reflect only those incidents reported by Monterrey's two leading newspapers, which are not a complete cataloguing of such incidents. Second, while some newspaper reports offered detailed listings of the neighborhoods involved in each incident, other reports simply grouped the neighborhoods anonymously into categories, as in "the northwest neighborhoods" or "various neighborhoods."

17. The Secretaría de Asentamientos Humanos y Planificación del Estado de Nuevo León classified all the neighborhoods of the Monterrey Metropolitan Area according to average income level. The tables in this chapter that categorize the neighborhoods according to income are based on data provided by the Secretaría. The Departamento de Estadística del Estado de Nuevo León also contributed some helpful income data. In fact, most neighborhoods in Monterrey are not homogeneous with regard to income. Upper-middle and upper-income families live side by side, as do lower-middle and lower-income families, and lower-income with marginal-income families. Even in the most impoverished neighborhoods, there are usually a few families that could be considered lower-middle income or even higher. In a neighborhood classified as lower income on average, the actual range of incomes may run from middle-income to impoverished. Nevertheless, it is possible to identify a predominant income group in most neighborhoods. For classification purposes, planners in the Monterrey and Nuevo León governments labeled each neighborhood according to the predominant income group.

18. The income of 15.4 percent of the population was unknown (Pozas Garza 1991: 69).

19. The number of strategies used in each incident of protest was counted in the following manner. The newspaper account of each incident described what each neighborhood, or group of neighborhoods, did, step by step. If one neighborhood blocked a street to demand water, that was counted as one strategy-use. If ten neighborhoods blocked the same street together, that one strategy was counted ten times to reflect the decision on the part of each neighborhood to employ that strategy. In another example, if three neighborhoods protested in front of the Governor's Palace, that counted as three strategy-uses. If those three neighborhoods were then joined by four other neighborhoods to move on to protest at the Water Service, that was counted as seven strategy-uses. The total for that one incident (three neighborhoods protesting together in the morning at the Governor's Palace and then moving on in the afternoon to protest along with four other neighborhoods at the Water Service) would have been counted as ten strategy-uses. Thus the data in table 4.7 reflect the sum total of all strategies used by each neighborhood that participated in each incident.

20. Mexico has a long tradition of creating public spaces for its citizens. Even before the Spanish invasion, the cities of pre-Columbian civilizations featured public plazas. During the colonial period, every town in Mexico built under the Royal Ordinances of King Philip II of Spain was mandated to have a public plaza. There is, thus, a tradition of citizens incorporating public space into their daily lives. For more on this subject, see Herzog 1992.

21. See, for example, *El Norte*, 7-19-1979, 7-20-1979, 11-11-1980, 5-22-1983; and *El Porvenir*, 4-28-1983.

22. See for example, *El Norte*, 6-5-1974, 5-10-1975, 6-2-1976; and *El Porvenir*, 6-1-1976 and 6-15-1977.

23. Residents of lower-income neighborhoods incorporate public space into their lives on a more routine basis than do upper-income residents. From using public transportation to seeking each other out as members of reciprocal exchange networks, lower-income residents are less isolated from one another than are upper-income residents, who live principally within the privacy of their homes and cars.

24. Centro de Investigaciones Económicas, Universidad Autónoma de Nuevo León *Boletín Trimestral* no. 87 (junio 1977), as quoted by Servicios 1977; Banco de México, *Boletín Mensual*, as quoted in Villatoro et al. 1983: 31.

25. Servicios 1977: 9. Here we use the average of the increase in rates for the first four categories of residential water service, which included 80 percent of Monterrey's population.

26. Eckstein (1989: 46) suggests that public protest can cause "contagion," spreading to groups in society that on their own have not reached the point of public protest. Protest is therefore threatening to the elite who defend the status quo, both for the actual disruption it causes and for its potential to be contagious.

27. For example, the World Bank's policy for water services in Third World cities is laid out in the booklet *Water Supply and Waste Disposal* (World Bank 1980: 15, 18). First, the bank explains that if the urban population of the Third World were served with house connections and the rural population with standpipes and hand pumps, then the total costs for providing water to everyone would exceed $600 billion (in 1978 dollars). If, on the other hand, urban areas were served by a greater mix of house connections and standpipes, the total cost would fall to $300 billion or less—still an unfeasible amount, in the World Bank's view. The authors suggest that "in urban areas . . . basic needs can generally be met at costs lower than that of many of the programs carried out in the 1970s by applying lower standards of service, such as standpipes in place of house connections, and simpler technology." Later, the document provides four reasons why "immediate implementation of full higher-grade delivery systems for all towns and cities in the developing countries is not sensible": 1) "many of the potential users are too poor to pay the full cost of house connections," 2) "the houses are often not suitably constructed for internal plumbing," 3) "the community is often unable to raise the capital to construct the facilities," and 4) "the costs . . . to dispose of the wastewater . . . would be high." Yet in Monterrey, which is typical of Latin American cities in terms of the quality of low-income housing and the standards of living and incomes of the poor, house connections were extended to all households in the poor neighborhoods.

5. GENDER, CLASS, AND WATER: THE ROLE OF WOMEN IN THE PROTESTS OVER WATER

1. Race was not a factor in the composition of the participants in the Monterrey protests. Monterrey has no local indigenous culture or black population.

2. Social reproduction refers to the tasks and processes that are necessary for an individual to be fully able to participate in society: eating, bathing, washing clothes, keeping healthy, learning, and so forth.

3. In well-off homes (where the woman works out of professional ambition, instead of or in addition to economic need), the mother or wife is still the manager of the household, even if she has paid help.

4. The data in table 5.2 vastly minimize the extent of women's participation in the

protests. The data come from the newspaper descriptions of the incidents. The newspapers' identification of the gender of participants was highly erratic; sometimes the text would explicitly refer to protesters as "350 housewives" or "irate housewives," while at other times the text would say "350 residents" or "irate residents" with the accompanying photo showing a large group of women and no men. Consequently, it is possible that in many cases when the textual description of the participants was gender-neutral, and there was no accompanying photo, the participants were mainly women.

5. We get fifty-nine by adding ten plus forty plus seven from the incidents that had multiple neighborhood participation plus two incidents that represented single neighborhood actions.

6. These examples are based on personal observations in Monterrey.

7. Newspaper reports in *El Norte* and *El Porvenir*.

8. Personal observation at the Water Service, Monterrey.

9. The engineers also had to avoid shutting off water service to a previously militant neighborhood to service a currently militant neighborhood—otherwise, they might provoke new protests.

10. Newspaper reports in *El Norte* and *El Porvenir*.

11. The protests over water in Monterrey did not receive support from organized labor, and workers did not use their unions or go on strike to demand better water services in their homes. Yet experience in other countries has shown this to be possible. In Italy, in the early 1970s, the response to the government's attempt to raise electricity rates nationwide took place both in the sphere of social reproduction and in the sphere of production. Housewives organized in urban neighborhoods, but industrial workers also organized in the factory, and the state electrical workers collaborated by refusing to disconnect residential electricity service even when ordered to do so. This simultaneous activity on all fronts resulted in the government withdrawing the rate increase and implementing instead a graduated system that was more equitable (Ramírez 1975). In Monterrey, mobilizing over water remained not only within the sphere of social reproduction but was primarily the terrain of women.

12. Interview, Lic. María de los Angeles Pozas Garza, director, Graduate School of Sociology, Universidad Autónoma de Nuevo León, Monterrey, November 21, 1985.

13. Interview, Lic. María de los Angeles Pozas Garza, director, Graduate School of Sociology, Universidad Autónoma de Nuevo León, Monterrey, November 21, 1985. In addition, conversations with Ana María Alonso (University of Arizona, Tucson) about her research in Namiquipa, Chihuahua, provide evidence in support of these ideas (conversations took place in 1987 at the Center for U.S.-Mexican Studies, University of California-San Diego, in 1987).

14. While the organization of the Fomerrey neighborhoods sounds similar to the Tierra y Libertad neighborhoods with their block-by-block organization and block leaders, the purpose was different. With Fomerrey, the government sought to regain control over the poor urban population in Monterrey. Tight neighborhood organization allowed government representatives to know about, control, or channel any mobilizing activity.

15. Interview, María de los Angeles Pozas Garza, director, Graduate School of Sociology, Universidad Autónoma de Nuevo León, Monterrey, March 17, 1987.

16. Interview, María de los Angeles Pozas Garza, director, Graduate School of Sociology, Universidad Autónoma de Nuevo León, Monterrey, March 17, 1987.

17. The survey used a random sample of neighborhoods in Monterrey and was carried out in ninety-three homes in twenty neighborhoods. Each home was surveyed once a month for six months.

6. AGUA PARA TODOS: THE GOVERNMENT'S RESPONSE TO THE WATER CRISIS

1. The centralized politico-administrative system imposed by the Spaniards coincided with the highly centralized form of governance in existence under Aztec rulers before the Spanish Invasion.

2. It is difficult to know whether reduced federal investment in major infrastructure projects for Ciudad Juárez and Chihuahua was the result of a bias in resource allocation or of decreased public spending due to the economic crisis the country was facing. However, it is notable that the most significant water infrastructure ever built for Monterrey was under construction during the same years that the PAN held the state government in Chihuahua and Ciudad Juárez. The federal government, therefore, was making major investment decisions for urban infrastructure even during the economic crisis, and even on behalf of a city with which it had sustained decades of hostile relations (Monterrey). This raises the question of whether the lack of major federal investment in Ciudad Juárez and Chihuahua from 1983 to 1986 was due, at least in part, to a political decision to underfund opposition governments.

3. BANOBRAS is the Banco Nacional de Obras; SEDUE is the Secretaría de Desarrollo Urbano y Ecología.

4. The discussion of government agencies involved in Monterrey's water sector highlights only the most significant agencies during the period under study in this chapter, 1970 to 1985.

5. While the Santa Catarina district also served sprawling poor urban neighborhoods, these could not benefit from the new investments if they were not connected to the water system—and mostly they were not.

6. This means that the Water Service supplied water to consumers but was not paid by consumers for all of it. Unaccounted-for water included water lost in leaks, water lost to illegal taps of the water main, and billing errors due to faulty meters. The figure of 45 percent unaccounted-for water is the average of the figures given in Comisión 1976d: 1 and Comisión 1977: 15.

7. From 1973 to 1977, water rates went up 252 percent, while the minimum wage in Monterrey increased only 157 percent (Servicios 1977: 6). Yet, from 1973 to 1977, water services for the population depending on the minimum wage (or less) had not improved.

8. Interview, Ing. Enrique Lavalle, Comisión de Agua Potable de Monterrey, Monterrey, Nuevo León, Mexico, November, 17, 1983.

9. Until 1966, the executive director of the Commission had been the SRH representative. From 1966 to 1976 Carlos Maldonado, who was the representative to the board from the chamber of real estate, was the executive director. Maldonado is a major industrialist and hotelier in Monterrey.

10. Interview, Ing. Enrique Lavalle, Comisión de Agua Potable de Monterrey, Monterrey, Nuevo León, Mexico, November, 17, 1983.

11. "Actas de la Comisión de Agua Potable de Monterrey," attendance lists.

12. The other two new ministries created by López Portillo were the Secretaría de Programación y Presupuesto (Programming and Budget), and the Secretaría de Patrimonio y Fomento Industrial (Patrimony and Industrial Development).

13. In March 1977, only four months after taking office and right in the middle of the conflicts in Monterrey's water sector, President López Portillo met with the Grupo Monterrey in Monterrey. In his diary (López Portillo 1988: 558), the president noted a good rapport with the businessmen and commented that one of the leading Monterrey industrialists gave a speech recognizing the value of harmonious relations. The *Wall Street Journal* (November

12, 1979: 1) underscores this point with the following article headline: "Mexican Magnates: role of industrialists of Monterrey grows as country develops; they and government bury old ill will and cooperate to put oil income to use."

14. Jacobi Neru (1987) demonstrates that protests over water in São Paulo, Brazil, were in fact stimulated by the perception of increased government willingness to finance improvements in neighborhood water service.

15. Interview, Ing. Enrique Lavalle, Comisión de Agua Potable de Monterrey, Monterrey, Nuevo León, Mexico, December 8, 1983.

16. In his diary, commenting on having picked Martínez Domínguez as the candidate for governor of Nuevo León in 1978, President López Portillo (1988: 786) wrote, "We need an experienced politician in Nuevo León . . . in order to get the state back in shape."

17. President López Portillo authorized six thousand million pesos for the Plan Hidráulico, which I have rephrased as six billion, following U.S. terminology for numbers. A Mexican billion (1,000,000,000,000) equals one U.S. trillion. When I use the word billion in the text I always mean the U.S. definition of billion (1,000,000,000). With the 1980 exchange rate, the 6,000,000,000 pesos initially authorized for the Plan Hidráulico equaled $257,953,560 U.S. (Nacional Financiera 1990: 710).

18. A description by the office of the president of a May 1983 trip by President de la Madrid to Monterrey states that a central theme of the visit was the scarcity of water (Presidencia 1985a: 157).

19. As shown in earlier chapters, most of the neighborhoods that participated in the protests over water were connected to the municipal water system and protested in response to the dramatic deterioration of their water service, either due to the onset of rationing or to the unreliability of the rationing system. These neighborhoods stood to benefit from the Plan Hidráulico because they were connected to the water system and could receive water from the new dam. However, up to three hundred thousand people, living in neighborhoods all around the Monterrey Metropolitan Area, were not connected to the water system. The government may have been concerned that protests would spread to these neighborhoods once the Cerro Prieto dam was inaugurated and there was no improvement in water service for neighborhoods not connected to the water system. The four-year publicity campaign waged by the government, which had reached into every last neighborhood of Monterrey, had promised a complete solution to the city's water problems. All of a sudden, in 1983, the government realized that its "complete" solution was leaving out three hundred thousand people. The fact that the Ministry of Planning and Budget emphasized the protests over water in its report on the water problems of Monterrey suggests that the protests themselves contributed to the government's endorsement of the Water Service's proposal for Water For All.

20. In Mexico, large infrastructure projects that are the pet projects of a particular government official are expected to be completed before the end of the term in office of the official who authorized or created the project.

21. It is very difficult to arrive at a dollar translation of the cost of the Plan Hidráulico and of Water For All. The Plan Hidráulico cost 36,000,000,000 pesos spent over the course of five years, from 1980 through 1984. In 1980 and 1981 the exchange rate of the peso was stable at 23.26 pesos to the dollar (Nacional Financiera 1990: 710–11). But starting in early 1982, the peso was devalued, and its value vis-à-vis the dollar deteriorated steadily throughout the 1980s. Averaging the monthly exchange rate for each year, and assuming that the Plan Hidráulico funds were disbursed equally over the five years (which they were not), we arrive at an estimate of 830 million dollars. It is probably fair to say that the Plan Hidráulico cost about one billion U.S. dollars, and Water For All about 25 million.

22. Without the water from Cerro Prieto, Monterrey would have had a water supply deficit of over 40 percent.

23. At the end of 1985 the new governor, Jorge Treviño, announced that water rates would increase 222 percent in 1986 (*El Norte*, 12-13-1985). In 1982, Governor Martínez Domínguez, responding to the requirements of the IDB, had decreed a 75 percent rate increase to be followed by yearly increases pegged to inflation. However, adjustments were not made in 1983, 1984, or 1985 despite the fact that inflation was close to 100 percent in each of those years. Consequently, by the end of 1985, the Water Service's rates were again out of line with the price index, necessitating the abrupt and heavy rate increase decreed by Governor Treviño. Meanwhile, from 1982 to 1985 the real minimum wage declined by 47 percent (*Proceso*, 9-6-1986: 21).

24. The El Cuchillo project had an estimated cost of $650 million dollars and was financed half by the Inter-American Development Bank and half by the Mexican government (Villatoro et al. 1990: 1). This was the IDB's fourth loan for water infrastructure for Monterrey; it had also helped finance the Plan Hidráulico and Water For All.

25. The El Cuchillo dam was the number one site selected after technical studies were carried out by the Commission during the 1960s and was the priority project that the Commission pushed for during its years of disagreements with the Ministry of Hydraulic Resources (Secretaría de Recursos Hidráulicos—SRH). The SRH, which never included the El Cuchillo dam on its list of potential dams, instead prioritized the Cerro Prieto dam. The fact that both dams were eventually built indicates that both were technically feasible and that both sets of studies had technical integrity. This supports the conclusions suggested in chapter 3 that the disagreements between the SRH and the Commission were based on larger political conflicts and not on technical incompetence by one side or the other. In short, the disagreements did not have technical merit. At the same time, during the years of conflict the federal government did not charge municipal water authorities for the water extracted from dams, wells, or other sources, so the cost of the water itself was not a factor in the decision not to build a particular dam. Since 1985 the SARH has begun charging for water in bulk, however, there has been strong opposition to the charges from municipal water authorities. In 1989, the SARH created the Comisión Nacional de Agua (National Water Commission, CNA), which is mandated, among other responsibilities, to manage the system of water fees. However, most urban water authorities in Mexico, including the Water Service in Monterrey, have not paid for water since the CNA was created and have instead formed the Association of Water and Sewerage Authorities to negotiate with the SARH for lower rates.

26. In other words, because the Water Service already uses the water from Cerro Prieto to substitute for other sources of water as the other sources recover from depletion, they will not need to do the same with the water from El Cuchillo. Therefore, the El Cuchillo water will be a real addition to the current total water supply.

7. CONCLUSION: THE POLITICS OF WATER

1. Within the industrial sector, federal spending prioritized the petroleum and energy industries. During the 1950s and 1960s, Veracruz and Tamaulipas were the most important petroleum producing states, which explains the unusually high level of federal investment in both states. For its part, the Federal District already concentrated the major share of import substitution industrialization (Palacios 1989: 163).

2. The three new ministries were the Secretaría de Asentamientos Humanos y Obras Públicas (Settlements and Public Works), the Secretaría de Programación y Presupuesto

(Programming and Budget), and the Secretaría de Patrimonio y Fomento Industrial (Patrimony and Industrial Development).

3. There are thirty-two states in Mexico, including the Federal District.

4. Social infrastructure includes rural and urban services; economic infrastructure includes roads, railroads, bridges, ports, airports, and telecommunications (Palacios 1989: 196).

5. In 1983 the federal bureaucracy alone (excluding state and municipal employees) employed more than three million people (Bailey 1988: 62).

6. For more on *camarillas*, see Smith 1979: 252–68; Bailey 1988: 75–77; and Cornelius and Craig 1991: 42.

7. Rodríguez (1987: 165) and Ward (1986: 40) both highlight the fact that policy making in Mexico is not fully understood because the process by which policy is formulated is "secret" and "takes place behind closed doors."

8. They also depended on federal government authorization to submit loan proposals to international development banks like the IDB.

9. The two representatives of the low-income neighborhoods were not from low-income families themselves. For example, one of them lived in Monterrey's wealthiest neighborhood and was the owner of three car and heavy-machinery dealerships. It seems that these representatives served as yes-men to the private sector representatives who came to control the board of directors.

10. The five municipalities were Monterrey, San Nicolás de los Garza, San Pedro Garza García, Santa Catarina, and Guadalupe. As of 1992, the Monterrey Metropolitan Area has expanded to include two more municipalities, General Escobedo and Apodaca.

11. One of the professionals who had worked for the Commission for many years told me that power on the board of directors was concentrated in the representatives of the private sector along with Elizondo, the Commission's general director (who was an engineer). Further, he claimed that the power of private sector representatives came not from the institutions they represented (for example, the chamber of industries or of real estate) but from their power as individuals within the Monterrey bourgeoisie (interview, Comisión de Agua Potable de Monterrey, November 17, 1983).

12. Chapter 3 documents the smaller projects that were agreed upon, authorized, and constructed from 1954 to 1976. However, besides the La Boca dam, no single large project that could make a serious dent in Monterrey's water deficit was authorized. Further, an engineer with the Secretaría de Agricultura y Recursos Hidráulicos told me that Governor Zorrilla Martínez had severely reduced the Water Service's budget because he thought that in extending the water distribution system the Service had favored developments owned by the Grupo Monterrey over new low-income settlements (interview, SARH local office, Monterrey, Nuevo León, November 18, 1983).

13. Only in four states do gubernatorial terms coincide with presidential terms: Chiapas, Morelos, Tabasco, and Yucatán. However, in all four cases the incoming governor is selected by the outgoing president, which means that these four governors serve their whole term under a different president than the one who selected them (Bailey 1988: 150–54).

14. President López Portillo did support Governor Zorrilla's actions to take back control of the Commission and the Water Service in 1977.

15. The Federal District, Mexico, Jalisco, and Veracruz were the four top-ranked states in terms of GDP. For all intents and purposes, the Federal District and Mexico can be considered as one unit, because Mexico's prominence in the GDP derives from the expansion of Mexico City out of the Federal District into the state of Mexico. The importance of Veracruz is tied to its role as a petroleum producing state. If the Federal District and the state of

Mexico are combined, and only contribution to the GDP from non–petroleum producing states is considered, Nuevo León would have ranked third in 1970, 1975, and 1980.

16. Occasionally, neighborhoods from one part of the city might organize a protest event together or, more spontaneously, take part in a protest together; but neighborhoods from different sectors of the city never organized together. Of course, if protest groups happened to show up at the same government office at the same time they would each continue on with the purpose of their visit, perhaps giving the appearance of protesting together. As regards leaders, in some neighborhoods natural leaders may have emerged during specific events, but no individual ever acted as an overarching leader attempting to unify or transform the protests into a planned, citywide set of actions.

17. Participation in social movements is possible when problems are addressed as strategic rather than practical. Then, it becomes more important to help build the social movement even if doing so means postponing household chores. Women have participated in social movements across Latin America, and in Mexico and Monterrey. What distinguishes social movement from protest is the focus on social transformation, and the explanation of immediate problems as based on relations of power that can be challenged and changed.

18. The Plan Hidráulico and Agua Para Todos had the effect of calming the protests in Monterrey. However, this is not an example of co-optation of entire neighborhoods; it is an example of successful protest. Precisely because the participants in the protests were acting out of practical interests, they had one goal: improving water service to their neighborhoods. Therefore, a government response that gave them improved service meant their goal was reached.

19. On occasion, women were forced to leave government offices by being pushed or pulled outdoors, but never with the acute violence that has at times characterized government response to social movements, land invasions, and mass protests.

20. The city of São Paulo, Brazil, experienced a phenomenon similar to Monterrey: water services were extended in one massive program to all unserved neighborhoods after citywide protests over inadequate water service (Watson 1992).

21. In a similar vein, Ward (1990: 81) says, "From central government's viewpoint, good city management in the Metropolitan Area [Mexico City] requires that social unrest be contained and appeased. This may be achieved through political mediation as well as through successful and efficient systems of delivery of public goods."

22. I first discussed these ideas in Bennett 1992b.

23. For example, the city of Aguascalientes has turned management of the city's water system over to a private company managed by a board of directors with representatives from both the private sector and the government.

24. In most cases, private extraction of water draws from the same sources as government extraction of water. For proper water management, it is necessary that there be a comprehensive tally of all water removed from each source. Depletion of the source can occur if more water is extracted than is returned through natural replenishment.

25. It would have been very difficult for the government planners of 1909 to imagine the industrial development that took place in Monterrey after the Revolution, the growth of the population, and the higher per capita water requirements for the city as a whole. In addition, since this was Monterrey's first municipal water system, and one of the first in any Mexican city, it is understandable that not all dimensions of regulating private ownership of the service were foreseen.

26. Private sector control of the Commission's board began in the mid-1960s. In 1966, two eminent members of the Grupo Monterrey who were on the Commission's board of directors formed an executive committee composed of just the two of them to make deci-

sions in between board meetings. In addition, while the local representative of the Secretaría de Recursos Hidráulicos was one of the few government board members to attend almost all meetings from 1954 to 1971, after 1971 he practically stopped attending.

27. After 1976, the Commission's board of directors continued to include representatives from the private sector; however, they stopped attending meetings.

28. These concerns were expressed equally by the government and the private sector representatives on the Commission's board.

29. This example of the private sector resorting to the private, individual provision of a public service is not unique. In other cities, private firms have provided their own electricity, mail service, and mass transportation for employees (Coing 1991: 8).

30. The withholding of federal government funds was not due to negative technical evaluations by the government of the water infrastructure projects prioritized by the Commission. Funding was not denied because the Commission was proposing technically unsound or unfeasible infrastructure. As shown in chapter 6, the priority projects of both the Secretary of Hydraulic Resources and the Commission were eventually constructed in the 1980s and 1990s. In short, both were technically viable. The disagreements between the Commission and the SRH were rooted in politics, not technology.

31. Standards also include setting tariff levels and, if necessary, providing subsidies for low-income or impoverished users.

32. Urban water provision consists of a series of steps, which could be broken down and contracted out individually to the private sector. For example, purification of water at each source could be sold to private firms, while the distribution of water to different sectors of the city could be franchised out for management by different private sector firms. This could be feasible in a city like Monterrey before 1985, when the city was divided into three sectors, each receiving water from a different source. After 1985, when the Transfer Ring connected all the sources of water for the city, a different involvement of the private sector would have been necessary.

33. Coing (1991: 18) raises the point that there is a real problem with trying to achieve the complete provision of public services in cities that do not have a base of mass consumption (that is, in cities where there is a large population base with no discretionary income). Drawing from Massiah and Tribillon (1987), Coing suggests an alternative model of service provision. Instead of using the service level of the wealthiest sectors of the population as the model of service that individuals as well as planners aspire to, Coing suggests taking the minimum needs of the poorest of the poor as a starting point. This most basic level of infrastructure should be provided by the public sector across the city. Each neighborhood would have the opportunity of improving its level of service, but the cost of doing so would be borne completely by the consumer. This system would make basic infrastructure the model (instead of the most elaborate infrastructure) and would remove from the government the need to fund and subsidize the construction of neighborhood infrastructure.

BIBLIOGRAPHY

"Actas de la Comisión de Agua Potable de Monterrey 1954–1979." Handwritten minutes of the meetings of the Comisión de Agua Potable de Monterrey.

Alonso, Ana María. 1988. "U.S. Military Intervention, Revolutionary Mobilization, and Popular Ideology in the Chihuahuan Sierra, 1916–1917." In *Rural Revolt in Mexico and U.S. Intervention*, ed. Daniel Nugent. La Jolla: Center for U.S.-Mexican Studies, University of California-San Diego, Monograph Series no. 27.

Alvarez, Sonia. 1990. *Engendering Democracy in Brazil: Women's Movements in Transition Politics*. Princeton: Princeton University Press.

Andreas, Carol. 1985. *When Women Rebel: The Rise of Popular Feminism in Peru*. Westport, Conn.: Lawrence Hill and Co.

Annis, Sheldon, and Peter Hakim, eds. 1988. *Direct to the Poor: Grassroots Development in Latin America*. Boulder: Lynne Rienner.

Anson, Ricardo. 1978. *Implicaciones socioeconómicos de la marginación en el Area Metropolitana de Monterrey*. Monterrey: Instituto Tecnológico de Estudios Superiores de Monterrey, Departamento de Economía, Serie de Trabajos de Investigación Económica.

"Anteproyecto de abastecimiento de agua potable para la ciudad de Monterrey." 1949. Author unknown, manuscript in the archives of Servicios de Agua y Drenaje de Monterrey, Nuevo León.

Arizpe, Lourdes. 1990. "Foreword: Democracy for a Small Two-Gender Planet." In *Women and Social Change in Latin America*, ed. Elizabeth Jelin. London: Zed Books; Geneva: UNRISD.

Babb, Florence E. 1989. *Between Field and Cooking Pot: The Political Economy of Marketwomen in Peru*. Austin: University of Texas Press.

Bailey, John J. 1988. *Governing Mexico: The Statecraft of Crisis Management*. London: Macmillan; New York: St. Martin's.

Barrig, Maruja. 1989. "The Difficult Equilibrium Between Bread and Roses: Women's Organizations and the Transition from Dictatorship to Democracy in Peru." In *The Women's Movement in Latin America*, ed. Jane S. Jaquette. Boston: Unwin Hyman.

Benería, Lourdes, and Martha Roldán. 1987. *The Crossroads of Class and Gender:*

213

Industrial Homework, Subcontracting, and Household Dynamics in Mexico City.
Chicago: University of Chicago Press.

Bennett, Vivienne. 1989. "Urban Public Services and Social Conflict: Water in Monterrey." In *Housing and Land in Urban Mexico*, ed. Alan Gilbert. La Jolla: Center for U.S.-Mexican Studies, University of California-San Diego, Monograph Series no. 31.

———. 1992a. "The Origins of Mexican Urban Popular Movements: Political Thought and Clandestine Political Organizing of the 1960s and 1970s." Paper presented at the 17th International Congress of the Latin American Studies Association, Los Angeles, September.

———. 1992b. "The Evolution of Urban Popular Movements in Mexico Between 1968 and 1978." In *The Making of Social Movements in Contemporary Latin America: Identity, Strategy, and Democracy*, ed. Sonia Alvarez and Arturo Escobar. Boulder, Colo.: Westview.

Beneveniste, Guy. 1970. *Bureaucracy and National Planning: A Sociological Case Study in Mexico.* New York: Praeger.

Blondet, Cecilia. 1990. "Establishing an Identity: Women Settlers in a Poor Lima Neighborhood." In *Women and Social Change in Latin America*, ed. Elizabeth Jelin. London: Zed Books; Geneva: UNRISD.

Borja, Jordi. 1975. *Movimientos sociales urbanos.* Buenos Aires: Ediciones Siap-Planteos.

Bourque, Susan C. 1985. "Urban Activists: Paths to Political Consciousness in Peru." In *Women Living Change*, ed. Susan Bourque and Donna Robinson Divine. Philadelphia: Temple University Press.

Bradley, David J. 1978. "Health Aspects of Water Supplies in Tropical Countries." In *Water, Wastes and Health in Hot Climates*, ed. Richard Feachem, Michael McGarry, and Duncan Mara. Chichester: English Language Book Society and John Wiley and Sons.

Braunstein, Fernando. 1985. "Acceso al agua potable y calidad del hábitat en el Gran Buenos Aires: Crónica de un proceso de deterioro." *Boletín de medio ambiente y urbanización* 3, no. 10 (April 1985), 19–27.

Burdick, John. 1992. "Rethinking the Study of Social Movements: The Case of Christian Base Communities in Urban Brazil." In *The Making of Social Movements in Latin America: Identity, Strategy, and Democracy*, ed. Sonia Alvarez and Arturo Escobar. Boulder, Colo.: Westview.

Butler Flora, Cornelia. 1984. "Socialist Feminism in Latin America." *Women and Politics* 4, no. 1 (spring): 69–93.

Cabrera, Luis, and Gustavo Molina Font. 1944. "Conflicto entre el gobierno de Nuevo León y la compañía de Servicio de Agua y Drenaje de Monterrey, S.A." Mexico City: Alegato del Gobierno de Nuevo León ante la Segunda Sala de la Suprema Corte de Justicia de la Nación.

Caldeira, Teresa Pires de Rio. 1990. "Women, Daily Life and Politics." In *Women and Social Change in Latin America*, ed. Elizabeth Jelin. London: Zed Books; Geneva: UNRISD.

Camacho, Daniel. 1990. "Los movimientos populares." In *América Latina, hoy*, ed. Pedro Vuskovic et al. Mexico City: Siglo XXI and Editorial de la Universidad de las Naciones Unidas.

Cámara Nacional de Comercio de Monterrey. 1946. "Estudio del problema de agua y drenaje en la ciudad de Monterrey." Monterrey.

Camp, Roderic. 1982. *Mexican Political Biographies, 1935–1981*. Tucson: University of Arizona Press.

———. 1989. *Entrepreneurs and Politics in Twentieth-Century Mexico*. New York: Oxford University Press.

Castells, Manuel. 1979. *City, Class, and Power*. London: Macmillan.

———. 1980. *The Urban Question: A Marxist Approach*. Cambridge: MIT Press.

———. 1982. "Squatters and Politics in Latin America: a Comparative Analysis of Urban Social Movements in Chile, Peru and Mexico." In *Towards a Political Economy of Urbanization in Third World Countries*, ed. Helen Safa. Oxford: Oxford University Press.

———. 1983. *The City and the Grassroots*. Berkeley: University of California Press.

Centro de Investigaciones Económicas. 1965. *El problema del agua en Monterrey*. Monterrey: Facultad de Economía, Universidad de Nuevo León.

CEPAL. 1980. *Agua, desarrollo y medio ambiente en América Latina*. Santiago de Chile: Comisión Económica para América Latina.

Cerutti, Mario. 1983. *Burguesía y capitalismo en Monterrey, 1850–1910*. Mexico City: Claves Latinoamericanos.

Chant, Sylvia. 1991. *Women and Survival in Mexican Cities: Perspectives on Gender, Labour Markets and Low-Income Households*. Manchester, Eng.: Manchester University Press.

Chávez Gutiérrez, José. 1992. Director of Administration and Finances, Servicios de Agua y Drenaje de Monterrey, Nuevo León, Mexico. Letter to author dated June 15.

Chávez Padrón, Martha. 1979. *Ley Federal de Aguas*. Mexico City: Editorial Porrúa, S.A.

Chodorow, Nancy. 1979. "Mothering, Male Dominance, and Capitalism." In *Capitalist Patriarchy and the Case for Socialist Feminism*, ed. Zillah R. Eisenstein. New York: Monthly Review Press, 1979.

Chuchryk, Patricia M. 1989. "Feminist Anti-Authoritarian Politics: The Role of Women's Organizations in the Chilean Transition to Democracy." In *The Women's Movement in Latin America*, ed. Jane S. Jaquette. Boston: Unwin Hyman.

Coing, Henri. 1991. "Revisando los servicios urbanos." Paper presented at the 8th

Encuentro de la Red Nacional de Investigación Urbana, "Servicios Urbanos y Privatización," Ciudad Juárez, Chihuahua, Mexico, February 7–8.

Collier, David. 1976. *Squatters and Oligarchs: Authoritarian Rule and Policy Change in Peru*. Baltimore: Johns Hopkins University Press.

Comisión de Agua Potable de Monterrey. 1976a. "Agua potable a Monterrey."

———. 1976b. "Informe de actividades al 31 de diciembre de 1976."

———. 1976c. "Comentarios: actuaciones realizadas por su vocal ejecutivo Sr. Carlos Maldonado Elizondo y su gerente Ing. Leobardo Elizondo. Violaciones fundamentales al acuerdo presidencial que la creó."

———. 1976d. "Consideraciones sobre los ingresos que corresponden a Servicios de Agua y Drenaje de Monterrey."

———. 1977. "Abastecimiento de agua en Monterrey en 1977."

———. 1981. "Manual de organización."

Cook, Maria Lorena. 1990. "Organizing Opposition in the Teachers' Movement in Oaxaca." In *Popular Movements and Political Change in Mexico*, ed. Joe Foweraker and Ann Craig. Boulder, Colo.: Lynne Rienner.

Cornelius, Wayne. 1975. *Politics and the Migrant Poor in Mexico City*. Stanford: Stanford University Press.

Cornelius, Wayne, and Ann Craig. 1991. *The Mexican Political System in Transition*. La Jolla: Center for U.S.-Mexican Studies, University of California-San Diego, Monograph Series no. 35.

Cowan, L. Gray. 1990. *Privatization in the Developing World*. New York: Greenwood.

Craig, Ann. 1990. "Institutional Context and Popular Strategies." In *Popular Movements and Political Change in Mexico*, ed. Joe Foweraker and Ann Craig. Boulder, Colo.: Lynne Rienner.

Cusicanqui, Silvia Rivera, and the Andean Oral History Workshop (THOA). 1990. "Indigenous Women and Community Resistance: History and Memory." In *Women and Social Change in Latin America*, ed. Elizabeth Jelin. London: Zed Books; Geneva: UNRISD.

de la Madrid, Miguel. 1983a. *Primer informe de gobierno, 1983, informe complementario*. Mexico City: Presidencia de la República.

———. 1983b. *Primer informe de gobierno, 1983, sector desarrollo urbano y ecología*. Mexico City: Presidencia de la República.

El Diario. Monterrey, Mexico. 6-24-1980, 7-15-1980.

Diario Oficial. Nuevo León, Mexico. 5-7-1964, 2-28-1980, 12-21-1981.

Dresser, Denise. 1991. *Neopopulist Solutions to Neoliberal Problems*. La Jolla: Center for U.S.-Mexican Studies, University of California-San Diego, Current Issue Brief no. 3.

Eckstein, Susan. 1977. *The Poverty of Revolution: The State and the Urban Poor in Mexico*. Princeton: Princeton University Press.

———, ed. 1989. *Power and Popular Protest in Latin American Social Movements*. Berkeley: University of California Press.

La economía mexicana en cifras, edición 1986. 1986. Mexico City: Nacional Financiera.

Eisenstein, Zillah R., ed. 1979a. *Capitalist Patriarchy and the Case for Socialist Feminism.* New York: Monthly Review Press.

————. 1979b. "Developing a Theory of Capitalist Patriarchy and Socialist Feminism." In *Capitalist Patriarchy and the Case for Socialist Feminism,* ed. Zillah R. Eisenstein. New York: Monthly Review Press.

Elizondo, Leobardo. 1977. "Comisión de Agua Potable de Monterrey: abastecimiento de agua potable." Monterrey: Comisión de Agua Potable de Monterrey.

Enloe, Cynthia. 1989. *Bananas, Beaches, and Bases: Making Feminist Sense of International Politics.* Berkeley: University of California Press.

Escobar, Arturo, and Sonia Alvarez, eds. 1992. *The Making of Social Movements in Latin America: Identity, Strategy, and Democracy.* Boulder, Colo.: Westview.

Etherton, David. 1980. *Water and Sanitation in Slums and Shantytowns.* New York: UNICEF Water, Environment, and Sanitation Team.

Excelsior. Mexico City. 9-1-1978, 6-12-1979, 3-22-1980.

Fagen, Richard, and William Tuohy. 1972. *Politics and Privilege in a Mexican City.* Stanford: Stanford University Press.

Farías, Luis M. *Así lo recuerdo: testimonios políticos.* Mexico City: Fondo de Cultura Económica.

Feachem, Richard, Michael McGarry, and Duncan Mara, eds. 1978. *Water, Wastes and Health in Hot Climates.* Chichester: English Language Book Society and John Wiley and Sons.

Feijoó, María del Cármen. 1989. "The Challenge of Constructing Civilian Peace: Women and Democracy in Argentina." In *The Women's Movement in Latin America,* ed. Jane S. Jaquette. Boston: Unwin Hyman.

Feijoó, María del Cármen, and Monica Gogna. 1990. "Women in the Transition to Democracy." In *Women and Social Change in Latin America,* ed. Elizabeth Jelin. London: Zed Books; Geneva: UNRISD.

Fernández-Kelly, María Patricia. 1983. *For We Are Sold, I and My People: Women and Industry in Mexico's Frontier.* Albany: State University of New York Press.

Foweraker, Joe, and Ann Craig, eds. 1990. *Popular Movements and Political Change in Mexico.* Boulder, Colo.: Lynne Rienner.

Fox, Jonathon, and Gustavo Gordillo. 1989. "Between State and Market: The Campesinos' Quest for Autonomy." In *Mexico's Alternative Political Futures,* ed. Wayne Cornelius, Judith Gentleman, and Peter Smith. La Jolla: Center for U.S.-Mexican Studies, University of California-San Diego, Monograph Series no. 30.

Friedmann, John. 1987. *Planning in the Public Domain: From Knowledge to Action.* Princeton: Princeton University Press.

García, María Pilar. 1992. "The Venezuelan Ecology Movement: Symbolic Effectiveness, Social Practices, and Political Strategies." In *The Making of Social Movements in Latin America: Identity, Strategy, and Democracy*, ed. Sonia Alvarez and Arturo Escobar. Boulder, Colo.: Westview.

Garza, Gustavo, and Martha Schteingart. 1978. *La acción habitacional del Estado de México*. Mexico City: El Colegio de México.

Gaventa, John. 1980. *Power and Powerlessness: Quiescence and Rebellion in an Appalachian Valley*. Urbana: University of Illinois Press.

Gilbert, Alan, ed. 1989. *Housing and Land in Urban Mexico*. La Jolla: Center for U.S.-Mexican Studies, University of California-San Diego, Monograph Series no. 31.

Gilbert, Alan, and Peter M. Ward. 1985. *Housing, the State and the Poor: Policy and Practice in Three Latin American Cities*. Cambridge: Cambridge University Press.

González de la Rocha, Mercedes, and Agustín Escobar Latapí, eds. 1991. *Social Responses to Mexico's Economic Crisis of the 1980s*. La Jolla: Center for U.S.-Mexican Studies, University of California-San Diego.

Goodman, John, and Gary Loveman. 1991. "Does Privatization Serve the Public Interest?" *Harvard Business Review* (Nov.–Dec.): 26–38.

Graham, Lawrence S. 1971. *Mexican State Government: A Prefectural System in Action*. Austin: Institute of Public Affairs, University of Texas-Austin.

Grindle, Merilee S., ed. 1980. *Politics and Policy Implementation in the Third World*. Princeton: Princeton University Press.

Grindle, Merilee S., and John W. Thomas. 1991. *Public Choices and Policy Change: The Political Economy of Reform in Developing Countries*. Baltimore: Johns Hopkins University Press.

Haber, Paul. 1992. "Collective Dissent in Mexico: The Politics of Contemporary Urban Popular Movements." Ph.D. diss., Columbia University.

Hanke, Steve, ed. 1987a. *Privatization and Development*. San Francisco: International Center for Economic Growth, ICS Press.

———. 1987b. "Successful Privatization Strategies." In Hanke, Steve (ed.). *Privatization and Development*. San Francisco: International Center for Economic Growth, ICS Press.

Heclo, Hugh. 1974. *Modern Social Politics in Britain and Sweden: From Relief to Income Maintenance*. New Haven: Yale University Press.

Hellman, Judith Adler. 1983. *Mexico in Crisis*. New York: Holmes and Meier.

Herbert, John D. 1979. *Urban Development in the Third World: Policy Guidelines*. New York: Praeger.

Hernández, Luis. 1990. "Diez años de trincheras: las coordinadoras de masas." *El Cotidiano* 36 (julio–agosto): 34–46.

Hernández Terán, José. 1983. "Pasado, presente, y futuro del abastecimiento de agua de Monterrey, México." Speech presented at the Club Industrial de Monterrey, November 3.

Herzog, Lawrence A. 1990. *Where North Meets South: Cities, Space and Politics on the U.S.-Mexico Border.* Austin: University of Texas Press.

————. 1992. "Between Cultures: Public Space in Tijuana, Mexico." *Places* 8, no. 3 (spring): 54–61.

Hirschman, Albert O. 1984. *Getting Ahead Collectively: Grassroots Experiences in Latin America.* New York: Pergamon.

Hughes, Steven, and Kenneth Mijeski. 1984. *Politics and Public Policy in Latin America.* Boulder, Colo.: Westview.

Instituto Nacional de Estadística, Geografía, e Informática. 1983. *X Censo general de población y vivienda, 1980. Estado de Nuevo León.* Vol. 2, tomo 19. Mexico City: Secretaría de Programación y Presupuesto.

————. 1985. *Estadísticas históricas de México.* Mexico City: Secretaría de Programación y Presupuesto, Dirección General de Estadística.

————. 1990. *XI Censo general de población y vivienda: resultados preliminares.* Mexico City: Secretaría de Programación y Presupuesto, Dirección General de Estadística.

Inter-American Development Bank. 1988. *Economic and Social Progress in Latin America: 1988 Report.* Washington, D.C.: Inter-American Development Bank.

Jacobi Neru, Pedro Roberto. 1987. "Carencia de sanidad básica y demandas sociales: los movimientos por agua en la ciudad de San Pablo." *Boletín de Medio Ambiente y Urbanización* (March): 75–80.

Jaquette, Jane S., ed. 1989. *The Women's Movement in Latin America.* Boston: Unwin Hyman.

Jaramillo, Samuel. 1988a. "Crisis de los medios de consumo colectivo urbano y capitalismo periférico." In *Economía política de los servicios públicos: una visión alternativa,* ed. Luis Mauricio Cuervo et al. Bogotá: Centro de Investigación y Educación Popular.

————. 1988b. "Evolución del suministro de los servicios de agua potable y desagüe en Bogotá. Notas para su interpretación." In *Economía política de los servicios públicos: una visión alternativa,* ed. Luis Mauricio Cuervo et al. Bogotá: Centro de Investigación y Educación Popular.

Jelin, Elizabeth, ed. 1985. *Los nuevos movimientos sociales 1: Mujeres. Rock Nacional.* Buenos Aires: Centro Editor de América Latina.

————, ed. 1990a. *Women and Social Change in Latin America.* London: Zed Books; Geneva: UNRISD.

————. 1990b. "Citizenship and Identity: Final Reflections." In *Women and Social Change in Latin America,* ed. Jelin. London: Zed Books; Geneva: UNRISD.

Jones, E. *Towns and Cities.* 1966. Oxford: Oxford University Press.

Kirby, Andrew, Paul Knox, and Steven Pinch. 1984. *Public Service Provision and Urban Development.* New York: St. Martin's.

Kollar, K. L., and L. Brewer. 1975. "Industrial Development Through Water Resources Planning." *American Water Works Association Journal* 67, no. 12 (Dec.): 686–90.

Kusnir, Liliana, and Carmen Largaespada. 1986. *Women's Experience in Self-Help Housing Projects in Mexico."* In *Learning About Women and Urban Services in Latin America and the Caribbean*, ed. Marianne Schmink, Judith Bruce, and Marilyn Kohn. New York: Population Council.

Laboratorio e Ingeniería de la Calidad del Agua, S.A. 1979–1980. *Distrito de control de la contaminación y reutilización de aguas residuales del Area Metropolitana de Monterrey*. Monterrey, Mexico.

Lau, Rubén, and Victor M. Quintana Silveyra. 1991. *Movimientos populares en Chihuahua*. Ciudad Juárez, Chihuahua: Universidad Autónoma de Ciudad Juárez, Estudios Regionales 3.

Leon, Rosario. 1990. "Bartolina Sisa: The Peasant Women's Organization in Bolivia." In *Women and Social Change in Latin America*, ed. Elizabeth Jelin. London: Zed Books; Geneva: UNRISD.

Levine, Daniel, and Scott Mainwaring. 1989. "Religion and Popular Protest in Latin America: Contrasting Experiences." In *Power and Popular Protest in Latin American Social Movements*, ed. Susan Eckstein. Berkeley: University of California Press.

Linn, Johannes, F. 1979. *Policies for Efficient and Equitable Growth of Cities in Developing Countries*. Washington, D.C.: World Bank, Staff Working Paper no. 342.

———. 1983. *Cities in the Developing World: Policies for Their Equitable and Efficient Growth*. New York: Oxford University Press, published for the World Bank.

Logan, Kathleen. 1984. *Haciendo Pueblo: The Development of a Guadalajaran Suburb*. Tuscaloosa: University of Alabama Press.

Lomnitz, Larissa. 1975. *Como sobreviven los marginados*. Mexico City: Siglo XXI.

López Portillo, José. 1988. *Mis tiempos: biografía y testimonio político, parte primera y parte segunda*. Mexico City: Fernández Editores.

Mainwaring, Scott. 1987. "Urban Popular Movements, Identity, and Democratization in Brazil." *Comparative Political Studies* 20, no. 2 (July): 131–59.

Martínez Almazán, Raúl. 1988. *Las finanzas del sistema federal mexicano*. Mexico City: Instituto Nacional de Administración Pública (INAP).

Martínez Nava, Juan M. 1984. *Conflicto estado empresarios en los gobiernos de Cárdenas, López Mateos y Echeverría*. México City: Editorial Nueva Imagen.

Massiah, G., and J. F. Tribillion. 1987. *Villes en développement*. Paris: Ed. de la Découverte.

Massolo, Alejandra. 1988. *Memoria de pedregal, memoria de mujer. Testimonio de una colona*. Mexico City: Mujeres para el Diálogo.

Maxfield, Sylvia. 1990. *Governing Capital: International Finance and Mexican Politics*. Ithaca: Cornell University Press.

Maxfield, Sylvia, and Ricardo Anzaldúa Montoya, eds. 1987. *Government and Private Sector in Contemporary Mexico*. La Jolla: Center for U.S.-Mexican Studies, University of California-San Diego, Monograph Series no. 20.

Meyer, Lorenzo. 1986. "Un tema añejo siempre actual: el centro y las regiones en la historia mexicana." In *Descentralización y democracia en México*, ed. Blanca Torres. Mexico City: El Colegio de Mexico.

Middlebrook, Kevin. 1989. "The CTM and the Future of Government-Labor Relations." In *Mexico's Alternative Political Futures*, ed. Wayne Cornelius, Judith Gentleman, and Peter Smith. La Jolla: Center for U.S.-Mexican Studies, University of California-San Diego, Monograph Series no. 30.

Molyneux, Maxine. 1985. "Mobilization Without Emancipation? Women's Interests, State and Revolution in Nicaragua." In *New Social Movements and the State in Latin America*, ed. David Slater. Amsterdam: Center for Latin American Research and Documentation (CEDLA).

Montaño, Jorge. 1985. *Los pobres de la ciudad en los asentamientos espontáneos*. 5th ed. Mexico City: Siglo XXI.

Montemayor Hernández, Andrés. 1971. *Historia de Monterrey*. Monterrey: Asociación de Editores y Libreros de Monterrey A.C.

Mumford, Lewis. 1961. *The City in History*. London: Secker and Warburg.

Nacional Financiera. 1990. *La economía mexicana en cifras. 1990*. 11th ed. Mexico City: Nacional Financiera, S.N.C.

Navarro, Marysa. 1989. "The Personal Is Political: Las Madres de Plaza de Mayo." In *Power and Popular Protest in Latin American Social Movements*, ed. Susan Eckstein. Berkeley: University of California Press.

El Norte. Monterrey: Editorial El Sol, 1970–1985.

Nota informativa de la gira del Gobernador del Estado, Señor Alfonso Martínez Domínguez, 10 abril 1984. Press release from the office of the governor of Nuevo León.

Novedades. Mexico City. 5-24-1980, 5-25-1980.

Nuncio, Abraham. 1982. *El Grupo Monterrey*. Mexico City: Editorial Nueva Imagen.

Ortiz Monasterio, Fernando, and Marianne Schmink. 1986. "Women and Waste Management in Urban Mexico." In *Learning About Women and Urban Services in Latin America and the Caribbean*, ed. Marianne Schmink, Judith Bruce, and Marilyn Kohn. New York: Population Council.

Ostrom, Elinor. 1990. *Governing the Commons: The Evolution of Institutions for Collective Action*. New York: Cambridge University Press.

Palacios, Juan José. 1989. *La política regional en México: las contradicciones de un intento de redistribución*. Guadalajara: Universidad de Guadalajara.

Palerm, Angel. 1972. "Ensayo de crítica al desarrollo regional en México." In *Los beneficios del desarrollo regional*, ed. David Barkin. Mexico City: SEP-SETENTAS.

Penfold, Anthony. 1979. "Brazil (Minas Gerais) Water Supply and Sewerage Project III, Project Appraisal Mission." Report prepared for the World Bank, Washington, D.C.

Pérez Güemes, Efraín, and Alma Rosa Garza del Toro. 1984. "El movimiento de posesionarios en Monterrey 1970–1985." Monterrey: unpublished manuscript.

Perlman, Janice. 1976. *The Myth of Marginality: Urban Poverty and Politics in Rio de Janeiro*. Berkeley: University of California Press.

Philip, George. 1992. *The Presidency in Mexican Politics*. New York: St. Martin's.

Pinch, Steven. 1985. *Cities and Services: The Geography of Collective Consumption*. London: Routledge and Kegan Paul.

Piven, Frances Fox, and Richard Cloward. 1979. *Poor People's Movements: Why They Succeed, How They Fail*. New York: Vintage.

Portes, Alejandro. 1985. "Latin American Class Structures: Their Composition and Change During the Last Decades." *Latin American Research Review* 20, no. 3: 7–40.

Portes, Alejandro, and John Walton. 1976. *Urban Latin America: The Political Condition from Above and Below*. Austin: University of Texas Press.

El Porvenir. Monterrey. 1970–1985.

Pozas Garza, María de los Angeles. 1990. "Los marginados y la ciudad." In *La marginación urbana en Monterrey*, ed. Victor Zuñiga and Manuel Ribeiro. Monterrey: Facultad de Filosofía y Letras, Universidad Autónoma de Nuevo León.

———. 1991. "Evolución socio-económica del Area Metropolitana de Monterrey." Manuscript.

Presidencia de la República. 1985a. *Las razones y las obras, Gobierno de Miguel de la Madrid, crónica del sexenio 1982–1988, primer año*. Mexico City: Presidencia de la República, Unidad de la Crónica Presidencial, Fondo de Cultura Económica.

———. 1985b. *Las razones y las obras, Gobierno de Miguel de la Madrid, crónica del sexenio 1982–1988, segundo año*. Mexico City: Presidencia de la República, Unidad de la Crónica Presidencial, Fondo de Cultura Económica.

———. 1988. *Los presidentes de México: discursos políticos, 1910–1988*. Tomo 5, José López Portillo, Miguel de la Madrid Hurtado. Mexico City: Presidencia de la República, Dirección General de Comunicación Social, El Colegio de México.

Proceso. Mexico City. 4-2-1977, 9-6-1986.

Puente Leyva, Jesús. 1976. *Distribución del ingreso en un área urbana: el caso de Monterrey*. 3rd ed. Mexico City: Siglo XXI.

Ramírez, Bruno. 1975. "The Working Class Struggle Against the Crisis: Self-Reduction of Prices in Italy." *Zerowork, Political Materials* 1 (December).

Ramírez Saiz, Juan Manuel. 1986. *El movimiento urbano popular en México*. Mexico City: Siglo XXI.

Rich, Richard C. 1982. *The Politics of Urban Public Services*. Lexington, Mass.: D. C. Heath and Co.

Roberts, Bryan. 1978. *Cities of Peasants: The Political Economy of Urbanization in the Third World*. Beverly Hills: Sage.

Rodríguez, Victoria. 1987. "The Politics of Decentralization in Mexico: Divergent Outcomes of Policy Implementation." Ph.D. diss., University of California-Berkeley.

Rodríguez, Victoria, and Peter Ward. 1992. *Policymaking, Politics, and Urban Governance in Chihuahua: The Experience of Recent PANista Governments*. U.S.-Mexican Policy Report no. 3. Austin: Lyndon B. Johnson School of Public Affairs, University of Texas-Austin.

Rojas Sandoval, Javier, and María Elena Rodríguez. 1988. "La industria siderúrgica en Monterrey: HyLSA (1943–1985)." In *Monterrey: siete estudios contemporáneos*, ed. Mario Cerutti. Monterrey: Universidad Autónoma de Nuevo León.

Roth, Gabriel. 1987. *The Private Provision of Public Services in Developing Countries*. New York: Oxford University Press, published for the World Bank.

Rubin, Jeffrey. 1990. "Popular Mobilization and the Myth of State Corporatism." In *Popular Movements and Political Change in Mexico*, ed. Joe Foweraker and Ann Craig. Boulder, Colo.: Lynne Rienner.

———. 1992. "The Ambiguity of Resistance." Amherst: Rethinking Marxism Conference, University of Massachusetts-Amherst, November.

Safa, Helen Icken. 1988. "Towards a Theory of Women's Collective Action in Latin America." Paper presented at the Congress of Americanistas, Amsterdam, July.

Saldaña, José P. 1965. *Apuntes históricos sobre la industrialización de Monterrey*. Monterrey: Centro Patronal de Nuevo León.

Saragoza, Alex M. 1988. *The Monterrey Elite and the Mexican State, 1880–1940*. Austin: University of Texas Press.

Sara-Lafosse, Violette. 1986. "Communal Kitchens in the Low-Income Neighborhoods of Lima." In *Learning About Women and Urban Services in Latin America and the Caribbean*, ed. Marianne Schmink, Judith Bruce, and Marilyn Kohn. New York: Population Council.

Sargent, Lydia, ed. 1981. *Women and Revolution: A Discussion of the Unhappy Marriage of Marxism and Feminism*. Boston: South End.

Schild, Verónica. 1991. "Disordering Differences: Women and the 'Popular' Movement in Latin America." Paper presented at the 16th Congress of the Latin American Studies Association, Washington, D.C., April 4–6.

Schmidt, Samuel. 1991. *The Deterioration of the Mexican Presidency: The Years of Luis Echeverría*. Tucson: University of Arizona Press.

Schmink, Marianne, Judith Bruce, and Marilyn Kohn, eds. 1986. *Learning About Women and Urban Services in Latin America and the Caribbean*. New York: Population Council.

Schteingart, Martha. 1985–1986. "Movimientos urbano-ecológicos en la ciudad de México: el caso del Ajusco." *Estudios Políticos* 4/5 (October–March): 17–23.

Scott, Ian. 1982. *Urban and Spatial Development in Mexico*. Baltimore: Johns Hopkins University Press.

Scott, James C. 1985. *Weapons of the Weak: Everyday Forms of Peasant Resistance*. New Haven: Yale University Press.

Secretaría de Programación y Presupuesto. 1980. *Información sobre gasto público, 1969–1978*. Mexico City: Secretaría de Programación y Presupuesto, Coordinación General de los Servicios Nacionales de Estadística, Geografía e Informática.

———. 1985. *31 experiencias de desarrollo regional*. Mexico City: Secretaría de Educación Pública, SEP Cultura, Foro 2000.

Servicios de Agua y Drenaje de Monterrey. 1973. "Síntesis histórica de Servicios de Agua y Drenaje de Monterrey." Monterrey.

———. 1971–1976. "Informe de actividades de Servicios de Agua y Drenaje de Monterrey." Monterrey.

———. 1976a. "Informe al gobierno del estado." Monterrey.

———. 1976b. "Comentarios: actuación realizada por su gerente Ing. Leobardo Elizondo. Violaciones institucionales." Monterrey.

———. 1977. "Sistema tarifario propuesto." Monterrey.

———. 1980. *Monterrey: Servicios de Agua y Drenaje*. Mexico City: Reunión Internacional sobre Sistemas Hidráulicos en Grandes Urbes, Documento de Apoyo.

———. 1981. "Pasado, presente, futuro." Monterrey.

———. 1983. "Acciones tomadas para atenuar el problema de la escaséz de agua potable en el año de 1983." Monterrey.

———. 1984. "Nota informativa de la gira del Governador Alfonso Martínez Domínguez el dia 10 de abril de 1984." Monterrey.

———. 1985–1991. "Informe anual de operación, 1985–1991." Monterrey.

Sheahan, John. 1987. *Patterns of Development in Latin America: Poverty, Repression and Economic Strategy*. Princeton: Princeton University Press.

Slater, David, ed. 1985. *New Social Movements and the State in Latin America*. Amsterdam: CEDLA (Center for Latin American Research and Documentation).

Smith, Peter. 1979. *Labyrinths of Power: Political Recruitment in Twentieth Century Mexico*. Princeton: Princeton University Press.

El Sol. Monterrey: Editorial El Sol, 4-8-1983.

Starn, Orin. 1992. " 'I Dreamed of Foxes and Hawks': Reflections on Peasant Protest, New Social Movements, and the Rondas Campesinas of Northern Peru." In *The Making of Social Movements in Latin America: Identity, Strategy, and Democracy*, ed. Arturo Escobar and Sonia Alvarez. Boulder, Colo.: Westview.

Stephen, Lynn. 1989. "Popular Feminism in Mexico." *Z Magazine* 2, no. 12: 102–06.

Stevens, Evelyn P. 1974. *Protest and Response in Mexico*. Cambridge: MIT Press.

Stohr, Walter, and Fraser Taylor. 1981. *Development for Above or Below?* Chichester: John Wiley and Sons.

Tarrow, Sidney. 1989. *Struggle, Politics, and Reform: Collective Action, Social Movements, and Cycles of Protest*. Ithaca: Cornell University, Center for International Studies, Western Societies Program, Occasional Paper no. 21.

Tijerina Garza, Eliézer. 1965. *Análisis de demanda de productos alimenticios: el caso de Monterrey*. Monterrey: Centro de Investigación Económica.

Tirado Jiménez, Ramón. 1990. *Asamblea de barrios: nuestra batalla*. Mexico City: Editorial Nuestro Tiempo.

Torres López, Enrique, and Mario A. Santoscoy. 1985. *La historia del agua en Monterrey desde 1577 hasta 1985*. Monterrey: Ediciones Castillo.

Touraine, Alain. 1984. "Social Movements: Special Area or Central Problem in Sociological Analysis?" *Thesis Eleven* no. 9: 5–15.

La Tribuna. 1980. Monterrey.

Ugalde, Antonio. 1974. *The Urbanization Process of a Poor Mexican Neighborhood*. Austin: Institute of Latin American Studies, University of Texas-Austin.

El Universal. Mexico City. 10-28-1979.

Vargas González, Pablo E. 1991. "Agua potable: hacia la privatización del servicio en Pachuca." Paper presented at the 8th Encuentro de la Red Nacional de Investigación Urbana, Ciudad Juárez, Chihuahua, February 7–8.

Vellinga, Menno. 1988. *Desigualdad, poder y cambio social en Monterrey*. Mexico City: Siglo XXI.

Villarreal, Diana, and Victor Castañeda. 1986. *Urbanización y autoconstrucción de vivienda en Monterrey*. Mexico City: Centro de Ecodesarrollo, Editorial Claves Latinoamericas.

Villatoro, J., R. Arnaboldi, J. M. Fariña, E. Yáñez, A. Rionegro, and W. Pastor. 1983. *Project for the Expansion and Improvement of the Water Supply and Sewerage Service of the Metropolitan Area of Monterrey*. Washington, D.C.: Inter-American Development Bank, Project Report 1289-A, August 16.

Villatoro, J., R. Arnaboldi, C. Gómez, M. C. Price, B. Santacruz, and M. de Moya. 1983. *Proyecto de Agua Potable y Alcantarillado, Monterrey IV, Informe de Proyecto*. Mexico City: Banco Inter-Americano de Desarrollo.

Vizcaya Canales, Isidro. 1971. *Los orígines de la industrialización de Monterrey: una historia económica y social desde la caída del Segundo Imperio hasta el fin de la Revolución (1867–1920)*. Monterrey: Librería Tecnológico.

Walton, John. 1992. *Western Times and Water Wars: State, Culture, and Rebellion in California*. Berkeley: University of California Press.

Ward, Peter. 1986. *Welfare Politics in Mexico: Papering Over the Cracks*. Boston: Allen and Unwin.

———. 1990. *Mexico City*. London: G. K. Hall and Co.

Watson, Gabrielle. 1992. "Water and Sanitation in São Paulo, Brazil: Successful Strategies for Service Provision in Low-Income Communities." Master's thesis, Department of Urban Studies and Planning, Massachusetts Institute of Technology.

White, Anne U. 1978. "Patterns of Domestic Water Use in Low-Income Communities." In *Water, Wastes and Health in Hot Climates*, ed. Richard Feachem, Michael McGarry, and Duncan Mara. Chichester: English Language Book Society and John Wiley and Sons.

Wolf, Eric R. 1982. *Europe and the People Without History*. Berkeley: University of California Press.

World Bank. 1980. *Water Supply and Waste Disposal*. Washington, D.C.: World Bank.

Zermeño, Sergio. 1985. *México: una democracia utópica, el movimiento estudiantil del 68*. Mexico City: Siglo XXI.

Zolezzi, Mario, and Julio Calderón. 1985. *Vivienda popular: autoconstrucción y lucha por el agua*. Lima: DESCO, Centro de Estudios y Promoción del Desarrollo.

INDEX